Published for the
Organization of American Historians

THE CITIZEN SOLDIE

THE
CITIZEN
SOLDIERS

The Plattsburg Training Camp Movement, 1913–1920

John Garry Clifford

The University Press of Kentucky

To Wunderli, Larry, and Ruth,
who know all about magic

ISBN: 0-8131-1262-1

Library of Congress Catalog Card Number: 71-183350

Copyright © 1972 by The University Press of Kentucky

A statewide cooperative scholarly publishing agency serving Berea College, Centre College of Kentucky, Eastern Kentucky University, Kentucky State College, Morehead State University, Murray State University, University of Kentucky, University of Louisville, and Western Kentucky University.

Editorial and Sales Offices: Lexington, Kentucky 40506

Contents

Preface

Plattsburg, at first glance, does not seem to have changed much in the years since 1915. The same barracks, parade ground, and officers' quarters where Leonard Wood held benevolent command remain as they were a half-century ago. The old railroad station where Theodore Roosevelt once fulminated to newspaper reporters stands unchanged. The same beautiful surroundings are there—the rolling countryside, gray Adirondacks to the south, Green Mountains to the east, and Lake Champlain. Ferries still come across the lake from Burlington.

But Plattsburg has changed, just as America has changed. Hotel Champlain, where businessmen/soldiers once ate expensive dinners, is now a temporary community college. The interstate highway from Albany to Montreal has all but done away with passenger traffic on the Delaware and Hudson Railroad. Even more important are the military changes. The old army base has been converted into an air force base. In stark contrast to the sleepy barracks near the lake, shiny new hangars and long runways occupy the old farmland to the west along the Peru Road where rookies and regulars once engaged in mock battles. Sleek B-52 bombers, with jungle camouflage, have used the Plattsburg base to refit and reservice after missions to Vietnam—a far cry from the 1,200 enthusiasts who demonstrated for military preparedness in 1915.

It is always tempting to blame present troubles on past mistakes, and there will be some historians who will trace the difficulties of the 1970s back to World War I. In the sense that all things have a beginning, it is certainly worthwhile to look again at the debates and demonstrations that marked the development of American military policy more than a half-century ago. It is well to remember, in this present atmosphere of concern about military institutions and controversy over volunteer or draft armies, that the issues are not new.

In preparing this manuscript for publication I have incurred obligations which I should like to acknowledge. The librarians and archivists at many institutions have unflaggingly kept up with my requests for books and man-uscripts — Indiana University Library, Chicago Historical Society, University of Tennessee Library, University of Connecticut Library, Columbia Oral History Office, Ster-ling Library of Yale University, Widener Library of Har-vard University, Baker Library of Dartmouth College, Har-vard University Archives, Manuscripts Division of the Li-brary of Congress, Army War College Library, Boston Pub-lic Library, New York Public Library, University of North Carolina Library, and the Buffalo Historical Society. In-diana University provided me with a university fellowship in 1967-1968, and the University of Connecticut graciously made available a summer faculty research grant in 1970.

Many individuals generously gave their time to aid in my research. The following Plattsburgers talked with me about their training camp experiences: Horace W. Frost, John R. Tunis, Thomas W. Miller, Landon Thomas, and Richard A. Newhall. Newhall read and commented on sev-eral draft chapters as well. Colonel Milton S. Heilfronn was kind enough to send me a detailed tape recording of his experiences at the Monterey training camps in 1913-1914; I am very grateful. Mrs. Catherine Drinker Bowen talked with me about her father, Henry S. Drinker, and let me read his unpublished autobiography. And I must thank Mrs. Mary D. C. Dimond for allowing me access to the Grenville Clark papers, without which the story of the Plattsburg camps would be incomplete. In this regard, too, I would be remiss in not thanking Mrs. Ruth Wight, Gren-ville Clark's longtime secretary and now cataloger of the Clark papers at Dartmouth. Mrs. Wight is a historian, al-though she might deny such an allegation.

Friends, colleagues, and teachers also provided much

helpful criticism during the various stages of writing. At Indiana University, John E. Wiltz, Irene D. Neu, and Chase C. Mooney patiently and wisely performed the task of dissertation readers. Russell H. Bastert, Irving B. Holley, Jr., Charles W. Johnson, Eugene Trani, Ronald J. Jensen, Philip L. Cantelon, and David M. Pletcher also commented on one or more chapters. I owe a great debt to Robert H. Ferrell. This fine historian is the perfect dissertation adviser, giving excellent criticism throughout the long ordeal, instilling confidence and enthusiasm when they wane, and keeping after his students until that dissertation becomes a book. Lastly, I give my thanks to my wife Dale, who is a better historian than I am. She may never know how much she helped.

I.
General Wood— The Beginnings

In hot, dusty Gettysburg during July 1913, on the same battlefield where Union and Confederate armies had clashed fifty years earlier, some 160 students from sixty-one schools and colleges spent six weeks learning how to shoulder arms, clean a rifle, march in formation, and, in general, act like soldiers. In California a similar camp opened at the Presidio of Monterey, attended by sixty-three young men from twenty-nine schools. These Students' Military Instruction Camps, as they were called, did not capture the public imagination that summer of 1913. One or two pacifists raised a protest, but the camps scarcely seemed important enough to divert popular attention from the baseball pennant race or Jack London's latest novel.[1]

What went on at Gettysburg and Monterey did interest Major General Leonard Wood, then in his final year as chief of staff of the United States Army. So far as his duties permitted, Wood made himself personally responsible for the camps. He wrote letters to college presidents, persuaded a reluctant War Department to sponsor the project, and handpicked the officers and Regular Army units that would supervise training. Wood even visited both camps, an experience which increased his enthusiasm. There was something about bright young men in khaki that stirred the general's soul. At Gettysburg he was impressed by the students' eagerness to learn and thought it a good sign that so many were attending voluntary chapel.[2] At his later Monterey inspection Wood again marveled at the military results and noted that the student regiment "looks much like a regular organization."[3]

The chief of staff had discovered something that summer for which he had been searching a long time. These student camps were to provide the machinery — or, as one later writer put it, a "most subtle engine" — which Wood could use to reform the army and radically alter American defense policy.[4] "I think we have opened up a field of wonderful possibilities," he exulted to a friend, "in a way which will in the end be far reaching and result in a far better understanding than has ever before existed of what the country needs and what the true purposes of any army are."[5]

ONE

Secretary of War Newton D. Baker once observed that Leonard Wood was "the most prodigiously busy man you ever saw."[6] It was an accurate description. Wood was fifty-three years old in 1913 and in the midst of an extraordinarily full career. A young graduate of Harvard Medical School, he had joined the army in 1885 as a contract surgeon; twenty-five years later he became chief of staff. The intervening years saw him win the Congressional Med-

[1]Edwin M. Meade, "Wood's Military Camps for College Men Denounced," *New York Sunday Times,* July 20, 1913, 4: 14. On the day that camp opened in Gettysburg the press in nearby Harrisburg was more interested in the problem of nude swimmers in the Susquehanna River than it was in student soldiers. *Harrisburg Patriot,* July 8, 1913.

[2]Diary of Leonard Wood, July 13, 1913, Leonard Wood MSS, Library of Congress.

[3]Wood Diary, July 29, 1913. Colonel Milton S. Heilfronn (ret.), a trainee at Monterey in 1913, was able to recall Wood's visit vividly over a half-century later. Wood, Heilfronn remembered, was dressed in civilian clothes, with a straw hat and rather gaudy red tie. The general gave only a short speech. Heilfronn to John Garry Clifford, December 1967, tape recording in my possession.

[4]Walter Millis, *Road to War* (Boston, 1935), p. 94.

[5]Wood to Theodore Roosevelt, September 27, 1913, Wood MSS. See also Wood to J. St. Loe Strachey, December 9, 1913, ibid.

[6]Diary of Josephus Daniels, March 23, 1917, quoted in E. David Cronon, ed., *The Cabinet Diaries of Josephus Daniels, 1913-1921* (Lincoln, Nebr., 1963), p. 120.

al of Honor for helping capture the Apache chieftain Geronimo, rise to national prominence as colonel of the "Rough Riders" in 1898, and prove himself an able colonial administrator, first, as governor of Cuba's Santiago Province and, in 1899, as military governor of the whole island. With his close friend and fellow Rough Rider Theodore Roosevelt in the White House, Wood transferred to the Philippines, where in 1903 he became governor of the Moro Province and three years later commanding general of the Philippines Division. His tenure as chief of staff began in July 1910.

He was an interesting person, this man whom the secretary of war in 1911–1913, Henry L. Stimson, regarded as "the finest soldier of his acquaintance until he met another Chief of Staff thirty years later." A muscular man of medium height who had a benevolent, somewhat hawk-nosed profile, Wood believed completely in the strenuous life. As a young officer in California and in the South, he had coached and played for some of the finest amateur football teams in the country. When he went to Cuba, he had made it a point to learn the Cuban national sport of jai alai and, indeed, had become an expert. In later years he was still an accomplished fencer and horseman, and while stationed at Governor's Island in 1914–1917, he would amuse himself by taking the elevated trolley up to 125th Street and then "walk all the way to South Ferry at a brisk pace."[7] Wood also practiced a kind of primitive isometrics, which one of his aides described as "a combination of Hindu cult, *jiu jitsu* and internal acrobatics."[8] The general sometimes forgot himself and would startle people in the middle of a conversation with his grimaces and contortions. He suffered one physical disability, a persistent lameness in the left side of his body, which resulted from a large tumor

[7]Henry L. Stimson and McGeorge Bundy, *On Active Service in Peace and War* (New York, 1947), p. 33. Stimson was referring to General George C. Marshall—the "other" chief of staff; Gordon Johnston to Hermann Hagedorn, January 12, 1931, Hermann Hagedorn MSS, Library of Congress.

[8]Johnston to Hagedorn, January 12, 1931, as quoted in Hagedorn, *Leonard Wood: A Biography*, 2 vols. (New York, 1931), 2:172.

pressing on the brain. He had undergone surgery in 1909 and for a time was able to check the problem without eliminating it. But this lameness was more annoyance than handicap. It did not interfere with his activities. Few men could work around the clock or travel so many miles with so little rest as Leonard Wood.[9]

On the surface, then, Wood seemed to resemble his good friend Roosevelt. The comparison should not be pushed too far. Wood's interests were more narrow and he had few of the mannerisms and facial expressions which made Roosevelt such a favorite of cartoonists. Though Wood was blunt and owned a quick temper, he was less volatile than Roosevelt; he had stronger prejudices and could hold grudges longer. Like the former president, however, Wood was able to attract a large following among younger people, particularly junior officers who shared his views on military reform. Such later well-known army personalities as George S. Patton, Douglas A. MacArthur, Frank R. McCoy, George Van Horne Moseley, John McAuley Palmer, Johnson Hagood, and James G. Harbord owed much of their military success to service under Wood. The general made it a practice in Cuba, Washington, and elsewhere to delegate considerable authority to capable subordinates. As one officer put it, he acted "more like a football captain than . . . a military martinet."[10]

It was in the role of a professional soldier taking part in politics that Wood gained a reputation which was uniquely his. Resented by many army people for his non-West Point background and civilian friendships, he aroused suspicion outside the service by his vigorous assertion of military objectives. He was a disturbing figure for pre-1917 America. "When I am away from him [Wood]," President Taft's military aide wrote, "I have a deep suspicion of him and see where he schemes too much for the good of anyone, but when I am with him I find myself quite swept off my feet

[9]Wood's diaries, which detail his daily routine from the 1880s until his death in 1927, give an accurate picture of the man's great capacity for work.

[10]Johnson Hagood, "Leonard Wood," unpublished manuscript (ca. 1928) in Hagedorn MSS.

by his engaging personality."[11] Because he possessed definite ideas about the role of the soldier in a democracy and was willing to bring these ideas into public debate, Wood became as controversial a personality in his time as Douglas MacArthur was a generation later.

When Wood took over as chief of staff in 1910, the army was changing from a small, loosely organized collection of garrisons left over from the Indian Wars into an efficient, centrally controlled professional structure on the European model. Elihu Root, as secretary of war under Presidents McKinley and Roosevelt, had begun the metamorphosis a decade earlier with such innovations as the General Staff, Army War College, and special service graduate schools. The purpose of these reforms had been to rouse the military establishment from its peacetime lassitude to the point where it might be able to defend the country in case of war. Despite Root's efforts, the 75,000-man army had no such capability when Wood arrived in Washington in 1910.

The new chief of staff wanted an army that could fight a major war. He scorned current illusions about international brotherhood. "Wars," he once wrote, "are not matters of impulse of the moment but . . . are brought about by great underlying causes which are almost as uncontrollable as the seasons, and the best way to make them as infrequent as possible, and short and humane when they do come, is to be reasonably ready for them."[12] Like Roose-

---

[11]Archie Butt, *Taft and Roosevelt*, 2 vols. (New York, 1930), 2:764. Gordon Johnston, an officer who served under Wood for many years, gave the following interesting appraisal: "Wood had two distinct sides to him. On the one hand he was the big doer, the man who delighted in the difficult job and savoring it, as few other men of his time could; the strong robust man of action. On the other hand, he was a man of intense ambition, hungry for power and not above doing things to get it which he later regretted—cultivating men who could help him along—or pushing aside others who stood in his way. Between these two conflicting elements, the soul of Leonard Wood seemed to beat back [and forth]. Normally he was the big doer. But even in the midst of his biggest undertakings in which he was most deeply interested, the other element would thrust itself to his momentary benefit, but never to his lasting satisfaction." Johnston to Hermann Hagedorn, February 1, 1929, Hagedorn MSS.

[12]Wood to Bernard I. Bell, December 8, 1913, Wood MSS. Another time Wood wrote that "the suppression of war . . . is about as difficult as to effectively neutral-

velt, Alfred Thayer Mahan, and others of the new imperialist school in America, Wood believed that force should
rightly be a part of foreign policy and that military strength
should be sufficient to back up overseas commitments, as
well as to protect the homeland from invasion.[13] Wood's
was a strident philosophy, and he was not inclined to be
charitable toward those of a different persuasion. He ab-
horred pacifists; he looked upon David Starr Jordan as "a
vaporing fool" and Oswald Garrison Villard as "an emascu-
lated traitor."[14] When told that the botanist Luther Bur-
bank was speaking in opposition to military preparedness,
the general is reported to have asked: "Isn't he the man
who developed spineless cactus?"[15] Pacifism meant laziness
and cowardice; worst of all, its military weakness made
inevitable the wars it professed to abolish. Wood was certain of this.

If the general sometimes waxed hot against civilians, he
found just as many targets within the military. There were
those who did not agree that the army's primary task was to
ready itself for war, and there were some who did agree
but differed with Wood as to means. The first attitude was
representative of the army's bureau chiefs, those senior
officers in Washington who were in charge of Ordnance,
Signal Corps, Engineers, and the like. The most powerful
of these was the adjutant general, Major General Fred C.
Ainsworth. Wood liked to tell the story of a bureau chief
who in 1898 supposedly exclaimed: "This is awful. I just
had my office in the best shape it was ever in; and along
comes this war and upsets everything."[16] Such bureaucrats
were engrossed in day-to-day detail—keeping records,

---

ize the influence of gravitation or to revise the general law which governs all
things, namely, the survival of the fittest." Wood to L. S. Rowe, September 30,
1915, ibid.

[13]See Robert E. Osgood, *Ideals and Self-Interest in America's Foreign Relations*
(Chicago, 1953), chaps. 1–3, 7, 10.

[14]As cited in Jack C. Lane, "Leonard Wood and American Defense Policy,
1900–1920" (Ph.D. diss., University of Georgia, 1962), p. 96; Wood to Sydney
Brooks, October 12, 1915, Wood MSS.

[15]Hagedorn, *Leonard Wood*, 2:173.

[16]Wood, "Why We Have No Army," *McClure's Magazine* 37 (April 1912): 678.

meeting payrolls, feeding, housing, and clothing troops. Many of these officers had served in Washington for two decades or more; and some, like Ainsworth, had established close relations with Congress. Believing that they had a stake in the army's civilian functions, they set out to thwart reorganization through such petty devices as refusing to pay officers who had been transferred to new posts by authority of the General Staff alone. Wood had to face this challenge, and the ensuing "Battle of the Doctors" between himself and Ainsworth (also a graduate of the Medical Corps) occupied the better part of his first two years as chief of staff. With strong backing from Secretary of War Stimson, Wood finally established his authority and forced Ainsworth's resignation in the spring of 1912. But it was a costly victory which brought resentment both in the army and in Congress.[17]

The second point of view that Wood had to combat was what one historian has termed "Uptonian pessimism."[18] The reference is to Emory Upton, a brilliant officer whose major work, *The Military Policy of the United States,* was published posthumously in 1904 by Elihu Root, twenty years after Upton had committed suicide.[19] Upton's ideas dominated American military doctrine in the years before the First World War. The critical analysis that he drew of democracy's reluctance to finance a defense establishment in peacetime, the unreliability of state militia, and the average citizen's ostrich-like ignorance of military realities was both persuasive and accurate. Upton was on shakier ground when it came to solutions. He wanted the United States to adopt a large regular army along Prussian lines with a minimum of civilian control. This professional force would then double or triple itself during wartime through

[17]For the best accounts of the Wood-Ainsworth controversy, see Mabel E. Deutrich, *Struggle for Supremacy: The Career of General Fred C. Ainsworth* (Washington, D.C., 1962), pp. 105–27; and Elting E. Morison, *Turmoil and Tradition: The Life and Times of Henry L. Stimson* (Cambridge, Mass., 1960), pp. 144–68.

[18]Russell F. Weigley, *Towards an American Army* (New York, 1962), pp. 156–62.

[19]Upton's career is traced in Stephen E. Ambrose, *Upton of the Army* (Baton Rouge, La., 1965).

a "cadre" system, and thus eliminate the useless militia or National Guard. But of course 150 years of tradition were not to be reversed by an Uptonian snap of the fingers. Since American society prior to 1917 never would have permitted a sizable standing army, Uptonians could only despair. As one officer remarked in 1906 regarding an essay contest that queried how democracy could be effectively adapted to military purposes: "There is no answer."[20]

Wood no doubt considered himself a disciple of Upton; he invariably recommended his works to anyone seeking information about the army.[21] Nevertheless, the general's Rough Rider background and natural exuberance prevented him from being painted into an Uptonian corner. Although he may have concurred with the Uptonian argument that the militia was worthless under conflicting state and federal jurisdiction, he qualified his disapproval. "I have always believed in the Militia," Wood wrote to the adjutant general of New Jersey in 1913, "because I know that in it is a strong soldier element (as well as a rotten political one), and for the further reason I am certain the soldier element is going to dominate eventually. . . . If this is not to be the case, all of us who are really interested in military preparedness will have to look to some other method of security."[22] It was here that Wood parted company from the professionals. He had faith in the citizen soldier. He said he could make civilians into soldiers in six months — instead of the customary two or three years. And Wood meant to put such principles into practice. He meant to breathe life into a citizen reserve.

The National Guard seemed the logical place to begin. This traditional source of ready-armed "minutemen" had

---

[20]As quoted in Russell F. Weigley, *History of the United States Army* (New York, 1967), p. 336.

[21]Wood's references to Upton were particularly evident in his correspondence with the military writer Frederic L. Huidekoper, whose book *The Military Unpreparedness of the United States* (New York, 1915) was written at Wood's request as a conscious updating of Upton's work. See numerous letters from Wood to Huidekoper in the Wood MSS.

[22]Wood to W. F. Sandler, Jr., October 15, 1913, ibid.

been evolving since 1900 into the kind of organization that could make professional soldiers forget the sins of its state-oriented past. The Dick Act of 1903, another of Elihu Root's reforms, had asserted federal control over state militia by having the War Department issue arms and equipment without charge, in return for which Guard units were required to hold a minimum number of drills and target practices each year, plus a summer encampment of not less than five days in the field. The law also recognized the president's power to call militia troops into national service for nine months. Additional legislation in 1908 struck out any time limit for federal service and stated explicitly that this service could be ordered "either within or without the Territory of the United States."[23] But the army — and General Wood — remained skeptical of the militia. Notwithstanding joint maneuvers and inspection by regular officers, Guard units of different states varied greatly. Some welcomed increased military responsibility; others, particularly in the South, resented federal supervision. The General Staff and the National Guard Association lobby in Washington regarded one another with mutual distrust. Therefore, when Attorney General George W. Wickersham obligingly decided in 1912 that it was unconstitutional to require militia service beyond the borders of the United States, Wood was forced to do what he wanted to do anyway.[24] He had to look elsewhere for a reserve.

This quest for a reserve plan operated on several different levels. Wood may have known where he wanted to go by 1912, but because of the army's outdated organization he was uncertain how to proceed. (For example, that same year Wood and Stimson tactically reorganized the army's forty-nine scattered outposts into four "paper" divisions, a move which proved successful when American forces had to mobilize on the Texas border in February 1913.)[25] On a fundamental level the chief of staff could

[23]*U. S., Statutes at Large*, vol. 35, pp. 339–403.

[24]For the battle between the National Guard and General Staff, see Martha Derthick, *The National Guard in Politics* (Cambridge, Mass., 1961), pp. 29–32.

[25]Morison, *Turmoil and Tradition*, p. 138.

urge more Americans to take up rifle-shooting.[26] More quixotically, he could advocate that 100,000 Americans of East European descent take their military training firsthand by fighting in the Balkan Wars.[27]

Wood's favorite scheme suggested a simple change in army recruitment policy. Instead of a five-year enlistment, he wanted two years of active duty or less, after which the soldier would pass into a national reserve. The idea was to cut down on reenlistments so that the army would cease to be a self-sustaining collection of veterans and become, in Wood's phrase, "a great mill through which the population is passed and trained to bear arms."[28] Wood pushed this plan hard and tried to translate it into legislation. An elaborate outline for even more sweeping reorganization was prepared by three younger staff officers and appeared as a supplement to the annual report of the secretary of war for 1912, entitled "The Organization of the Land Forces of the United States."[29] As part of the Army Appropriation bill of that year, Congress did pass a law which allowed recruits to accept furlough to the reserve after three years with the colors. But the conditions attending the new enlisted reserve were such that few men (only sixteen by 1915) chose to join; and, try as he might, Wood could not make further changes in this direction.[30] Friends of General Ainsworth in Congress, men like Congressman James Hay of Virginia, chairman of the House Committee on Military Affairs, opposed any plan by the chief of staff. National Guard partisans fought anything that might undercut the militia. Even

[26]Wood, "Rifle Practice for Public Schools," *Collier's* 46 (December 7, 1910): 16. Wood also encouraged rifle-shooting in his annual reports; see *War Department Annual Reports, 1911* (Washington, D.C., 1911), 1:177.

[27]Wood to Sherman Miles, May 29, 1913, Wood MSS.

[28]Wood, "Why We Have No Army," p. 682.

[29]*War Department Annual Reports, 1912* (Washington, D.C., 1912), 1:67–128.

[30]The problem with the new reserve law was that three years was simply too long to give much incentive to the men to go into a reserve; soldiers preferred to reenlist. Out of 21,000 enlistees in the period from November 1, 1912, to August 31, 1913, only sixty-one applied for furlough to the reserve after three years. Wood and Garrison tried to alter the system so as to allow enlistees to take examinations at six-month intervals for furlough, but Congress never acted on their suggestions. See John Dickinson, *The Building of an Army* (New York, 1922), p. 14; see also Wood to James G. Harbord, May 22, 1913, Wood MSS.

regular officers were not very happy at the prospect of short enlistments, of continually training inept civilians.[31] Wood had to devise a more oblique approach.

TWO

A source of inspiration appeared early in 1913 in the person of Lieutenant Henry T. Bull, a cavalry officer detailed as professor of military science at Cornell University. Bull had read of a Navy Department scheme to take college students on board battleships for a two-month summer cruise and thought that such an idea might be adapted to army purposes. He went to Washington during Cornell's spring recess and suggested to Wood that qualified students be attached to Regular Army units for four or five weeks in the summer without any formal enlistment contract. Bull was certain substantial numbers would respond. The idea intrigued Wood, who thought that such a scheme might work better in special camps. He set Bull to work with Captains Robert O. Van Horn and Douglas A. MacArthur in preparing a detailed program. Wood obtained the backing of Lindley M. Garrison, secretary of war in the new Wilson administration. Finances were arranged, and sites chosen. By the end of April the wheels were ready to turn.[32]

The chief of staff on May 10, 1913, addressed the following circular letter to the country's college and university presidents:

[31]The army opposition to Wood's reforms is portrayed in the memoir of George Van Horne Moseley, "One Soldier's Journey," 4 vols. (unpublished), 1:90–105. Moseley served on the General Staff when Wood was chief of staff; Moseley MSS, Library of Congress.

[32]For Bull's role, see Preston Brown, "The Genesis of the Military Training Camps," *Infantry Journal* 37 (December 1930): 609–11; see also Wood Diary, April 7, 1913, and Bull to Wood, June 12, 1920, Wood MSS. Other individuals made similar suggestions about summer training at about the same time as Bull; see Mortimer E. Cooley to Woodrow Wilson, March 24, 1913, and J. A. Miller, Jr., to Garrison, March 29, 1913, Record Group 94, AG2023393, Adjutant General files (National Archives). Both Cooley and Miller derived their ideas from the proposed naval cruises. As it turned out, the naval cruises were not held in 1913 because of a diplomatic crisis with Japan.

1. The Secretary of War has decided to hold two experimental military camps of instruction for students of educational institutions during the coming summer vacation period. Should these camps prove a success, it is intended to hold them annually, one in each of the four sections of the country.

2. The object of these camps is, primarily, to increase the present inadequate personnel of the trained military reserve of the United States by a class of men from whom, in time of a national emergency, a large proportion of the commissioned officers will probably be drawn, and upon whose military judgment at such time, the lives of many other men will in a measure depend.

The object sought is not in any way one of military aggrandizement, but a means of meeting a vital need confronting a peaceful, unmilitary, though warlike nation, to preserve that desired peace and prosperity by the best known precaution, viz.: a more thorough preparation and equipment to resist any effort to break such peace.[33]

There had been inklings of such an experiment for the past year. "Camps of instruction" were nothing new in regard to the militia, and the special "Report on the Organization of the Land Forces of the United States" had explicitly mentioned such camps in connection with a proposed national reserve. Wood had already conferred with one or two college presidents, but he wanted to make sure that the new administration approved before going ahead.[34]

That Wood should look to the colleges was almost inevitable. They were a resource which the army had neglected for too long. In 1913 more than thirty thousand students in schools and universities were undergoing some kind of military training.[35] This training ranged from the West Point-like discipline at Norwich and the Virginia Military Institute to the courses in drill and tactics required at

[33]As quoted in Ralph Barton Perry, *The Plattsburg Movement* (New York, 1921), p. 2.

[34]*War Department Annual Reports, 1912*, 1:121; Wood to Arthur Hadley, May 7, 1913, Wood MSS.

[35]Perry, *Plattsburg Movement*, p. 8.

all land-grant colleges.[36] Unfortunately, the War Department had only slight contact with these potential reserve officers. Since 1904 a section of the General Staff had made inspections of schools with military departments, but it did little more than observe and report. Those institutions given highest rank could designate a certain number of "honor graduates," who would then be placed on the preferred list for commissions in the Regular Army. The War Department did not keep records of the thousands of other students with military training.[37]

The situation was at its worst in the land-grant colleges. Here the army's hands were tied. Administration of the Morrill Act, the legislation of 1863 that had established land-grant colleges, was legally the responsibility of the Interior Department. Army officers who taught drill at these schools generally regarded their assignment as akin to Siberia, and their instruction usually reflected their disposition. With the War Department powerless to set standards, the quality of military training at land-grant institutions became a haphazard proposition, dependent on the whims of the university president, the character of the instructor, and the enthusiasm of the students. Of the last there was usually very little.[38]

To Wood such a state of affairs was intolerable. He was a college man with college instincts. When he had lunch, it was at the "Club"—the Harvard Club in New York, the University Club in Washington. He liked the college boy, and he got along well with university presidents. His oldest son was preparing for Harvard, not West Point. The army

[36]Two good studies of military education prior to the First World War are Ira L. Reeves, *Military Education in the United States* (Burlington, Vt., 1914); and L. R. Gignilliat, *Arms and the Boy* (Indianapolis, Ind., 1916).

[37]Edward Orton, "Our Land Grant Colleges as a Military Asset," *National Service* 1 (June 1917): 317-18; H. C. Hale, "Military Instruction in Colleges," *Infantry Journal* 10 (March-April 1914): 688-91; Richard Stockton, Jr., "Military Schools and the Nation," *Infantry Journal* 11 (July-August 1914): 24-32.

[38]There were, of course, exceptions to this rule. The University of Minnesota, the University of California at Berkeley, and Cornell University each had excellent military programs. Nonetheless, the general quality of military training under the Morrill Act was not very high. See *War Department Annual Reports, 1913* (Washington, D.C., 1913), 1:151-52, 188-91; see also Gene M. Lyons and John W. Masland, "The Origins of the ROTC," *Military Affairs* 23 (Spring 1959): 3-4.

should not ignore this untapped source of trained man-power but should exploit it to full potential and include the nonmilitary Ivy League schools as well. Military training did not have to be something tedious, dull, and ineffectual.[39]

The summer camp scheme fitted in perfectly. Wood first pictured it as a device for coordinating instruction in the land-grant schools.[40] If the army could get these boys out voluntarily during vacation, standardization would become inevitable. Once successful, the camps would attract greater numbers, and step by step there would emerge a reserve officer program independent of the militia.

Wood's initial object was not entirely military. He knew that six weeks of summer training would not go far toward making soldiers. He did feel, though, "that a great deal can be done in the implanting of a sound military policy, and that this year will be only a beginning of the real work."[41] Here was an opportunity to show youth what the army was all about. Wood informed a Boston acquaintance:

> In addition to the practical instruction there will be a series of lectures on our military history, and others outlining our military policy. We do not want to preach militarism, but we do want to establish in each college, university and school throughout the country some true conception of what our military history has been and what we need in the way of a sound military policy for the future. We do not wish ... to teach militarism or to preach large standing armies, but we do want to revivify or perhaps recreate that sense of person-al and individual responsibility for one's preparedness to

[39]Wood's main effort at reform in the years 1913 to 1915 concentrated on military training in the colleges. Of course, this objective did not eliminate other attempts at reform, such as changing curriculum at the United States Military Academy, urging reorganization of Regular Army units, and advocating more intensive training methods in the army itself. Wood concentrated on the colleges because he saw them as the best hope for changing public opinion on military matters—a prerequisite for any meaningful reform of American defense policy. For an excellent short summary of Wood's ideas, see Weigley, *Towards an American Army*, pp. 200-222. The most concise statement by Wood of his aims is in a four-page letter to J. St. Loe Strachey, December 9, 1913, Wood MSS.

[40]*War Department Annual Reports, 1913*, 1:188-91.

[41]Wood to General Thomas H. Barry, May 26, 1915, Wood MSS.

discharge efficiently the duties of a soldier in case the Republic should become involved in war.[42]

There would be nightly lectures around the Gettysburg campfire with the ghosts of Lee, Meade, and Longstreet in attendance. Students would see graphic illustration of America's inadequate defenses, of what could happen when a nation was unprepared for war. They would see the army the way Wood saw it, because the general personally assigned several of his staff officers and other officers then serving in the colleges as instructors.[43] "The whole official personnel," Wood told the commanding general of the Eastern Department, "have [*sic*] got to be of the right sort, or the thing won't work out smoothly."[44]

Though farther away and thus unable to receive Wood's personal supervision, the West Coast camp proceeded along lines similar to Gettysburg.[45] The department commander, Major General Arthur Murray, shared Wood's enthusiasm for the project; so did the younger officers, most notably the camp commander, Major Herman Hall.[46] The actual training site was at Pacific Grove, some two miles from the Monterey Presidio.[47] And while this camp may have lacked the historical setting of Gettysburg, it had the attraction of being situated in the beautiful Big Sur country.[48]

[42]Wood to Henry L. Higginson, May 9, 1913, ibid.

[43]Wood to Barry, May 13, 1913, ibid.

[44]Wood to Barry, May 26, 1913, ibid.

[45]See Adjutant General to Commanding General, Western Department, April 22, 1913, RG 94, AG2023393.

[46]For Murray and Hall, see their reports to the Adjutant General, dated, respectively, September 15 and August 11, 1913, RG 94, AG2023393.

[47]Pacific Grove was chosen because "it was near the street car line, near places of amusement and recreation and was in a quiet, prohibition town." Hall's report, ibid.

[48]Major Hall commented, "The climate hereabouts is wonderful. . . . Carmel, Monterey, Pacific Grove are all nice (quiet) places and Carmel seems especially attractive — four miles from here. There is quite a literary and artistic crowd there and they seem to enjoy life in a semi-Bohemian way." Hall to James G. Harbord, June 8, 1913, Harbord MSS, Library of Congress. Colonel Heilfronn's recollections (tape recording in my possession) also go into detail in regard to the amusements and physical atmosphere at Pacific Grove. One might add at this point that the physical attractions of the college training camps had much to do with their success. Arthur Stanwood Pier's book, *The Plattsburgers* (Boston, 1917), a

THREE

Wood knew that the 1913 camps were an experiment and conducted them accordingly. He did not want to ask for extra appropriations, not with a new Democratic administration in power and Congress generally hostile to his views. Students who volunteered had to pay their own expenses. Not counting transportation, the cost amounted to approximately $27.50 ($10 for uniform, $17.50 for food). In selecting Gettysburg as one of the sites, Wood could take advantage of the tents and equipment assembled there for the Grand Army of the Republic's fiftieth anniversary of the battle. At both the Gettysburg and Monterey camps Regular Army units did the cooking and handled all maintenance.[49]

The course of instruction was rigorous. Trainees rose with the 5:15 bugle and went through a series of supervised calisthenics. Then came breakfast, followed by several hours of drill and theoretical work. Afternoons were given over to sports or voluntary exercises, at the student's option; evenings were for quiet talks and recreation. Training progressed from the manual of arms to close order formation, open order, the use of cover and entrenchment, range estimation, and patrols. Once over their initial awkwardness, students became so eager to learn that they would devote free afternoons to putting one another through their drill exercises. Officers occasionally had to order the boys to swim and play ball.[50]

---

novel about the college camps, presents as the leading protagonist a young man who had never camped in the open or fired a rifle. It was the novelty of these experiences that attracted him to the camp. And, once there, the young man's enthusiasm grew with each passing day. Pier, who was editor of *Youth's Companion,* attended the Business Men's Camp at Plattsburg in 1915.

[49]Another example of economy at Gettysburg was the presence of Sigmund Eisner, a clothing merchant from Red Bank, New Jersey. Eisner was able to supply regulation uniforms at low cost, and as a result he became the unofficial tailor for training camp men, not only at Gettysburg, but also at subsequent camps at Plattsburg and elsewhere. See Brown, "The Genesis of the Military Training Camps," p. 611; see also James H. McRae, "Report of the Students' Military Instruction Camp at Gettysburg, Pa., 1913," September 23, 1913, RG 94, AG2023393.

[50]See Henry S. Drinker, "The Students' Military Instruction Camp at Gettysburg," *New York Times,* August 17, 1913.

Fundamentals digested, the trainees turned to other tasks. At Gettysburg a full battery of artillery, company of engineers, cavalry troop, infantry battalion, and signal corps company were present to furnish combat instruction in each of the army's five main branches. After two weeks student companies took to the fields and woods for daily maneuvers—with regular troops as the "enemy." The fourth week at Monterey saw intensive training on the rifle ranges,[51] where each student received personal attention. The week ended with a battery of tests, each individual being ranked and the student company with the highest total score winning a prize.

Then came the "hike," where everything taught previously took on greater relevance. Under thirty-pound packs, trekking up to fifteen miles a day, camping under the stars, the trainees spent seven days working out a continuous military problem. There were daily skirmishes with blank cartridges. Students learned camp sanitation and how to read a contour map. Cemeteries were stormed and farmhouses captured. It was grueling work; and when the young men finally returned to camp, they had sore feet, aching backs, and considerable acquaintance with the business of soldiering. As the commander of the Gettysburg camp put it: "They worked hard, were quick and eager to learn, and maintained their interest and enthusiasm to the end."[52]

The military accomplishment pleasantly surprised General Wood. The army was so attuned to the average uneducated recruit that it had overlooked the "elite" possibilities of the college man. After only two days Wood's adjutant at Gettysburg, Captain Van Horn, was reporting "a most encouraging, enthusiastic, and willing bunch. I have never seen a more promising set of young men."[53] As soon as he heard the results on the rifle range, Wood boasted to Stim-

[51]There were no rifle ranges at Gettysburg; thus the hike out to Mount Gretna took place prior to the rifle instruction. At Monterey, it was the other way around. At later camps, rifle instruction always preceded the hike.

[52]Major James H. McRae, "Report . . . ," September 23, 1913, RG 94, AG2023393.

[53]Robert O. Van Horn to Wood, July 9, 1913, Wood MSS.

son that "something like 90% became marksmen." He was impressed that so many young men from the larger universities, men without any previous military training, performed so well. He told Stimson that "they illustrated how it is that Switzerland, with only short intense periods of training, has such a good army."[54]

However impressive these military results may have been, they were secondary to the larger task of selling the training camp idea.[55] The fact that the trainees were civilians and not servicemen was uppermost in the minds of the officers. The commandant at Monterey told how "one student was reported by members of the company as returning to camp slightly intoxicated and was given [only] a reprimand." Because of age and circumstance the army chose to "tighten discipline gradually."[56] One of the Gettysburg trainees, a student from South Carolina, wrote home about the men who were his officers, telling what regular fellows they were, how they invited students to eat at their table, how they played baseball with the trainees, and how they went out of their way to bring girls and musicians from Harrisburg for a Saturday night dance.[57] The idea of carefully selecting the officer-instructors seemed to be paying off. While on the West Coast during August, Wood received word from his aide of the large number of laudatory letters about Gettysburg, from students, parents, even congressmen.[58] One father after visiting the camp wrote Wood that nearly every trainee he talked with had picked out an officer as his "idol."[59]

Perhaps even more important than the impression of the camps on those attending was their equally strong impact on the college presidents. Without the support of

[54]Wood to Stimson, September 19, 1913, ibid.

[55]These first camps were productive, militarily. Of the 159 students at Gettysburg, eighty-four later served as commissioned officers during the World War. See Brown, "Genesis of the Military Training Camps," p. 611.

[56]Hall, "Report . . . ," RG 94, AG2023393.

[57]G. Buist Rivers, letter in *Charleston* (S. C.) *Evening Post,* July 29, 1913.

[58]Frank R. McCoy to Wood, August 13, 1913, Frank R. McCoy MSS, Library of Congress.

[59]E. C. Rice to Wood, August 13, 1913, Wood MSS.

these men the chief of staff could not have gathered even a hundred trainees in 1913; nor could he further his reserve plans without their help. This group of educators, which included such outspoken pacifists as Columbia's Nicholas Murray Butler and Stanford's David Starr Jordan, endorsed military training. But Butler and Jordan were not typical. For every ultrapacifist there seemed to be at least five like burly Jacob Gould Schurman of Cornell, who in 1914 would persuade the New York state legislature to build a $350,000 armory for his university's cadet corps.[60] Another individual who liked to see his students in uniform was Benjamin Ide Wheeler of the University of California at Berkeley. General Wood met Wheeler during an inspection tour of the Far West in 1912 and noted in his diary that the president had a "fine photograph" of Germany's Kaiser Wilhelm II hanging in his office.[61] The two men hit it off splendidly, and Wheeler encouraged the men from Berkeley's student corps to attend the camp at Pacific Grove. Wood's friendships also included Arthur Hadley of Yale and Lawrence Lowell of Harvard. Since neither institution had a military department, Wood found it easy to convince both men of the advantages of supervised summer instruction for their otherwise indolent charges. Then, too, with a former president of Princeton in the White House, the general took pains to keep that university's present incumbent, John Grier Hibben, informed. Hibben responded favorably.[62]

The most influential advocate turned out to be Henry Sturgis Drinker, president of Lehigh University. Drinker was one of those white-haired fatherly figures who seemed to epitomize American higher education at the turn of the

[60]Schurman, "Military Training at Cornell University," *National Service* 1 (May 1917): 217–20.

[61]Wood Diary, October 18, 1912.

[62]There are literally hundreds of letters between Wood and Hibben, Schurman, Hadley, Lowell, and other university presidents in the Wood MSS. Although the various college histories and biographies of prominent educators do touch on this involvement of the colleges in preparedness, it remains a neglected chapter in the history of American higher education. See Lyons and Masland, "Origins of ROTC," pp. 1–12.

century. He had served as head of this small Pennsylvania college since 1905 and was an engineering scholar of some repute. Fellow educators respected him.[63] Though of Quaker background and a member of the Carnegie Foundation for International Peace, Drinker believed with Wood that the best insurance against war was military strength. The summer camps fascinated him. College youth needed discipline, and the camps would provide it. Lehigh's young engineers could only benefit from firsthand knowledge of camp sanitation and the mechanics of field artillery. Drinker's efforts at recruiting resulted in a larger contingent, proportionately, at Gettysburg from his university than from any other.[64]

Nor was Drinker content with mere encouragement. His son Philip, a Lehigh student, was going to Gettysburg, so Drinker accompanied him.[65] He slept on army cots, listened to campfire lectures, watched the *fours left* and *fours right*. He even visited the students on their hike out to Mount Gretna, some sixty-five miles away. Drinker was captivated. "I can think of no six weeks," he wrote to the *New York Times,* "that could be spent by our boys to better advantage to themselves and with better promise to our country of development of good manly men and gentlemen."[66]

President Drinker's involvement became official near the end of the training course. One day during the march to Mount Gretna the entire training body decided to hold a meeting. Not far from the small town of Hershey's Mill these 159 students formally constituted the Society of the National Reserve Corps of the United States: they pledged to ready themselves for any future military obligation, to

[63]Drinker later described his role as a kind of buffer between Wood and the ultrapacifist college administrators. They would listen to him but not to the army. See Drinker, "The Story of the College Camps," *National Service* 2 (September 1917): 76.

[64]Yale and Cornell led with thirteen representatives apiece. Lehigh, a much smaller school, had eleven students at Gettysburg. See Brown, "Genesis of the Military Training Camps," pp. 610–11.

[65]In later years Philip Drinker invented the "iron lung."

[66]Drinker, "The Students' Military Instruction Camp at Gettysburg," *New York Times,* August 17, 1913.

promote the system of summer camps, and to urge and support a sound national defense policy. George H. Gaston, Jr. (Princeton, '13), became secretary-treasurer, and the elder Drinker was elected president.[67]

This was no honorary appointment. At General Wood's encouragement Drinker began correspondence with other university presidents, collecting their reactions and urging continued cooperation. In September 1913 he wrote a careful letter to Woodrow Wilson seeking endorsement of the camps. Wilson did not disappoint him. "I am very much interested," the President of the United States replied,

> in the successful working out of the idea of these college camps. I believe the students attending will derive not only a great deal of physical benefit from the healthful, open air life, but also that they will benefit from the discipline, habits of regularity and the knowledge of personal and camp sanitation. . . . The camps will also tend to disseminate sound information concerning our military history and the present policy of the Government in military matters, in addition to giving the young men themselves a very considerable amount of practical military instruction, which will be useful to them in case their services should ever be required.[68]

Wilson's words could have been written by Leonard Wood.[69] Drinker seized upon the statement and incorporated it as a frontispiece to the Reserve Corps yearbook that he and Gaston were preparing.[70]

Later that autumn at the Century Club in New York City, Drinker organized an Advisory Board of University Presidents for the National Reserve Corps. John Grier Hib-

[67]Brown, "Genesis of the Military Training Camps," pp. 610–11; Perry, *Plattsburg Movement,* p. 13.

[68]Perry, *Plattsburg Movement,* p. 16.

[69]In point of fact, the statement was drafted by Secretary of War Garrison. It is doubtful that Wilson ever paid much attention to the training camps until they became controversial in 1915. See Lindley M. Garrison to Woodrow Wilson, September 22, 1913, enclosing the "draft of a letter from you [Wilson] to him [Drinker] which I would like to have you sign if it meets with your approval." Woodrow Wilson MSS, Library of Congress.

[70]See Drinker to Wilson, August 20, November 21, 24, 1913, and January 27, 1914, Wilson MSS. There is a yearbook in the Wilson MSS.

ben was named chairman and Drinker secretary. Presidents Hadley, Lowell, Wheeler, and four others comprised the Board.[71]

For Wood these were happy times. Not only could he tell an English friend "what a splendid field all this has opened up" in the colleges, but he saw encouragement on other fronts as well.[72] He had undertaken a crosscountry tour of military installations that summer with Secretary Garrison, and the former New Jersey judge had agreed to support Wood's ideas concerning the reserves, short enlistment, and improvement of the militia. The chief of staff even thought for a time that Congressman Hay, General Ainsworth's good friend, was going to cooperate.[73] Wood began quietly to plan special training regiments for regular recruits, to prove to the army that soldiers could be properly trained in six to eight months. One of these, an infantry regiment, was to begin work early in 1914 at the Plattsburg Barracks on the shore of Lake Champlain in upstate New York.[74] Then, too, with revolution and civil war boiling in Mexico, Wood had to make preparations for possible military intervention—a duty which he did not find altogether unwelcome.[75]

Wood still managed to devote considerable energies to the college camps. With Captain Van Horn working full time as his assistant, he stepped up efforts at publicity. In October 1913 he announced through the secretary of war that four separate camps would be held the following summer. He did not specify where, so the ensuing deluge of letters from interested chambers of commerce gave ample

[71]The original Board consisted of Hibben of Princeton, Drinker of Lehigh, Hadley of Yale, Lowell of Harvard, George H. Denny of the University of Alabama, Wheeler of the University of California, H. B. Hutchins of the University of Michigan, Superintendent E. W. Nichols of the Virginia Military Institute, and New York Commissioner of Education John H. Finley. Perry, *Plattsburg Movement*, pp. 16–17.
[72]Wood to J. St. Loe Strachey, December 9, 1913, Wood MSS.
[73]Wood to Henry L. Stimson, September 19, 1913, ibid.
[74]See Merch B. Stewart to Wood, January 15, 1914; C. G. Morton to Wood, April 15, 1914; J. T. Dickman to Wood, August 19, 1914, Wood MSS.
[75]Hagedorn, *Leonard Wood*, 2:134–37.

evidence of the camps' extramilitary ramifications.[76] The chief of staff gathered press clippings to show congressmen.[77] He urged President Drinker to rush three thousand camp yearbooks to press in time to be distributed with the War Department annual reports at the end of the year.[78] He wrote letters and articles, always careful to stress the nonmilitary benefits to trainees and the fact that he was not advocating a large standing army.[79] He even tried to entice Nicholas Murray Butler by pointing out that "we should have a much lower criminal rate" with more extensive military training.[80]

More and more, Wood went directly to the colleges. In November 1913 he spoke to the presidents of the land-grant universities at their annual convention in Washington. He was in New York City a week later for Drinker's first meeting of the Advisory Board of University Presidents. He visited Princeton in October, Lehigh in December. In February 1914 he returned to Princeton, while Captain Van Horn spoke at Ann Arbor. That spring saw him give talks on the camps at Yale, Harvard, and Catholic University in Washington, D.C.[81]

The general was not a polished speaker, but somehow he got results. He would clump up to the platform and stand square with his hands clasped behind him. Then he would talk, in short sentences, epigram following epigram, with no pauses. Always there were historical allusions — quotations from Demosthenes, George Washington, Thomas Jefferson, Lord Roberts, and others. He would speak of the citizen's obligation to prepare himself personally for possible military service. He would outline the coming summer program and urge that as many students

[76]There are numerous letters of this sort in the Wood MSS for 1913.
[77]Wood to Desha Breckinridge, November 18, 1913, Wood MSS.
[78]Wood to Drinker, January 19 and 21, 1914, ibid.
[79]Wood complained to one magazine that an interview he had granted was mistitled "How to Have a Bigger Army," and that he was not in favor of this at all. Wood to editor of *Leslie's Weekly*, December 16, 1913, ibid.
[80]Wood to Butler, February 5, 1914, ibid.
[81]The general's itinerary is easily traced in his diary, October 1913–May 1914.

as possible attend. The speech would then conclude, no peroration, no elaborate gestures.[82] It was Spartan stuff, and it seemed to appeal. Six hundred and sixty-seven students were to turn out for the camps of 1914, more than triple the number for the first year.

Wood became more precise as to the military use that should be made of college instruction. During the meeting of land-grant college representatives in November 1913 he had observed that "undeveloped military resources are just about as useful in time of war as an undeveloped gold mine during a panic on Wall Street."[83] He went on to suggest a program whereby five hundred graduates of the land-grant colleges would be selected each year for commissions as "provisional" second lieutenants and assigned to regular units for one year's training, after which they would pass into a special officer reserve. Wood published this plan in his annual report for 1913 and gave it coverage in the articles he wrote about the college camps.[84] At that same meeting Edward Orton, dean of the Engineering School at Ohio State University, advanced a plea that the War and Interior departments jointly produce a standard course of military instruction. He agreed with Wood about commissioning graduates and urged that the General Staff detail more able officers as military professors. The majority of delegates echoed Orton's sentiments.[85] General Wood was pleased. In the course of the next three years, there was considerable discussion between Wood, the War College Division of the General Staff, and representatives of

[82]"His soldierly appearance, his sturdy figure, his fine, grim face, his earnestness, the short sentences, the simple English words, the clear enunciation, all combined to make a tremendous effect." Landon Thomas to Hermann Hagedorn, January 18, 1929, Hagedorn MSS. Thomas was aide-de-camp to Wood in 1918–1919; see also Hagedorn, *Leonard Wood*, 2:341–42. Several of Wood's standard speeches are collected in Leonard Wood, *The Military Obligation of Citizenship* (Princeton, N. J., 1915).

[83]"Stenographer's Notes on General Wood's Talk before the Association of American Agricultural Colleges and Experiment Stations," December 8, 1913, Wood MSS.

[84]*War Department Annual Reports, 1913*, 1:151–52; and Leonard Wood, "Students' Military Instruction Camp," *Harvard Illustrated Magazine* (April 1914), copy in Wood MSS.

[85]Wood Diary, November 13, 1913.

land-grant, military, and nonmilitary institutions, in which the details of a permanent reserve officer training program were threshed out. This program, the present-day ROTC, would become law as part of the National Defense Act of June 1916.[86]

Meanwhile, Wood had the 1914 camps to worry about. It was during the winter and spring of 1914 that he established a close personal friendship with President Drinker, a relationship which gained immediate support for the training camps and one which lasted until Wood's death in 1927. By writing to other college administrators and using the machinery of the Society of the National Reserve Corps, Drinker did yeoman work and took some of the burden off the General Staff.[87] Wood chose sites for the forthcoming camps, trying to find areas that were not only healthful and centrally located but near recognized vacation resorts. He settled again on Monterey for the West Coast. Ludington, Michigan, where the local Board of Trade provided special facilities, was the selection for the army's Central Department. He almost picked White Sulphur Springs, West Virginia, for the South, but decided on Asheville, North Carolina, near the foot of the beautiful Pisgah Mountains. And in the East, after considerable pressure from Senator Frank L. Greene and President Guy Potter Benton of the University of Vermont, Wood chose Fort Ethan Allen in Burlington.[88] Publicity was far more extensive than in 1913.[89] Again officers were carefully se-

[86]See Lyons and Masland, "Origins of ROTC," pp. 1–12.

[87]The correspondence between Wood and Drinker, which usually ran to fifteen or twenty letters a year apiece, reveals Drinker as a modest and willing instrument of Wood's policies. Far more than Grenville Clark, who headed the businessmen's side of the training camp movement after 1915, Drinker became genuinely close to the general.

[88]See Benton to Wood, November 18, 1913; and Greene to Wood, October 1, 1913, Wood MSS.

[89]In the Western Department, for example, "All universities, colleges, high schools, and the principal private educational institutions west of the Mississippi River, and the leading newspapers in all cities and many towns in the States of Arizona, New Mexico, California, Nevada, Utah, Montana, Idaho, Oregon and Washington, were communicated with and several articles prepared here regarding the camp were widely published by the newspapers of the Pacific Coast. The objects and aims of the student camp movement seem to be well received generally

lected, many having been at Gettysburg and Monterey the previous summer. The camps were to begin on July 6 and end on August 7, 1914—all except Monterey which would open and close two weeks earlier because of the different California school vacations.[90]

Wood was making these preparations during a period of acute military crisis. The policy of "watchful waiting" toward Mexico which President Wilson had inaugurated in December 1913 had nearly turned into war by the following spring. Wood was due to step down as chief of staff on April 22, 1914, but just a few days prior to this date there occurred the Tampico-Veracruz incident—what one historian has termed Woodrow Wilson's "affair of honor."[91] With American marines going ashore at Veracruz in retaliation for a supposed insult to the flag, Secretary Garrison designated Wood to command the mobilization of a mixed expeditionary force of militia and regulars.[92]

The general, however, was doomed to disappointment. When he and Captain Frank R. McCoy went to the White House on April 23, carrying maps and reports, all set to discuss possible invasion plans, they were ushered out after five minutes. Wilson, with his own ideas about the use of force, was unwilling to plan for such a contingency. He thought it inappropriate and unneutral.[93] For the remainder of the spring Wood puttered around Washington, organizing a force which he would never lead into battle and pouring frustration into his diary.[94] Before long the ambassadors of the ABC powers, Argentina, Brazil, and Chile, offered to mediate, and the crisis passed. On July 10, 1914, the ex-chief of staff assumed command of the Eastern

by educational institutions, the press and prominent citizens." General Arthur Murray, "Report of Student's Military Instruction Camp, Presidio of Monterey, California, 1914," August 17, 1914, RG 94, AG2084744.

[90]Wood was following Major Herman Hall's recommendations of the previous year. Hall, "Report . . . ," RG 94, AG2023393.

[91]Robert E. Quirk, *An Affair of Honor: Woodrow Wilson and the Occupation of Veracruz* (Lexington, Ky., 1962).

[92]Hagedorn, *Leonard Wood*, 2:141.

[93]Ibid., 2:144–45.

[94]See Wood Diary, April-June 1914.

Department of the army, with headquarters at Governor's Island in New York harbor.

Wood at the time was not displeased with his new duties. He could easily have obtained assignment to the Southern Department which included Texas and most of the southwestern border, a command in which Brigadier Generals Frederick Funston and John J. Pershing were soon to see action. Wood preferred the populous East with its larger area and its unparalleled opportunities for publicity.[95] Here he could hope to have some effect on public opinion, the transformation of which was a prerequisite to any meaningful reform of defense policy.[96]

Wood and President Drinker kept busy during the summer of 1914, crisscrossing each other's paths, inspecting student regiments. Both Fort Ethan Allen and Asheville fell under the general's jurisdiction, and the former camp with 350 students was the country's largest. Wood visited both camps and again was charged with enthusiasm. The Burlington inspection came in July; his crisp diary notes record: "Student battalion in early morning. Excellent. 350 men. Appearance fully up to if not better than regular organization. Whole thing a revelation to officers concerned."[97] Similar laudatory comments were coming from Drinker at Ludington and Asheville, where at the latter camp the Lehigh president reported seeing student companies march twenty-seven miles in nine hours.[98] Perhaps the highest tribute came from the camp commander at Burlington. "If I ever had to organize and train a regiment of volunteers for war," Captain Oliver Edwards wrote, "I would at once ask for all the men I could get . . . from this year's camp."[99]

[95]Wood to Elbert F. Baldwin, January 22, 1914, Wood MSS.

[96]For Wood's attitude on army reform at this time, see Wood to George Van Horne Moseley, March 28, July 3, 1914, Moseley MSS.

[97]Wood Diary, July 30, 1914.

[98]Drinker to Wood, August 22, 1914, Wood MSS. The twenty-seven mile march was made during a rainstorm. See Preston Brown, "Report on the Students' Camp of Military Instruction, Asheville, North Carolina, 1914," August 15, 1914, RG 94, AG2084744.

[99]Edwards to Henry S. Drinker, August 12, 1914, Wood MSS.

There seems little doubt that these 1914 camps were eminently successful. The commandant at the Ludington camp reported that "of the 112 [trainees] in attendance all but 2 joined the Society of the National Reserve Corps before leaving."[100] The reports from Monterey were even better. "As to the worth of this training from the point of view of benefit to the student," General Murray wrote, "there is no dissenting opinion; nor can there be any doubt as to its great value to the government and the Nation." The "broadening" influences of the student camps "as compared with the narrowing influences of purely local ideas, associations and interests, especially in matters military, constitute an element of especial value in the National life." Murray told how the adjutant general of California had succeeded in securing state funds so that some fifty "High School Cadets" could take the course at Monterey, and urged that "if other states and the general Government will make similar provisions, the success of . . . the movement will be fully assured."[101] In his own report, Wood was uncharacteristically cautious. "The young men who have attended these camps," he wrote,

> have done so at considerable personal expense, thereby indicating their sincerity of purpose, and interest. The general character of the students has been excellent, the discipline admirable in all the camps, and the increase in attendance this year has been marked. I believe next year there will be an even greater increase. I think that after three years' successful work, we can properly ask Congress for some assistance. I believe this assistance should be given cautiously and should be limited at first to furnishing rations, and perhaps transportation . . . not to exceed ten dollars per man.[102]

If circumstances changed, then the general might act more boldly.

[100]Captain George H. Shelton to the Adjutant General, November 15, 1914, RG 94, AG2084744.

[101]Murray, "Report . . . ," August 17, 1914, ibid.

[102]Wood to Adjutant General, October 16, 1914, ibid.

FOUR

General Wood spent July 31, 1914, riding the train between Burlington and Ludington. He rated the Michigan camp as excellent, but en route had heard disturbing rumors. In Chicago these rumors were soon confirmed as fact: Germany had declared war on Russia and within a few days would be invading Belgium. Wood was back in Washington by August 5, asking Secretary Garrison to send him to Europe as a military observer.[103]

[103]Wood Diary, July 31–August 5, 1914.

II.

World War I
& Preparedness

"A general European war is unthinkable," the *New York Times* observed on July 28, 1914. "Europe can't afford such a war, and the world can't afford it, and happily the conviction is growing that such an appalling conflict is altogether beyond the realm of possibility."[1] But within a week Europe was at war, and an astonished American public watched the beginnings of a conflict so terrible and far-reaching that in three years the United States, too, would become embroiled.

ONE

With the outbreak of the war the issue of military preparedness took on new importance. What had been the almost exclusive preserve of Wood and a handful of military reformers, now became a focus of national attention. As soon as the congressional elections in November 1914 were over, Theodore Roosevelt began to attack the Wilson administration for not preparing the country militarily. Others followed Roosevelt's lead, and the debate between pacifists and preparedness advocates intensified accordingly. Books and articles, some scholarly, some sensational, came off the presses urging Americans to rearm. Reorganization of the army, reform of the National Guard, universal military training, citizens' training camps, congressional appropriations—all became part of the public debate.[2] Although few important changes occurred in the military establishment before April 1917, the logic of the preparedness movement was such that, when war came, the country accepted the need for conscription, raised an army of some five million men, and sent an expeditionary force to Europe to "make the world safe for democracy."

Because the United States did go to war in 1917, strengthening the armed forces prior to intervention should have been a natural process. American diplomacy during the neutrality years carried the risk of war, and it would have made sense to prepare for such a possibility. But preparedness was not as simple or natural as it might appear in retrospect. The political scientist Robert E. Osgood has emphasized what he calls "the vagueness of preparedness." Military reform meant different things to different people and brought up issues which were not always military in essence. Some pro-Allied extremists envisioned preparedness as a first step toward intervention; so did pacifists, who opposed such steps. Others saw preparedness primarily in terms of self-defense, a measure to preserve American neutrality. If the United States could build up its military strength, so the argument went, no European aggressor would dare attack. Rural progressives suspected sinister motives on the part of munition-makers and Wall Street bankers, while civil libertarians opposed any abandonment of the volunteer system as a bastion against militarism. Supporters of preparedness such as Wood and Roosevelt often overreacted to their critics, calling them cowards and "mollycoddles" with a deficiency of red blood. Amid all the rhetoric, the issue of making military reforms to better defend the national interest, while not lost, often became obscure.[3]

[1]As quoted in Walter Lord, *The Good Years* (New York, 1960), p. 315.

[2]The literature of preparedness, 1914–1917, is extensive. The following represent a sampling: Howard D. Wheeler, *Are We Ready?* (Boston, 1915); Theodore Roosevelt, *Fear God and Take Your Own Part* (New York, 1916); Hudson Maxim, *Defenseless America* (New York, 1915); Owen Wister, *The Pentecost of Calamity* (New York, 1915); and John B. Walker, *America Fallen!* (New York, 1916). A useful, week-by-week survey of the preparedness movement can be found in William H. Tinsley, "The American Preparedness Movement, 1913–1916" (Ph.D. diss., Stanford University, 1939).

[3]According to Osgood, "there was little in the preparedness movement or its

There were several reasons for vagueness. A realistic military policy presupposes a realistic foreign policy, and such was lacking in 1914–1917. Viewing American interests and ideals as different from those of Europe, the Wilson administration never adopted a strict *Realpolitik* approach toward the war. Notwithstanding that several of Wilson's advisers sympathized with the Allied cause, there was never a serious thought, not even in the House-Grey Memorandum of 1916, of intervening to redress the balance of power, out of fear that a German victory would endanger American security.[4] War came in 1917 over the larger issue of neutral rights—not in defense of a sharply perceived national interest. Even interventionists outside the administration like Roosevelt favored war with Germany, not because American security was threatened, but because they felt a sense of righteousness, because Belgium had been invaded, and because Americans were being murdered on the high seas.[5] Preparedness did not fit easily into such a context. If neither the administration nor pro-Allied interventionists emphasized American interests and security, military policy could only be couched in fuzzy terms. This was especially true with regard to the administration. When Wilson finally gave his backing to preparedness in the summer of 1915, both the naval and military programs which passed Congress looked toward some vague postwar threat several years hence.[6] Preparedness was a long-range proposition at best for Wilson, and he personally discouraged the General Staff from even considering plans for a European expeditionary force prior to 1917.[7]

---

opposition to enlighten the nation on the fundamental bases of American security." See Osgood, *Ideals and Self-Interest*, pp. 208–11; see also William H. Harbaugh, "Wilson, Roosevelt, and American Interventionism, 1914–1917" (Ph.D. diss., Northwestern University, 1953), p. 261.

[4]Osgood, *Ideals and Self-Interest*, chaps. 8–9.

[5]See Russell Buchanan, "Theodore Roosevelt and American Neutrality, 1914–1917," *American Historical Review* 43 (July 1938): 775–90.

[6]Walter Millis, ed., *American Military Thought* (Indianapolis, Ind., 1966), pp. 304, 311.

[7]John A. S. Grenville and George Berkeley Young, *Politics, Strategy, and American Diplomacy: Studies in Foreign Policy, 1873–1917* (New Haven, Conn., 1966), p. 335.

The climate of opinion was thus a barrier to preparedness. When the European war broke out, the initial American response was that armaments and military preparations had been a prime cause of the conflict and that this country should not follow the same path.[8] Although preparedness did become a major issue within a few months, a large majority of Americans continued to oppose any steps toward war. Advocates of preparedness were forced to justify military increases in terms of defense, not intervention. The arguments were sometimes misleading. When opponents asked what the country was preparing for, the response all too often was a lurid picture of some foreign power invading New York or San Francisco. Sensational movies like the "Battle Cry of Peace" obscured the fact that military reform could have purposes other than repelling spike-helmeted soldiers.[9] There was exaggerated talk of militarism, and William Jennings Bryan uttered his famous statement of December 1914: "The President knows that if this country needed a million men, and needed them in a day, the call would go out at sunrise and the sun would go down on a million men in arms."[10] General Wood (who knew how long it would take to train a million men) could call Bryan "an ass of the first class" and curse American ignorance of military matters, but because of the widespread aversion to war even Wood had to tailor his arguments.[11] As late as March 1917, he told a leading pacifist, "Of course I did not urge our fighting Germany. Heaven knows that none of us in the army want war because we know what it means. We realize, however, that it may be forced upon us in defense of our rights, or of humanity."[12]

[8]Tinsley, "The American Preparedness Movement," pp. 12–14, Harbaugh, "Wilson, Roosevelt, and American Interventionism," pp. 15–16.

[9]Even Wood, when he saw this film version of Hudson Maxim's *Defenseless America,* thought it had "a little too much of the melodrama" and that it should emphasize "general training and preparedness" more. Wood to J. Stuart Blackton, August 25, 1915, Wood MSS. For another soldier's reaction, see George S. Patton to Wood, February 27, 1916, Wood MSS.

[10]Quoted in Merle Curti, "Bryan and World Peace," *Smith College Studies in History* 16 (April-July 1931): 233.   [11]Wood Diary, November 9, 1914.

[12]Wood to David Starr Jordan, March 23, 1917, Wood MSS.

The fact that preparedness became involved in politics also hindered discussion. Augustus P. Gardner, a Republican congressman from Massachusetts and the son-in-law of Senator Henry Cabot Lodge, fired the first gun of the preparedness assault by declaring in October 1914: "For a dozen years I have sat here like a coward, and I have listened to men say that in time of war we could depend for our defense upon our National Guard and our Naval Militia, and I have known all of the time that it is not so."[13] Although he tried to avoid partisanship by blaming Congress as a whole for the nation's inadequate defenses, Gardner's call for a public investigation of the military and naval establishments seemed to be aimed at the Wilson administration. And when such opponents of Wilson as Lodge and Roosevelt added their voices after the November elections, suspicion of partisanship increased.[14] New preparedness organizations were being formed: the American Defense League, Army League, National Security League; and the presence of such Republicans as Henry L. Stimson, Robert Bacon, and Elihu Root on the boards of directors seemed to have political implications.[15] This was the interpretation of President Wilson, who in his annual message in December 1914 dismissed the movement: "We shall not alter our attitude toward the question of national defense because some amongst us are nervous and excited. . . . If asked, 'Are you ready to defend yourselves?' we reply, 'Most assuredly, to the utmost.' . . . Let there be no misconception. The country has been misinformed. We have not been negligent of the national defense."[16]

In point of fact, partisanship was less a motive in preparedness than Wilson thought. The majority of Republicans in Congress (and Theodore Roosevelt) did not begin to press for military reform until after the 1914 elections, suggesting perhaps that once the ballots were counted prin-

[13]U.S., Congress, House, *Congressional Record,* 63rd Cong., 2d sess., 16745–47.

[14]Harbaugh, "Wilson, Roosevelt, and American Interventionism," pp. 29–33.

[15]Tinsley, "The American Preparedness Movement," pp. 32–36.

[16]As quoted in Hagedorn, *Leonard Wood,* 2:151; see also Arthur S. Link, *Wilson: The Struggle for Neutrality, 1914–1915* (Princeton, N.J., 1960), pp. 138–40.

ciple became more important than politics. Roosevelt told Lodge that he had held back for fear of hurting the Progressives at the polls, "but that after the election I should smite the administration with a heavy hand."[17] It was the same story in 1916 when Roosevelt, returning to the Republican party, tried to commit the GOP to a strong preparedness platform. He reported to Lodge: "They all admitted, readily enough, that we must come to universal military training, but they did not think the people were ripe for it, and were afraid to risk it."[18] The final stage of the preparedness movement, the push for compulsory military training, did not come until December 1916, again after the November elections.[19] If Republicans backed preparedness for political reasons, they were noticeably reluctant during the campaigns. Then, too, there were prominent Democrats in positions of leadership in the movement, men like S. Stanwood Menken, a New York attorney and founder in December 1914 of the most powerful of all the preparedness societies, the National Security League. Although the National Security League became deeply involved in politics during and after the war, Menken served as a moderating influence prior to 1917.[20] Mayor John Purroy Mitchel of New York and Colonel Robert M. Thompson, president of the Navy League, were two other Democrats who lent their talents to preparedness causes.[21] More often than not, partisanship was secondary. General Wood was being sincere when he told a fellow officer in 1915 that "the preparedness movement around here [New York] is entirely nonpolitical."[22]

Further complicating the issue was a general lack of coordination. Preparedness organizations often worked at

[17]Roosevelt to Lodge, December 8, 1914, Roosevelt MSS, Library of Congress.

[18]Roosevelt to Lodge, June 14, 1916, as quoted in Harbaugh, "Wilson, Roosevelt, and American Interventionism," p. 161 n.

[19]For Republican strategy in 1916, see ibid., pp. 219–20.

[20]See Robert D. Ward, "The Origin and Activities of the National Security League, 1914–1919," *Mississippi Valley Historical Review* 47 (June 1960): 51–65.

[21]On Thompson, see Armin Rappaport, *The Navy League of the United States* (Detroit, 1962), p. 50.

[22]Wood to Henry T. Allen, March 16, 1915, Henry T. Allen MSS, Library of Congress.

cross-purposes, competed for funds, disagreed on strategy and tactics. Special groups like the Navy League and the Aero Club of America were not particularly interested in compulsory military training, while other groups like the Association for National Service, the Universal Military Training League, the Business Men's National Service League, the Army League, and the Military Training Camps Association became dedicated to that very object. Divergence of opinion occurred during the debates over the National Defense Act of 1916: some organizations supported the War Department's plan for a federal reserve or Continental Army; others demanded much larger military increases.[23] Although some informal coordination did take place through individual leaders prior to 1917, it was no substitute for planning. General Wood, who might have provided effective leadership, tended to encourage any and all efforts at preparedness, thus making it difficult to focus on a single strategy.[24] Not until February 1917 was there organized the National Committee of Patriotic Societies, a central bureau in Washington which disseminated information and tried to coordinate activities.[25]

Was there, then, little more to preparedness than "parades, flag-waving, patriotic exhortation, and fervent appeals for [national] unity?" To conclude, as Osgood does, that "by the summer of 1916 preparedness had been adopted by so many groups that it bore the aspect of a patriotic reawakening more than a rational response to some vital and practical need"[26] would be too harsh an indictment. Despite its ambiguity, lack of cohesion, and political complications, the preparedness movement did look toward necessary reforms. If preparedness advocates talked too much about foreign invasions and the defense of

[23]Harbaugh, "Wilson, Roosevelt, and American Interventionism," pp. 130–35.

[24]"You know how he [Wood] is. He endorses practically every military enterprise on general principles without much regard as to how it will affect something else." Grenville Clark to Horace C. Stebbins, December 14, 1916, Grenville Clark MSS, Dartmouth College Library.

[25]Perry, *Plattsburg Movement*, pp. 152–54.

[26]Osgood, *Ideals and Self-Interest*, p. 211.

rights (instead of interests), they spotlighted the inferiority of the American military establishment. Although Roosevelt and others were not always candid about their interventionist aims, they continually pointed out that the American military, as constituted, could not fight a war on the European scale. When opponents charged them with trying to glorify force and turn the country into an armed camp, the preparedness groups argued that it was foolish to talk of peace and disarmament in a world at war. To charges that preparedness was undemocratic and would mean an end to reform at home, they responded by pointing to the American tradition of a citizen army and contending that military service, like taxation, was an obligation of citizenship.[27] Compulsory training and service were stressed more and more as war approached, and the debates helped condition the country to conscription after April 1917. For all its vagueness the preparedness movement made the United States question its isolationist belief in invulnerability and begin thinking, however awkwardly, of the role of force in international society.

Finally, there is the question of what might have happened if preparedness had been more successful. Colonel Edward M. House noted in 1915 that if war came with Germany, "it will be because we are totally unprepared and Germany feels we are impotent." What would have occurred if the United States had had 1,000,000 trained men to commit to foreign shores when Wilson asked for war, instead of a mere 24,000? American power would have asserted itself more quickly on the Western Front, and the war might have ended a year sooner, and with fewer casualties. There is the tantalizing possibility, as preparedness advocates argued at the time, that effective military reform could have prevented American entrance into the war. If

[27]A real weakness in the position of some conservative Republicans who supported preparedness was that they opposed progressive taxation to pay for military increases. Antipreparedness leaders like William Jennings Bryan pointed to this inconsistency as evidence that the preparedness movement was undemocratic. The issue itself became obscured. See Harbaugh, "Wilson, Roosevelt, and American Interventionism," p. 149.

the United States had possessed a sizable army trained and ready in 1917, Germany might not have risked renewing unrestricted submarine warfare. As it was, the German minister of marine declared that the likelihood of early intervention by the American army was "zero, zero, zero!" Whether preparedness could have deterred Germany or not, it would have given a more realistic base to American foreign policy.[28]

TWO

It was as the founder of the training camps and champion of preparedness that General Wood became so controversial in 1914 – 1917. The military historian Russell F. Weigley has written that "because he was the kind of man he was, Leonard Wood would have infuriated [people] if he had done no more than urge that infantrymen go on carrying rifles."[29] Wood did much more than talk about infantrymen and rifles.

Unlike most Americans, the general was not shocked by the coming of war in Europe; he had expected it. "Wars do not have their origin in personal likes and dislikes," he wrote in September 1914, "but are brought about by commercial and race influences; and until competition for trade and land, and all questions of race expansion are settled, I do not believe they will pass off the field. Readiness to defend one's interests tends to preserve the peace."[30] Moreover, Wood rather admired the war. As he wrote to a friend: "I would not speak of the war in Europe as a reversion to barbarism, as it really represents the highest development of organized effort, and a most superb sacrifice for the purpose of national integrity and policy. I think it would be better to speak of it as illustrating

---

[28]As quoted in Robert H. Ferrell, *Frank B. Kellogg—Henry L. Stimson* (New York, 1963), p. 148; Diary of Edward M. House, July 14, 1915, House MSS, Yale University.

[29]Weigley, *History of the United States Army*, p. 327.

[30]Wood to Hamilton Holt, September 26, 1914, as quoted in Hagedorn, *Leonard Wood*, 2:149.

the necessity of even the most highly civilized nations resorting to war to determine great issues which cannot be settled otherwise."[31]

Underneath the general's Darwinist philosophy there was, of course, strong sentiment in favor of the Entente powers. He glumly noted the early course of the war in his diary: "gradual withdrawal of Allies. English struggling to get men and train them in a hurry. No reserves. Old Anglo-Saxon story. All that saves England today is her navy."[32] Inasmuch as the United States probably would be drawn in, Wood was determined that the country should profit from England's mistakes.

While the German army rolled toward the Marne, the general did his best to push preparedness. He asked permission to go to Europe as an observer and was refused; the president did not want senior officers leaving the country.[33] Letters asking for information flooded into Governor's Island. Wood answered all of them. Congressman Augustus P. Gardner asked for data on the army, and Wood sent it: "Our people do not appreciate the suddenness with which modern war develops. . . . Our condition is one which invites attack."[34] The general talked constantly — to visitors, club luncheons, university banquets. He talked to Theodore Roosevelt, who in November began a series of syndicated articles on national defense. Colonel Edward M. House visited Governor's Island on more than one occasion. "Lunch with Col. and Mrs. House," Wood noted in his diary on November 9, 1914,

> Says he had a very pleasant talk with the President, and that he gave him my memo on short enlistments, reserves, etc., and while he wanted to go slow he seemed to think very well of it. Col. [House] lunched with us last week, and told me that he thought Bryan thoroughly discredit[ed] among all

[31]Wood to Oliver Edwards, October 16, 1914, Wood MSS.
[32]Wood Diary, September 5, 1914.
[33]Ibid., August 5, 1914.
[34]Wood to Gardner, October 16, 1914, Wood MSS; Wood Diary, October 24, 1914.

thinking people; that he, House, has told everybody in Europe—the Kaiser, the President of France, Sir Richard Gray [*sic*]—that they must not judge the President by Bryan; that he, the President was absolutely different and would shirk no risk or responsibility if necessary to take it.[35]

The general got along well with House, but he could not share his confidence in Wilson. The president was doing nothing about preparedness; in fact, he had referred to Gardner's call for congressional hearings on the army and navy as "good mental exercise."[36]

Wood tried to get the War Department to act and urged his successor as chief of staff, General William W. Wotherspoon, to show his reports to the president. He encouraged the assistant chief of staff, General Hugh L. Scott, a friend of Wilson, to intercede at the White House. When Secretary Garrison asked his opinion on what to say in the War Department annual report, Wood wrote in his diary: "Advised him to see the President . . . to put in a full, frank statement of conditions. . . . Tell the truth. The S[ecretary] of W[ar] much afraid of the Bryan yellow crowd upsetting his work."[37]

There were individuals in the War Department who shared Wood's sentiments. Although no military mission was sent to Europe for the express purpose of observing the war, the department did become involved in an effort in early August 1914 to rescue American citizens stranded in the war zones. The leader of this relief mission, which visited Berlin, London, Vienna, and Paris, was the thirty-year-old assistant secretary of war, Henry Breckinridge. Already disposed toward preparedness, Breckinridge witnessed firsthand the German drive toward Paris and came away convinced of the need for military reforms in the United States. In a world of predators, America was the "fatted calf."[38] When Breckinridge and his professional

[35]Wood Diary, November 9, 1914.
[36]*New York Times*, October 20, 1914.
[37]October 19, 1914.
[38]Breckinridge, "Memoir" (Columbia Oral History Project), p. 183.

aide, Colonel Henry T. Allen, returned to Washington in October they tried to press their views on Wotherspoon and Garrison. Wotherspoon, who had succeeded Wood in June and was due to retire at the end of the year, had considered not even writing an annual report, but after much persuasion from Breckinridge he agreed to do so. The report, full of facts and figures, was published in December, and Breckinridge called it the "most adequate treatment of the question that any responsible official had dared put forth up until that time."[39] Wotherspoon's main conclusion was "that we cannot, with our present strength, rapidly assemble a sufficient force, fully equipped for field operations, to meet such an expedition as might be dispatched against our shores."[40]

Wotherspoon's report was important, but Wood had written four such reports as chief of staff and little had come from them. What was needed was an equally candid report from the secretary of war, and this Breckinridge tried to bring about. He told Garrison that the way to publicize military reform was not the traditional recommendations amid a hundred pages of statistics; Garrison should let the reports of the adjutant general and the chief of staff speak for themselves and write a fifteen-page statement that would be "a nugget of gold in a bin of sawdust."[41] Garrison was receptive. He accepted the need for preparedness, but worried about writing a report which might contradict the policy of the president. He knew that Wilson was preparing a message to Congress about national defense and feared it would not be strong enough. But Wilson had not asked Garrison for advice. The former New Jersey judge and the former president of Princeton did not find it easy to talk to each other. ("I was never able to understand Mr. Wilson," Garrison recalled years later. "He was the most extraordinary and complex character I

[39]Breckinridge Diary, June 16, 1915, Henry Breckinridge MSS, Library of Congress.
[40]*War Department Annual Reports, 1914* (Washington, D.C., 1914), 1:131.
[41]Breckinridge Diary, June 16, 1915.

ever encountered.")[42] So the secretary asked Colonel House for advice, saying that he feared a frank report "would be like a bomb." House told Garrison not to "pussyfoot," that it was his "absolute duty" to tell the truth.[43] The secretary proceeded to draw up his report, giving a copy to the president's secretary, Joseph Tumulty. He hoped that Wilson would either permit publication of the report prior to his own message to Congress so as to avoid having the secretary of war seem to contradict the president, or, simply, make his own message conform to Garrison's report.[44] Wilson did neither.

The president went before a joint session of Congress on December 8, 1914, and a few days later Garrison's report was published. The contrast was striking. While praising the student military training camps, Wilson's message made clear that he would not support fundamental change. The country would not rely for defense upon a standing army, not even a reserve army, but "upon a citizenry trained and accustomed to arms." It was the old American military doctrine which reached back to the Revolution of 1775. Wilson had not departed a whit from it and seemed to be anticipating an attack by the British on Nassau Hall. "More than this," the president declared, "carries with it a reversal of the whole history and character of our polity. More than this . . . would mean merely that we had lost our self possession, that we had been thrown off our balance by a war with which we have nothing to do, whose causes cannot touch us, whose very existence affords us opportunities of friendship and disinterested service which should make us ashamed of any thought of hostility or fearful preparation for trouble."[45]

The report of the secretary of war evoked a different philosophy. "Those who are thoughtful and have courage," Garrison wrote, "face the facts of life, take lessons from

---

[42]Lindley M. Garrison to Ray Stannard Baker, November 16, 1928, Ray Stannard Baker MSS, Library of Congress.

[43]Notes of an interview with Garrison, November 30, 1928, ibid.

[44]Ibid.; and Breckinridge Diary, June 16, 1915.

[45]As quoted in Link, *Wilson: The Struggle for Neutrality,* p. 139.

experience, and strive by wise conduct to attain the desirable things, and by prevision and precaution to protect and defend them when obtained. It may be truthfully said that eternal vigilance is the price which must be paid in order to obtain the desirable things of life and to defend them." Arguing that "no reasonable person in this country today has the slightest shadow of fear of military despotism," he ridiculed pacifists who "have reached the conclusion that a nation today can properly dispense with a prepared military force, and therefore . . . apply the word [militarism] to any preparation or organization of the military resources of the nation." Antipreparedness "disregards all known facts, flies in the face of all known experience, and must rest upon faith in that which has not yet been made manifest." Although Garrison limited his recommendations to building up the Regular Army to full strength and training more men for the reserve ("absolutely imperative"), the differences between him and Wilson were altogether obvious.[46]

Those persons who had been disappointed by Wilson's message took heart in the War Department report. "It is a most courageous thing for him [Garrison] to do," Lodge observed to Roosevelt, "and I have seldom seen a better or stronger argument than he has made in regard to all the humbug talk about militarism."[47] The *New York Times,* by then a convert to preparedness, gave Garrison's statement full publicity, as did other Eastern papers.[48] One of the newly formed defense groups, the American Defense League, even endorsed universal military training.[49]

General Wood construed the secretary's report as an invitation to speak openly. In a speech before the Merchants Association of New York on December 15, Wood repeated Wotherspoon's assertion that the United States

[46]*War Department Annual Reports, 1914,* 1:1–14; see also Garrison, "America Unready," *Outlook* 108 (December 30, 1914), 997–99.

[47]Lodge to Roosevelt, December 11, 1914, Roosevelt MSS.

[48]*New York Times,* December 10, 1914; and Tinsley, "The American Preparedness Movement," pp. 55–56.

[49]Ibid., pp. 56–57.

was unprepared to fight a first-class power. He quoted "Lighthorse Harry" Lee, the Revolutionary commander, who once remarked when a detachment of raw recruits came to him: "That nation is a murderer of its people which sends them unprepared to meet those mechanized and disciplined by training." Wood added that the statement "was absolutely true at that time and it is just as true today."[50] The speech elicited protests from Democrats; and Garrison, at the president's prompting, sent the general a tactful rebuke. Since certain individuals were trying to make politics out of national defense, the secretary said, and since newspapers were misrepresenting everyone's views, it would be best for Wood at present to avoid public statements.[51] Wood took the hint, although he read between the lines. A few weeks later he reported to Roosevelt: "I have been doing all I can here to interest people and have the papers call attention to preparedness. Of course, I cannot proceed beyond a certain point in my activities. Just at present it has come down to talking where there are no reporters and giving the best advice I can to those who are writing on the subject."[52]

THREE

If differences of opinion over national defense were thus becoming obvious by the end of 1914, the attitude of President Wilson remained puzzling. Not only had he given blithe assurances to Congress which were at odds with the statements of his secretary of war and chief of staff, but he also tried to suppress the contrary views of Wood and other officers. As late as January 22, 1915, the president favored cutting back military and naval expenditures for the coming fiscal year.[53] Why was he so opposed to preparedness

---

[50]Hagedorn, *Leonard Wood,* 2:151; *New York Times,* December 16, 1914.

[51]Garrison to Wood, December 16, 1914, Wood MSS. "Better let the momentum come from without."

[52]Wood to Roosevelt, December 30, 1914, ibid. "They do not want any of us officers of the Army to do any more public talking for the press at present. However, this does not prevent us talking where there are no reporters, and it is there most good is done." Wood to Roosevelt, January 8, 1915, ibid.

during 1914 and early 1915? Was he simply ignorant of defense requirements? Was he playing politics with national defense, as some of his opponents suspected? Or was his position on preparedness part of a more broadly defined policy vis-à-vis the European war?

When Colonel House approached Wilson in November 1914 and urged Wood's ideas on a Swiss-type reserve army, the president balked. He wanted nothing which might compromise American neutrality. Besides, Wilson argued, military increases would alienate organized labor and shock the country as a whole. Even if the Germans were able to win the war, he told House, they would be too exhausted "seriously to menace our country for many years to come."[54] There was no point in antagonizing anyone. Opposed to intervention, hopeful that the United States might mediate the European conflict, the president saw no need for military preparations; he feared that such moves by the administration would "destroy the calm spirit necessary to the rescue of the world from a spell of madness."[55]

Like most Americans in 1914, Wilson did not know very much about military matters. He had prejudices against militarism, but little expert knowledge. Although in his long scholarly career prior to 1910 Wilson had studied the power and responsibilities of the presidency, he had focused almost exclusively on domestic considerations. In his textbook on comparative government, *The State* (1889), he devoted a mere four pages to the functions of the State Department, and four each to the army and the navy. As one historian has put it: "Wilson . . . was not particularly interested in the problems of the Commander-in-Chief of the armed forces of the United States. Indeed it is doubtful if he ever thought much about them."[56] When he began to

---

[53]Wilson's hostility toward preparedness and his suppression of Wood and Admiral Austin M. Knight are discussed in some detail in Link, *Wilson: The Struggle for Neutrality*, pp. 141–43.

[54]Diary of Colonel Edward M. House, November 4, 1916, as quoted in Charles Seymour, *The Intimate Papers of Colonel House*, 4 vols. (Boston, 1926), 1:298.

[55]Ibid., 1:32.

[56]Edward H. Brooks, "The National Defense Policy of the Wilson Administration, 1913–1917" (Ph.D. diss., Stanford University, 1950), p. 23.

consider candidates for secretary of war in 1913, he thought in terms of a good equity lawyer, someone capable of administering the Philippines—this being, in the president-elect's mind, the central task of the War Department.[57] Wilson's choice, Lindley M. Garrison, was a man he did not know personally and never really came to know during Garrison's three years in the Cabinet. This unfamiliarity with the military, combined with a belief that morality and principle were more important than force, made the president reluctant to view international affairs in terms of power. He had, moreover, the typical Southern progressive's aversion to preparedness; he saw that the jingoes, the big navy imperialists, Eastern bankers, and big industrialists favored military increases, and his first inclination was to oppose. America's mission was to purify itself, to save European civilization from its madness. This could be done only through neutrality and mediation, not by preparing for war.[58]

There was one other ingredient: Wilson's personality. Righteous, stubborn, a person who did not find it easy to listen to advice, the president had a difficult time overcoming his prejudices. Not until the late summer of 1915 did he give support to preparedness measures, and even then his decision was more a response to diplomatic and political pressures than from a change of intellectual conviction. Individuals like Colonel House, General Scott, and Garrison's successor as secretary of war, Newton D. Baker, could influence Wilson only by not pushing too hard. Committed to preparedness, these men could remain sympathetic and loyal to the president. But other advocates whose commitments were more urgent could not understand Wilson, whose belated advocacy of preparedness seemed to smell of hypocrisy and cowardice. And when Wilson proved ready to compromise in the winter of 1915–1916, these preparedness advocates thought that he lacked prin-

[57]See Morison, *Turmoil and Tradition,* p. 176 n.
[58]See the excellent discussion of Wilson's progressive attitude in Link, *Woodrow Wilson and the Progressive Era,* pp. 180–81.

ciples. By emphasizing morality, the president enraged opponents who believed they were more righteous than he. Justified or not, this antipathy to Wilson was very real. "Why is Mr. Wilson like an hour glass?" ran one query. "The longer he runs the less sand he has left."[59] Another comment was that "Wilson is similar to the white rabbit, with the sex instinct strongly developed but unwilling to protect its young."[60] A suspicious man himself, the president aroused suspicion in others.

The lack of communication between Wilson and Garrison was symptomatic. A former federal judge from New Jersey, Garrison showed a strong sense of responsibility as secretary of war. Although loyal to Wilson, he believed it his duty to present the facts as he saw them. He was distressed by public differences between himself and the president. Using Breckinridge as a go-between, he offered to resign in early February 1915. Wilson reassured Garrison and urged him to remain, saying that his resignation would probably cost the Democrats two million votes in the next election.[61] Garrison stayed at his position for another year, but his relations with the president were never smooth. He could not play the "schoolboy" to Wilson's "schoolmaster."[62] Breckinridge later attributed the difficulty to similarities in temperament, training, and background:

> Each had spent the major part of their [*sic*] adult life in telling it to others and not being answered back. Wilson never was one to accept opposition, with much grace, whether in the academic shades of Princeton or elsewhere. For a generation he had been giving forth his polished, graceful, erudite and oracular outgivings to the passing generations of Princeton students who sat more or less agog under the spell of his charming oratory. Garrison had been telling off lawyers and litigants. He spoke without much grace but with

[59]Frederick L. Huidekoper to Wood, November 7, 1916, Wood MSS.
[60]Willard Straight to Henry P. Fletcher, February 24, 1916, Henry P. Fletcher MSS, Library of Congress.
[61]Breckinridge Diary, February 4, 1916.
[62]Interview with Garrison, November 30, 1928, Baker MSS.

complete candor and downrightness, not only on matters which pertained to his own department but on any other question of national policy. . . . [In] the Cabinet he would tread on many toes—about as many toes as there were under that table.[63]

FOUR

Wood was also a man of strong will, and no one could expect him to remain quiet for long. After his reprimand in mid-December 1914 he had lunch with Garrison and was told to confine his efforts to areas outside the public spotlight.[64] He interpreted the secretary's warning to mean avoidance of unwanted publicity. "I am stirring up interest among the better class of men in New York," Wood told a friend in January 1915, "and through them I shall hope to accomplish something. Through dinners, lunches, and meetings with men in law, business or finance, one has a chance to push things a little in a way of disseminating information about the army."[65] Continuing his close ties with President Drinker and the National Reserve Corps of the United States, Wood pressed hard for increased enrollment in the student military training camps.[66] He encouraged the formation of the National Security League, the Army League, and other preparedness organizations. And he continued to request permission to go to Europe as an observer and to urge reform in the War Department.[67]

Patience was not one of Wood's virtues, and he was convinced that the United States would be forced into war with Germany within a year.[68] Although careful not to say anything publicly, he began to consider compulsory service as the means for obtaining necessary manpower. "There is one thing . . . none of our own people understand," he

---

[63]Breckinridge, "Memoir," p. 191.   [64]Wood Diary, December 23, 1914.

[65]Wood to James G. Harbord, January 13, 1915, Harbord MSS.

[66]Wood Diary, November 18, 1914.

[67]Wood to Hugh L. Scott, January 27, 1915; Wood to Sidney Brooks, January 9, 1915, Wood MSS.

[68]See conversation recorded in Diary of Chandler P. Anderson, March 22, 1915, Anderson MSS, Library of Congress.

observed to Frederic R. Coudert, "that is, what they describe as 'conscription.' We are all 'conscripts' under the constitution, from 18 to 45 years of age. The only difference in Europe is that the responsible fighting men (in our case from 18 to 45) are thoroughly trained and ready to serve intelligently and efficiently in defense of their country; we, with a fake humanity based upon profound conceit and ignorance, send our people to war to be slaughtered like sheep."[69]

Wood suggested to military writers that they push the idea of "universal training" and a "nation in arms," perhaps a modified version of the Swiss and Australian practice of a small professional army backed by yearly classes of citizen reserves.[70] The general prevailed upon his friend Frederick L. Huidekoper, a Washington attorney and founder of the Army League, to write an updated account of Emory Upton's classic studies of American military policy. The result of Huidekoper's efforts appeared in the summer of 1915, *The Military Unpreparedness of the United States,* a book which emphasized Wood's schemes for a large citizen reserve based upon the principle of universal military obligation.[71]

Since a system of universal training could not come into existence overnight, Wood gave approval to a program which could be of use in the short run. A group of volunteers had come to Governor's Island in early February 1915 with plans for what they called the American Legion. Their idea (not to be confused with the post-1918 Legion) was to establish an unofficial reserve composed of men of military age who had had military training or possessed some other skill that would be of military benefit. The reserve was to be strictly voluntary; members would pay dues of twenty-five cents a year; and all would pledge to serve in time of war. Wood probably should have steered clear of such an extra-

[69]Wood to Coudert, January 18, 1915, Wood MSS.

[70]Wood to Hudson Maxim, February 27, 1915; Wood to Sidney Brooks, January 9, 1915, ibid.

[71]For Huidekoper, see Weigley, *Towards an American Army,* pp. 203-8.

legal organization, but it sounded too much like the Rough Riders. Already Theodore Roosevelt and his four sons had joined, as had three former secretaries of war—Jacob M. Dickinson, Luke Wright, and Henry L. Stimson. So Wood gave his assent unofficially and permitted his aide-de-camp, Captain Gordon Johnston (a former Rough Rider), to serve as adviser.[72]

At first everything went well. A public announcement in late February stimulated 20,000 enrollments the first week.[73] Editorials in the New York City area were favorable.[74] But then there arose a howl of protest from the antipreparedness ranks. Rabbi Stephen S. Wise and President Nicholas Murray Butler of Columbia denounced the American Legion.[75] There were rumors of a Republican plot, and Secretary Garrison sent an excited inquiry.[76] Bishop David H. Greer, head of the American League to Limit Armaments, telegraphed President Wilson that Wood was sponsoring an organization clearly unconstitutional: "such propaganda as that of the American Legion is subversive to the interests of democracy and a violation of the policy and tradition of the United States of America."[77] Wood tried to explain to Garrison, calling Greer's attack an "audacious misstatement." He contended that although "some effort will be made to twist this into a political move, I don't believe there is a tinge of politics connected with it." Roosevelt was only a volunteer in the Legion, not its leader, and the organization was compiling a card index instead of conducting propaganda.[78] The administration, however, decided to act. Garrison on March 11 ordered the American Legion offices removed from the Army Building on Governor's Island, where Captain John-

---

[72]Hagedorn, *Leonard Wood*, 2:155; Tinsley, "The American Preparedness Movement," pp. 100–105; *New York Times*, February 26, 1915.
[73]*New York Times*, March 1, 1915.
[74]Ibid., March 7, 1915.
[75]Tinsley, "The American Preparedness Movement," p. 103.
[76]Garrison to Wood, March 5, 1915, Wood MSS.
[77]*New York Times*, March 4, 1915.
[78]Wood to Garrison, March 4, 1915, Wood MSS.

ston had installed them, and told Wood to refrain from future involvements of this sort, however unofficial.[79] It was not a harsh reprimand, but enough to sting the general. "I did not think it inconsistent conduct in an army officer," he complained to a friend, "to support in a friendly and personal way a patriotic movement whose sole objective is the betterment of national defense."[80]

The episode marked a turning point in Wood's attitude toward preparedness and the administration. It was interesting that, two weeks before the controversy broke, Garrison had issued a general order for officers of the army to refrain "from giving out for publication any interview, statement, discussion or article on the military situation in the United States or abroad."[81] Obviously the order was aimed at Wood. In the months that followed the general would always insist that he was obeying both the letter and the spirit of Garrison's order. Being a righteous man, the general no doubt convinced himself that his conduct was a model of rectitude. He did not give out interviews for publication, nor did he speak on controversial matters when reporters were present. But he did continue to talk. He would not be silenced. Prior to the American Legion episode the preparedness movement had sputtered along. Antipreparedness groups like the Women's Peace Party and the American League to Limit Armaments had been formed specifically to combat military propaganda, and President Wilson had thwarted any action by Congress or the War Department. The American Legion, too, was a failure, but it had demonstrated to Wood that certain elements in the New York area were eager to do something. If a sudden change should occur in the general American attitude toward the European war and toward preparedness, Wood was not about to sit back and remain silent. He might even risk his career.

[79]Garrison to Wood, March 11, 1915, ibid.

[80]Wood to James T. Williams, March 13, 1915, ibid.

[81]General Order No. 10, February 23, 1915, Hugh L. Scott MSS, Library of Congress.

FIVE

The sudden change in American attitudes took place some two months later. At a few minutes after two o'clock on the afternoon of May 7, 1915, at a point about twelve to fifteen miles off the south Irish coast near the Old Head of Kinsale, the German submarine U-20 fired a torpedo which struck "starboard side right behind bridge" of the Cunard liner *Lusitania*. An "unusually heavy detonation" followed, and within eighteen minutes the huge vessel had sunk, stern-first. Of 1,959 passengers and crewmen on board, 1,195 were drowned, including 94 children. One hundred and twenty-four of the victims were American.[82]

A country that had not seen any close connection between itself and the war across the Atlantic became indignant overnight. Newspaper headlines blazing with horror and outrage greeted Americans on the morning of May 8. Theodore Roosevelt let it be known that "this represents not merely piracy but piracy on a vaster scale of murder than the old-time pirates ever practised."[83] A few voices urged an immediate declaration of war against Germany; nearly everyone could agree with the *New York Times* that "there must go to the Imperial Government at Berlin a demand that the Germans shall no longer make war like savages drunk with blood." As the *Literary Digest* put it: "Condemnation of the act seems to be limited only by the restrictions of the English language."[84]

According to the historian Arthur S. Link, "the sinking of the *Lusitania* had a more jolting effect upon American opinion than any other single event of the World War.... [It] was their first real introduction to total war—to war as much against civilians as against armed forces, against women and children as well as men."[85] It did not mean a declaration of war, because, as former

[82]Millis, *Road to War*, pp. 162–70.
[83]As quoted in Harbaugh, "Wilson, Roosevelt, and American Interventionism," p. 65.
[84]*Literary Digest* (May 15, 1915), p. 1135.
[85]Link, *Wilson: The Struggle for Neutrality*, p. 372.

President Taft argued, "war that . . . will not endure the test of delay and deliberation by all people is not one that should be yielded to."[86] But the series of stiff diplomatic notes that President Wilson subsequently sent to Berlin carried the danger of war. Segments of public opinion that had been hostile or indifferent to military preparations, such as organized labor, clergymen, rural and small town areas, now supported Wilson's demand that Germany put an end to unrestricted submarine warfare. For the first time preparedness became a popular issue outside the anglophile, upperclass Northeast.[87]

[86]As quoted in Harbaugh, "Wilson, Roosevelt, and American Interventionism," p. 68.
[87]Ibid., pp. 64–69.

III.

Plattsburg &
'Our Kind of People'

Grenville Clark and Elihu Root, Jr., partners in a small Manhattan law firm, had scheduled a round of golf for Sunday, May 9, 1915. But news of the *Lusitania* left them "too angry and horror stricken to play." The two men spent the morning in the St. Andrews clubhouse talking. "Mr. Clark," Root remembered, "felt that inaction was intolerable."[1] That afternoon Clark returned to his office on 31 Nassau Street where he found J. Lloyd Derby, a young associate in the firm.[2] Clark felt that "the opportunity was present for some concerted effort to combine the young men of the country in a new movement for greater unity and a firmer national policy." Clark later recalled that "as a first step and in order to form a small nucleus" he and Derby decided to ask a number of their friends to send a telegram to President Wilson "expressing their views and to consider later what more definite steps could be taken."[3]

Clark drafted a statement during the evening. Next morning he showed it to Root, Derby, and twelve other lawyers and professional men who had gathered in their downtown office. Approval was unanimous, and young Theodore Roosevelt, Jr., became the first to affix his signature.[4] That day, May 10, the following telegram was sent to the White House:

> The undersigned citizens of New York express their conviction that national interest and honor imperatively require adequate measures both to secure reparations for past viola-

tions by Germany of American rights and secure guarantees against future violations. We further express the conviction that the considered judgment of the nation will firmly support the government in any measures, however serious, to secure full reparations and guarantees.

The wire appeared in the New York press and aroused considerable comment.

The original fifteen then telephoned fifty more like-minded acquaintances and invited them to a luncheon the following afternoon at the Harvard Club "to talk over the *Lusitania*." They stipulated that "in case of hesitation the invited person should in no way be urged to come," thus assuring "a very representative and earnest group." A few days later there was a larger meeting, called in a similar manner, which resulted in the formation of a Committee of 100.[5] Modeling itself on the Union League Club of the Civil War period, the new movement intended, as Clark put it, "to get a crowd together so as to be in touch in case anything comes up and to educate ourselves, and . . . the public, to the international issues and our duties with respect thereto."[6] But this was a vague purpose. The hot-blooded New Yorkers preferred action to talk. Clark, Roosevelt, and Philip Carroll were designated to prepare a more definite program.

It was late May before the trio hit on an idea. The previous autumn Clark had talked of forming a small military reserve corps composed of young businessmen and lawyers, but had dropped the project when little interest

[1]Elihu Root, Jr., "The Showing Up of Grenny Clark," *Weekly Bulletin* (of the firm Root, Clark, Buckner, and Howland), Vol. 2, no. 1 (March 12, 1921), photocopy in the Grenville Clark MSS.

[2]Derby's older brother, Richard, had married Theodore Roosevelt's daughter Ethel.

[3]"The Plattsburg Camps," undated (probably ca. 1920) notes in Clark's handwriting, Clark MSS.

[4]The fifteen signers were Elihu Root, Jr., Cornelius W. Wickersham, Devereux Milburn, John G. Milburn, Jr., Hamilton Fish, Jr., George S. Hornblower, A. Perry Osborn, Theodore Roosevelt, Jr., Richard Derby, J. Lloyd Derby, Crawford Blagden, Arthur C. Blagden, Robert Low Bacon, Philip A. Carroll, and Grenville Clark.

[5]"The Plattsburg Camps," notes in Clark MSS.

[6]Clark to DeLancey K. Jay, May 29, 1915, ibid.

developed.[7] Then, after the *Lusitania,* he happened to read an article about the military instruction camp for college students, scheduled that summer for Plattsburg, New York. Perhaps this was what they were looking for—if these camps could be adapted for men his own age, men in their late twenties and thirties. Clark talked to Roosevelt and Carroll and found them both enthusiastic. What did General Wood think? Carroll took the ferry over to Governor's Island, and the general proved cooperative. If as many as a hundred professional and businessmen signed up for such a camp, he would provide the officers and equipment.[8] No one realized what was about to begin.

ONE

A training camp for older men was not entirely a new idea for Wood. Just a month earlier one of his former staff officers, Captain Harry S. Howland, had reported from San Francisco that several men there between the ages of thirty and forty wanted to attend the student camp at the Presidio during June and July. Howland thought the proposal excellent and suggested that the camps be broadened to include both the students and the older men.[9] Indeed, there were a few persons past college age who had marched and fired rifles with the students in 1913 and 1914.[10] Although

[7]Clark to Theodore Roosevelt, November 19, 1914, Roosevelt MSS. In many instances, this seven-page letter is a remarkable forecast of how the Plattsburg camps would develop. In proposing a "reserve corps" to Roosevelt, Clark talked about men twenty-five to thirty-five years of age taking cavalry drills twice a week, rifle practice, "a reasonable amount of book study. . . . I would also have a short expedition into the country for possibly a week each year. . . . The plan would have in mind two general objects—first, actually to give . . . some sort of familiarity with military matters, so that [the men] would be of some . . . use in any emergency; second, to furnish as example by showing that some of us, at least, recognize the lack of preparedness of the country for any emergency and our willingness to take some protective step . . . to remedy the situation." There does not appear to have been any written reply by Roosevelt to Clark's plan; presumably, any response was oral. See also Henry S. Hooker, "National Defense Has Made Great Advance from 1914 to 1916," *Rangefinder* (August 8, 1916), copy in Clark MSS.

[8]Interview with Gordon Johnston (ca. 1928–1929), Hermann Hagedorn MSS; Clark to Jack C. Lane, March 19, 1963, Clark MSS.

[9]Howland to Wood, April 11, 1915, Wood MSS.

[10]For example, at the Ludington camp in 1914, there were two trainees

these had been isolated cases, the logic of extending the program must have occurred to Wood prior to the spring of 1915.[11] It remained only for some energetic group to prod him into action.

Nor was it mere coincidence that the young New Yorkers should do the prodding. "The center of the movement," one of these men remembered, was the stately old Harvard Club on West 44th Street.[12] It was here that Clark and his friends held their first meetings; and it was here that Wood had been coming two or three times a week since assuming command of the Eastern Department the previous summer. Wood liked the Harvard Club. He could have lunch, relax, sit down and talk with lawyers, bankers, and other civilians who shared his views; here he could free himself of Secretary Garrison's constraints on public speaking and discuss preparedness with all the frankness at his command.

Along with President Lowell and Assistant Secretary of the Navy Franklin D. Roosevelt, Wood had given a formal talk to a gathering of five hundred on January 29, 1915, and had remarked at the time to Langdon Marvin, secretary of the Harvard Club, that he wished to speak more intimately to a select group of fifty or sixty. Marvin arranged a dinner for February 18, attended by Clark, Theodore Roosevelt, Jr., and several others who later signed the *Lusitania* telegram. The discussion must have been a fierce one, with allusions to past and present blunders and hard talk about a citizen's military obligation in a democracy. As Marvin remembered years afterward, it was Wood's strictures about personal service and personal preparedness which started his friends to thinking about a Business Men's Camp.[13]

---

twenty-eight years of age and three who were twenty-six. Report of Captain George H. Shelton, November 15, 1914, RG 94, AG2084744.

[11]A. L. Boyce, one of the first Plattsburgers, later recalled a conversation with Wood in the fall of 1914 when the idea of an older men's camp was, supposedly, first brought up. See Boyce to Wood, July 17, 1918, Wood MSS.

[12]Langdon P. Marvin, "Memoir" (Columbia Oral History Project), pp. 31–32.

[13]Notes of interview with Langdon P. Marvin, March 8, 1930, Hermann Hagedorn MSS; see also Marvin to Wood, February 19, 1915, Wood MSS.

The general made disciples at the Harvard Club, and it is not difficult to understand why. These were young men, newly established in the law and other downtown professions, sons of men Wood had known for years. In a time when certainty and conviction were attributes of the educated, these university graduates looked upon such things as "right" and "duty" as tangible imperatives. Their background and sympathies were with the Allies. Philip Carroll and Richard Derby had been in France when the war began, and each had spent several months driving ambulances and working in the hospital service. Robert L. Bacon's father, former secretary of state and ambassador to France, Robert Bacon, was in Paris as director of the American Field and Hospital Service, an outspoken advocate of American intervention on the side of the Allies. There was also a physical appeal. Men like Hamilton Fish and Crawford Blagden, two of Harvard's most famous All-American linemen in recent years, could not help being stirred by the repeated comparisons of General Wood (an old football player himself) between athletic and military training.[14] Preparedness meant more than armaments and patriotic propaganda. To Wood and most of these younger men, it became a kind of moral reawakening, a demonstration of national service. There was no doubt as to the acknowledged leader. In military matters, even the Roosevelt tribe looked as much to Governor's Island as they did to Oyster Bay.

The *Lusitania* incident brought everything to a crisis. Though never as vociferous an interventionist as Theodore Roosevelt, Wood could have gone to war out of sheer outrage. "Rotten spirit in *Lusitania* matter," he told his diary on May 11, "yellow spirit everywhere in spots."[15] To make matters worse, there was an announcement that same day from Washington that all preparations were to be suspended for the forthcoming student camps. Wood ex-

[14]The number of outstanding sportsmen who went to Plattsburg in 1915 was one of the distinguishing features of the camp, as well as a commentary on the nature of athletics in the United States at this time.

[15]May 11, 1915.

ploded. Phoning and telegraphing General Bliss, he learned that the cancellation order originated in the Treasury Department where the comptroller arbitrarily had cut off appropriations without consulting the General Staff. Wood urged that the army hold these camps outside government reservations and said that he would undertake to raise money from private sources. (In the next few days both Theodore Roosevelt and financier Martin L. Schiff offered substantial contributions.)[16] Bliss told his former chief not to worry, tracked down what had happened, and saw that the camps were restored.[17] But bureaucracy being what it was, the rectification process took several weeks, during which time Wood fumed and muttered about conspiracies.[18]

In such a context, the timing of the Business Men's Camp was fortunate, since it could serve as an outlet for Wood's frustration. Enrollment had begun the last week in May, but it was going slowly with only twenty-five applications in the first two weeks. Then Wood spoke at the Harvard Club on the evening of June 14. Word had spread through professional and alumni associations, and over a thousand persons were crammed inside. "Great crowd," the general noted in his diary, "From all parts. Great interest in summer camps. Older type."[19] Wood explained fully the plan of operation, what four weeks of training would entail, why each man should avail himself of the opportunity.

[16]Schiff to Wood, May 13, 1915; Roosevelt to Wood, May 24, 1915, Wood MSS.

[17]The comptroller's decision was based on the fact that "camps of military instruction," as defined in War Department regulations, and under which the 1913 and 1914 camps had been authorized, specifically referred only to participation by the Regular Army. Any expenses which could be traced in the slightest way to the presence of students would be disallowed. As it was, the General Staff and the Judge Advocate General worked out a compromise whereby the 1915 camps could be held without any extra appropriations—a kind of "gentleman's agreement." Hence, it became a central object of both the War Department and the training camp movement to secure explicit recognition of these camps in the 1915–1916 Congress. See memorandum for the Adjutant General, March 13, 1915, RG 94, AG2237428; Tasker Bliss to Wood, May 13, 1915; George E. Downey to Lindley Garrison (copy), June 5, 1915; and Wood to Garrison, June 26, 1915, Wood MSS.

[18]Wood's relations with Secretary Garrison at this time had degenerated to the point where Garrison was sending back correspondence because Wood's aide had inadvertently misspelled the secretary's name; see Wood Diary, May 29, 1915.

[19]Ibid., June 14, 1915.

He finished his address with a subtle touch, by quoting from President Wilson's message to Congress the previous December. "We must depend in every time of national peril," the president had said, ". . . not upon a standing army, nor yet upon a reserve army, but upon a citizenry trained to arms. It will be right enough, right American policy, based upon our accustomed principles and practices, to provide a system by which every citizen who will volunteer for the training may be made familiar with the use of modern arms, the rudiments of drill and maneuver, and the maintenance and sanitation of camps."[20] Wood, by this late date, privately scorned the volunteer system, but he was not averse to paying lip service—especially when the administration had not yet authorized camps for older men. The packed audience responded enthusiastically, and each man received an application blank.

The June 14 meeting was a turning point. Wood found the response so gratifying that he decided to hold a separate training camp for businessmen, to take place after the student course, from August 8 to September 6.[21] He directed his aides, Captains Halstead Dorey and Gordon Johnston, to work full time with the civilians on enrollment; Dorey and Johnston were to be commander and adjutant, respectively, at the Plattsburg camp. General John F. O'Ryan, commander of the New York National Guard division, gave his immediate and unqualified endorsement.[22] In the next few weeks Wood and his officers spoke to groups in Boston, Baltimore, Philadelphia, and Chicago. Everywhere prominent men turned out. "We have really got a movement started here," the general informed Captain Frank R. McCoy. "We had a big crowd in Baltimore. Redmond Stewart is head of the movement there and W. J. Clothier and a lot of other good men in Philadelphia,

[20]*New York Times,* June 30, 1915. See also Perry, *Plattsburg Movement,* pp. 28–29.
[21]Wood to Philip Carroll, June 17, 1915, Wood MSS.
[22]O'Ryan's statement, dated June 17, 1915, was displayed prominently in the various circulars which the enrollment committees sent to prospective trainees. It was an early attempt to prevent controversy between the training camp idea and the militia system. There are several such circulars in the Clark MSS. See also RG 94, AG2310060.

[George R.] Fearing in Boston . . . and a number of other good men at the Harvard Club here."[23] Less restrained, Captain Johnston told McCoy that "the General is the hero of the hour and the whole country is looking to him."[24]

Wood secured authorization for the Business Men's camp under War Department General Order 38, June 22, 1915. This order was actually intended to provide for that summer's five college camps, but neither Secretary Garrison nor General Scott raised any objection. Wood also received a three thousand dollar check to cover extra expenses from Bernard M. Baruch, the Wall Street financier and friend of President Wilson.[25] Thirty dollars from each trainee would cover the cost of food and equipment.

The program thus launched, the commander of the Eastern Department left to spend the latter part of July and early August at the Plattsburg Barracks. There he kept an eye on the student camp, talked with visitors, and made an occasional speech. He could even relax and do a little fishing in the Saranac River just south of Plattsburg. Leonard, Jr., was taking the student course, and it pleased Wood when the boy made marksman rank.[26]

TWO

If Wood seemed to dominate the proceedings in 1915, it was because he was Leonard Wood. He did not do it all by himself. Working quietly behind the scenes, doing the little things while the general attracted crowds, the civilian organizers were giving the Plattsburg venture a style and coloring which was as much theirs as his. The leader of this group was still Grenville Clark, a man like Wood in some ways, unlike him in others.

Clark was thirty-two years old in 1915, a sturdy six-footer with a handsome, square-jaw New England face marred only by a slight birthmark above the left eye. Al-

[23]Wood to McCoy, July 9, 1915, Wood MSS.
[24]Johnston to McCoy, June 19, 1915, McCoy MSS.
[25]Wood to Baruch, June 29, 1915, Wood MSS.
[26]Wood Diary, August 8, 1915.

ready he was beginning to show qualities that would make him one of the most extraordinary Americans of the twentieth century. Born to wealth and social standing, he was a member of Harvard's Class of 1903 and had graduated from the Law School in 1906. Like many in this Harvard generation, he had been impressed by President Charles W. Eliot's urging of university-trained men to involve themselves in public service whether or not they held public office. All his life Clark heeded this advice, beginning in 1912 as a Bull Moose progressive and ending in the 1950s and 1960s as an articulate proponent of world peace and world federalism. A hard worker, he and Harvard classmates Francis W. Bird and Elihu Root, Jr., set up a small law office in 1909, which grew a few years later into the firm Root, Clark, Buckner, and Howland.[27] The law absorbed Clark during these early years, but not so much that he was unable to strike up a wide acquaintance among fellow lawyers, keep in touch with Harvard affairs, and inform himself on public issues. When it came time to recruit an organization following the *Lusitania* disaster, he knew just the right people.

Heir to a banking and railroad fortune, married to the former Fanny Dwight of Boston, a member of the ultraexclusive Porcellian and Somerset clubs, Clark moved in a rarified atmosphere. Most of his friends were part of the same aristocracy, sons of illustrious fathers. Philip Carroll, a Harvard classmate of Clark, was descended from the Carrolls of Carrollton. The individual who was to be Clark's closest collaborator in training camp matters was

[27]Emory R. Buckner and Silas Howland became partners in 1913, and after retiring from the Senate in 1916 Elihu Root, Sr., assumed the position of counselor. Over the years the firm would grow into one of the largest and most respected in the country, especially noted for the number of excellent young lawyers who were trained and then sent on to other positions. For example, Robert P. Patterson, later President Truman's secretary of war, was an associate at Root, Clark in 1915, as was Supreme Court Justice John M. Harlan in the 1920s; see the biography by Martin Mayer, *Emory R. Buckner* (New York, 1968). As for Grenville Clark, there has been little of importance published about him. He had a passion for anonymity. See "Grenville Clark: Statesman Incognito," *Fortune* 30 (March 1946): 110–15; and Irving Dilliard, "Grenville Clark: Public Citizen," *American Scholar* 33 (Winter 1963–1964): 97–104.

DeLancey K. Jay, a direct descendant of John Jay on his father's side and of John Jacob Astor on his mother's. Indeed, newspapers made much of this aristocratic background when the Plattsburg camp opened in August 1915, often giving the impression that these were merely millionaires out for a summer's lark. General Wood's biographer later wrote that "the butterflies of Newport and Bar Harbor complained that life was desolate, since the best of their young men were at Plattsburg"—a statement which Walter Millis quoted with appropriate sarcasm in his book *Road to War* and which has typecast the Plattsburg movement for historians ever since.[28]

But even if the civilian organizers were blue-bloods, even if Clark could boast to a friend that "the whole table at Delmonico's" had enrolled in the training course, the Plattsburgers were not aristocrats in the usual invidious sense.[29] The idea in Clark's mind was that the Business Men's Camp should be a demonstration by "our kind of people" that they were willing to do something personally about military preparedness.[30] In the beginning stages of the movement during late May and early June, the enrollment committee took care to contact only those persons most likely to cooperate actively. Clark traveled to Boston in June and persuaded fellow Harvard men John W. Farley and Benjamin Joy to organize recruitment along lines similar to New York.[31] When Wood expanded the movement with his June 14 address at the Harvard Club and subsequent speeches in other cities, he was building on a foundation already provided by the civilians. In mid-June the enrollment committee set up a make-shift recruiting bureau in the law office of William W. Hoffman at 15 Broad Street, where thousands of circulars and application blanks were mailed out to alumni lists, colleges, and professional

[28]Millis, *Road to War,* p. 210; Hagedorn, *Leonard Wood*, 2:160. For a recent view, see Francis Russell, "Plattsburg: The Camp by the Lake" in *The Great Interlude* (Boston, 1964), chapt. 1.
[29]Clark to Jay, May 29, 1915, Clark MSS.
[30]Ibid.
[31]Clark to Jay, July 10, 1915, ibid.

organizations.[32] Coordinating this work with the efforts of Wood and his staff on Governor's Island, the organizers were pleasantly surprised that by the second week in July between fifty and one hundred enrollment cards were pouring in daily.[33]

At this juncture, with less than a month before camp opened, Clark and his friends were encouraged to extend the movement to areas outside the anglophile Eastern seaboard. Recruitment continued to be selective. The *New York Times* ran an advertisement in the sports section appealing for Southern representation; bulletins went out to colleges and college graduates in the Southern states.[34] Roger Derby, brother of Lloyd Derby and a resident of North Carolina, promised to enlist a contingent from his region. And it was at this time that Philip Carroll went to Savannah on business, visiting and exhorting old acquaintances along the way. "Personal touch with the active men. That is the secret of the whole business," Clark told DeLancey ("Lanny") Jay as the latter prepared for an even more ambitious trip to the Midwest.[35] Armed with introductions to "the best & most desirable men," Jay undertook a three-day tour of Chicago, Cleveland, and Buffalo.[36] His object in Chicago was to explain Plattsburg to a small group of civic leaders and arrange for them to invite General Wood to deliver a speech. Jay succeeded. "It rather reminded me of poking a stick into an ant heap," he told his mother.[37] A few days later, July 21, Wood "made a straight

[32]These circulars contained a wealth of information: transportation routes, what equipment to buy, where to buy it, the cost, books to read in preparation for the training course, where to buy them, where to get a typhoid innoculation, a short description of the course, suggestions for members of the militia. There are a number of these bulletins and circulars in both the Wood and Clark MSS. In the Clark collection is one such circular with the notation in Clark's hand that this was the first and was "composed by Carroll, Roosevelt, Clark & Capt. Dorey after dinner at Carroll's room at Ritz Carlton early in June, 1915."

[33]Wood Diary, July 7–15, 1915.

[34]July 9, 1915.

[35]Clark to Jay, July 10, 1915, Jay Box, Clark MSS.

[36]W. W. Hoffman to Jay, July 14, 1915, ibid. See also Willard Straight to Clark, July 13; and David A. Goodrich to Jay, July 13—both these letters contain addresses and letters of introduction, ibid.

[37]Jay to Mrs. Augustus Jay, July 21, 1915, ibid. See also Jay to Gordon Johnston, July 16, 1915, ibid.

talk" to the Chicagoans "on preparedness, sane system, etc."[38] As a result, some fifty Midwesterners signed up for Plattsburg.

The surge in enrollment during July to more than a thousand persons precipitated a minor crisis in policy. Jay came back from Chicago eager to press a full-scale publicity campaign which he hoped would double or even triple the number of trainees in the remaining two weeks. Already he had suggested to Clark a friend of his, a public relations expert, who could write glowing newspaper articles and plan full-page advertisements for national magazines. Clark demurred. Some publicity had been inevitable, and stories such as Jay described were appearing in certain Eastern papers whose editors were sympathetic to the venture — the *New York Times, New York Sun, Philadelphia Public Ledger, Boston Herald, Boston Transcript.* "Experience shows," Clark said, that "the men who respond to such publicity . . . are not the type we want primarily to get, but [are] men of a type who want a cheap summer vacation." He had conferred with some of the other organizers and the consensus was to "keep the standard pretty high this first year so that we can form a homogeneous and compact organization to carry on the work another year." Too many recruits might complicate the army's training plans, and it was "very important not to have anyone disappointed in the quality of instruction he gets." Clark promised that "next year . . . we can loosen up and have all the publicity we can get."[39]

And so the policy of selective recruitment continued until the opening of camp in August. Of course, not all the men who went to Plattsburg in 1915 were millionaires or listed in the Social Register.[40] Far from it. Nonetheless, the

[38]Wood Diary, July 21, 1915.

[39]Clark to Jay, July 20, 1915, Clark MSS. For a representative sampling of pre-camp publicity in 1915, see Wood Scrapbooks, July-August 1915, Wood MSS.

[40]In an impressionistic examination of the descriptive cards of the 1915 trainees, located in the adjutant general's files in the National Archives, I was able to get a fair idea of the composition of camp personnel. Each of the 1,200-plus cards has the trainee's age, weight, height, residence, schooling, previous military experience, and remarks by his commanding officer. As evidenced by these cards and various printed rosters, probably less than 10 percent were men of national reputation; however, more than 90 percent were college graduates. Geographical-

lack of publicity and the requirement that each trainee pay his expenses meant a minimum of wage earners taking the course.[41] The men who went wanted to go and could afford to go. And there were enough individuals of national reputation to give the kind of impression that Clark desired. "I doubt," Wood wrote in his formal report to the adjutant general, "if there was ever assembled in a camp of instruction in this country as highly intelligent body of men or one more thoroughly representative of all that is best in our citizenry."[42]

In some ways this high quality of personnel made Plattsburg the success it became. Former Secretary of State Bacon was an applicant, all of fifty-five years old but in excellent physical condition. He had sent a wire to Wood just after the *Lusitania* disaster, offering his services in whatever capacity the general desired. Bacon returned from France early in the summer to preach preparedness and help his son enlist friends for Plattsburg. The one-time member of Theodore Roosevelt's Tennis Cabinet later told a newspaperman that his presence in camp represented "a protest . . . against the state of unpreparedness in this country."[43] Wood also found his former chief, Henry L. Stimson, "very warlike" that summer.[44] Stimson would have dearly loved to go to Plattsburg, but his attendance was required at the State Constitutional Convention in Albany through September. The former secretary of war did persuade his law partner, Bronson Winthrop, and his close

---

ly, the great majority of trainees came from the Northeast. The roster of Company G, a copy of which is in the Clark MSS, lists 137 of 148 company members as college graduates. From this sketchy record it would appear that although Plattsburg may not have been the exclusive "rich man's camp" pictured by some critics in 1915, it was still a fairly uniform collection of elites. Moreover, the large number of famous individuals who took the training gave this representation a symbolic value which is not easily measured. RG 94, AG2310061.

[41]There were rumors that the Philadelphia enrollment committee was actively discouraging applications from persons of more humble origin. Henry S. Drinker to Wood, August 10, 1915, Wood MSS.

[42]Wood, "Report on Military Instruction Camp," November 16, 1915, RG 94, AG2310060.

[43]James Brown Scott, *Robert Bacon: Life and Letters* (Garden City, N.Y., 1923), pp. 239–40; *New York Times*, August 12, 1915; Bacon to Wood (telegram), May 12, 1915, Wood MSS.

[44]Wood Diary, July 11, 1915.

friend, George Wharton Pepper, future United States Senator from Pennsylvania, to enroll. Both recruits were close to fifty.[45] Other earnest volunteers included Ralph Barton Perry, professor of philosophy at Harvard; Robert M. McElroy, the Princeton historian; Thomas W. Miller, a twenty-nine-year-old congressman from Delaware; Richard Harding Davis, war correspondent and old friend of Wood from Cuban days; Joseph Whitney Ganson, a wounded veteran of the French Foreign Legion; Police Commissioner Arthur Woods and forty of New York's finest; Henry H. Curran, New York alderman; Dudley Field Malone, collector of the Port of New York; Ralph W. Page, son of the ambassador to England; Henry James II, nephew of the novelist; former Rough Riders like Arthur F. Cosby and Frank Crowninshield; and Willard Straight, the youthful diplomat whose "dollar diplomacy" schemes had marked American policy in the Far East during the Taft administration. The involvement of Straight, then working for J. P. Morgan and Company in New York, was especially fortunate. Not only did this brilliant and engaging person have extensive contacts with the government and business communities, but it was he and his wife who had put up the money for the *New Republic* when that journal commenced publication in 1914. Close to editor Herbert Croly, Straight helped insure a favorable response to Plattsburg in Progressive intellectual circles.[46]

A prime example of Plattsburg's elitism in 1915 was the recruitment of a special "Motor Machine Gun" battery. The

[45]Stimson to Wood, July 26, August 25, 1915, Wood MSS; Winthrop to Wood, July 31, 1915, Wood MSS; Pepper, *Philadelphia Lawyer: An Autobiography* (Philadelphia, 1944), pp. 110 – 12.

[46]On Straight, see Herbert Croly's biography, *Willard Straight* (New York, 1924), and Charles Forcey, *The Crossroads of Liberalism* (New York, 1961), pp. 245-50. Before Straight married Dorothy Whitney, daughter of the railroad tycoon William C. Whitney, he had shared a bachelor's apartment in Washington with a number of intelligent and active young men, among them fellow diplomats Henry P. Fletcher and William Phillips, Frank R. McCoy, Wood's longtime aide, and future Plattsburgers Basil Miles and Roger Derby. Through McCoy, Straight was particularly friendly with Captains Dorey and Johnston, Wood's aides in 1915. McCoy's papers in the Library of Congress are a good source for Straight's role and the attitude of his friends. The Straight MSS in the archives of Cornell University, Ithaca, New York, are not complete for 1915.

organizers of this enterprise were Roger Derby, Raynal C. Bolling, and Harold B. Clark, all Harvard graduates in their early thirties. General Solicitor for the United States Steel Corporation and a former officer in the New York National Guard, Bolling took the lead in recruiting men and procuring cars and drivers from the automobile companies.[47] All told, the battery consisted of some seventy men, fifteen motorcycles, cars, and trucks of varying types, including one "superdreadnaught" which weighed eight tons fully loaded. Several of the vehicles carried armor-plating with machine gun mounts. The expenses, which Bolling and his men paid themselves, ran to nearly $5,000.[48] Personnel was very much a class affair, with eight to ten men being enrolled from each of several locales so as to "spread the idea."[49] From the New York area several of the original businessmen's group joined up: Philip Carroll, Elihu Root, Jr., Langdon P. Marvin, John G. Milburn, Jr. "All the best families seem to have been drafted into a machine gun platoon," one New Yorker wrote. "Socially, it is already a tremendous success, as people like myself are already going around apologizing for not being there. It remains to be seen what military results are coming out of it, as well as how many ancient warriors land in the hospital."[50]

Because of delays in securing equipment, the "mobile force" did not assemble in New York City until just a few days before camp was scheduled to open. Then, "loaded

[47]Bolling was an interesting person. Not only did he organize the machine gun troop in 1915, but he also arranged to have an airplane brought up to Plattsburg to participate in maneuvers. Altogether Bolling made eighty-two flights in this machine averaging about ten miles apiece. He subsequently devoted his military attentions to aviation, organizing an Aero Squadron in the New York National Guard. During the war he headed the first American air mission to France, where he was killed early in 1918, the first American officer of high rank killed in combat. Bolling was a colonel at the time of his death. See Bolling to Wood, September 14, 1915, Wood MSS; and Harvard College, *Class of 1900, Twentieth Anniversary Report* (Cambridge, Mass., 1922), pp. 57–62.

[48]Bolling to Gordon Johnston, November 22, 1915, RG 98, "Records of the Plattsburg Barracks, 1916," National Archives.

[49]Bolling, "Opportunity in Our National Defense," *Collier's* 56 (January 8, 1916): 74.

[50]George Marvin to Frank R. McCoy, August 7, 1915, McCoy MSS.

down with canned goods and all sorts of unnecessary paraphernalia," the trucks and cars took two days to reach Albany. "It was *that* mobile," Roger Derby remembered. Disgusted at such slowness, Derby, a wealthy plantation owner, suddenly decided to buy a Ford truck in Albany. (Bolling had refused to deal with the Ford company because of Henry Ford's outspoken pacifism.) Derby's purchase proved to be the swiftest of the lot—"the only mobile unit we had."[51] It still required two more days to reach Plattsburg. Nearly every bridge was too small for Bolling's eight-ton behemoth, and a three-inch gun caisson which the civilians were pulling up from New York kept coming loose on curves. Not until August 10, 1915, two days after the majority of trainees, did the grimy aristocrats finally straggle into camp.[52]

THREE

"And jeers, and cries of Bosh and Flubdub were heard in the land. And many Men of Peace there were, from the East, from the West, from the North and from the South, who waxed exceedingly sore. And they mocked the Doctrine of Peaceatanyprice. And they girded themselves as for battle and they turned their Faces toward a Place that is called Plattsburg."[53] Thus did one of the trainees write of his experience, in one of the many laudatory articles which appeared in the late summer and autumn of 1915. And there was indeed a mystique about this town of ten thousand inhabitants, the seat of New York's Clinton County.

Plattsburg had a historical setting athwart the old invasion route between Canada and the Hudson River Valley. Sixteen tiny ships under Benedict Arnold had fought an invading British flotilla to a standstill off Valcour Island,

---

[51]Roger Alden Derby, *Memoirs* (privately printed, 1959), pp. 273–74. Derby was much more enthusiastic in 1915 than he later remembered. See his "Lessons of the Plattsburg Camp," ca. Autumn 1915, newspaper clipping in Wood Scrapbooks; also Derby to Wood, October 7, 1915, Wood MSS.

[52]*New York Tribune*, August 10, 1915.

[53]H. D. Wheeler, "Plattsburg—Will It Work?" *Harper's Weekly* 61 (September 11, 1915): 248.

five miles from the site of Plattsburg, in the autumn of 1776. The area was again the scene of a combined land and naval engagement during the late summer of 1814 when a squadron of vessels under Master Commandant Thomas Macdonough routed a numerically superior British foe and sent them scurrying back toward Montreal. This was one of the few American victories in the War of 1812. The following year a regular army post was established, the Plattsburg Barracks. Some two miles south of town along the state road to Albany, the military reservation covered seven hundred acres and was usually garrisoned by a regiment of infantry. As chief of staff in 1914, General Wood had converted the post into a special training school for regular recruits.

It was an ideal spot for a civilian training camp. One hundred and fifty miles north of Albany, Plattsburg was accessible via rail and auto, with ferries running daily from Burlington and other points on Lake Champlain. Water was plentiful, and the surrounding countryside sparsely settled. The town was modern enough, carried metropolitan newspapers, and boasted adequate tourist accommodations — including the beautiful Hotel Champlain, situated on a bluff overlooking the lake, perhaps the finest hostelry in all of northern New York. Rolling terrain and numerous streams gave variety to military maneuver, and the fact that the garrison was essentially a training post, complete with rifle range and parade grounds, made it adaptable to a large influx of rookies.

Plattsburg had not catered to civilian trainees prior to 1915, the two previous student camps in the Eastern Department having been at Gettysburg and Burlington. It appears, however, that the college boys had disturbed too many Vermont cows and chickens during their forays. The Plattsburg chamber of commerce proved more understanding, and General Wood endorsed the change of scenery.[54]

[54]See J. A. Freeman to Wood, November 13; Wood to Freeman, November 15; and M. M. Cahill to Wood, November 28, 1914, Wood MSS.

The camp which twelve hundred businessmen called home for the first two weeks of training was bounded on three sides by tall groves of oak and maple. To the east lay that part of Lake Champlain known as Cumberland Bay, its broad expanse studded with small islands of pine and rock. Patches of poison ivy notwithstanding, the lakeshore became a haven in late afternoons as bonesore, perspiring recruits tried to splash a little feeling back into their bodies before retreat. The Albany Road ran through the middle of camp, and to the west was the mile-long parade ground. Officers' quarters, mostly brick bungalows marked individually with name and rank, were located at the far side of the drill field. Two-storied enlisted men's barracks occupied an area farther north, and behind them stood the workshops and stables. At the northernmost end of the reservation, separated from the rest of the camp by a white rail fence, a large pyramid tent stood at the edge of the trees with a flagpole to the front. This was General Wood's quarters.

The TBMs—"Tired Business Men"—were allocated an area half a mile long, three hundred yards broad, between the macadam road and the lake. On ground that sloped gently toward the water the army set up sixteen parallel rows of conical tents, in lines running north to south. Each of these brown-canvas marvels housed six men, and altogether they comprised two battalions of eight companies apiece. Single tents at the southern end of the sixteen company "streets" served as headquarters for the company commanders, all Regular Army lieutenants and captains. Much larger tents to the south were used as lecture halls, and beyond them were the tarred-roof, open-sided buildings in which Sergeant Harry Schwartz, "the best bean man in the Third Artillery," and his five assistant cooks served up army mess.[55]

The civilians began to arrive on August 8, the after-

[55]For descriptions of the Plattsburg camp, see *New York Times*, August 15, 1915; and Richard Harding Davis, "The Plattsburg Idea," *Collier's* 56 (October 9, 1915): 7. See also Russell, *The Great Interlude*, pp. 13 – 15.

noon before camp officially opened. And among these early khaki-clad arrivals was a tall, good-looking young man of thirty-six named John Purroy Mitchel. Archie Roosevelt, a holdover from the college camp, greeted him at the depot and led him through the registration ritual where he paid thirty dollars and was issued a canteen, poncho, eating utensils, pup tent, and other equipment. A doctor examined him, and Mitchel, being six foot three inches, was assigned to a tent in Company B, First Battalion. There Captain John R. Kelley demonstrated how to set up an army cot. Mitchel learned quickly and was soon teaching other rookies. Photographs and articles in the next morning's city newspapers pictured the young man straddling his cot as if it were a colt, jerking hard on the side ropes to get the legs up. It all seemed very funny, because John Purroy Mitchel happened to be the mayor of New York.[56]

The presence of Mitchel guaranteed national publicity for Plattsburg, though not always the kind that Wood and the civilian organizers would have preferred. A quiet, almost shy person, Mitchel believed intensely in the preparedness issue and worked hard at being a soldier.[57] He avoided interviews and did what he could to remain anonymous. But the New York press was too enterprising. The mayor's military vacation was good copy. Whatever Mitchel did at Plattsburg, the newspapers wrote it up. New Yorkers grinned as he made his bed, chuckled at his first manual of arms, watched him fire on the rifle range. It was especially humorous in late August when Mitchel pulled rank on fellow rookie Alderman Henry H. Curran and sent Curran back to New York to represent him on urgent city

[56]*New York Tribune*, August 10, 1915. The John Purroy Mitchel MSS at the Library of Congress have scrapbooks containing hundreds of articles, cartoons, and photographs of the mayor at Plattsburg.

[57]A graduate of Columbia, Mitchel had been elected mayor in 1913 as a "fusion" candidate, a reform-minded, anti-Tammany Democrat, elected with Republican support. It is the thesis of Mitchel's scholarly biographer that the mayor's obsession with the preparedness question undermined his popular support and led to his disastrous defeat in the 1917 election. Mitchel subsequently trained as a pilot in the air service. He was killed in a freak accident during the spring of 1918. Mitchel Field on Long Island was named after him. See Edwin R. Lewinson, *John Purroy Mitchel: Boy Mayor of New York* (New York, 1965).

business.[58] Despite the fact that Mitchel did well in the training course, being made a second lieutenant at the end of camp, the press chose to stress the less serious side of his military life.[59]

This lighter side of Plattsburg did exist, since the trainees were enjoying themselves. They appreciated the incongruity of a lowly New York patrolman putting Police Commissioner Woods through his paces; they had fun watching a cavalry sergeant show polo players and steeplechasers how to curry a horse. Untutored civilians found military science utterly fascinating. A disciple of William James tried to describe what it was like to maneuver in full battle dress: "You are wearing your hump, with its various outlying parts, such as the rifle in your hand and the canteen on your hip. By bending your body until your back is parallel to the ground, you are able to simulate running. The gait as well as the contour resembles the camel's; but alas! you enjoy no such natural adaptation for packbearing, nor for the rude contact with earth that awaits you."[60] Richard Harding Davis told how exhilarating it was to watch "the editor of *Vanity Fair* [Frank Crowninshield], the Collector of the Port of New York [Dudley Field Malone], and the diplomat who made Huerta famous [former Chargé d'Affaires to Mexico, Nelson O'Shaughnessy] jump up and race to the cook tent."[61] Unhorsed cavalry recruits joked about how it was "aviation" they were learning, not "equitation."[62] Wood reported to Captain McCoy that "Regis Post [former Governor of Puerto Rico] forgot he had insomnia and had to struggle to keep awake . . . Fred Huidekoper [the military writer] almost died of solemnity. Such a thought as shaking hands when you met him in the

[58]See Curran, *From Pillar to Post* (New York, 1941), p. 192.

[59]The clippings in the Mitchel scrapbooks bear out this interpretation. Even the *New York Times* tended to dwell on the humorous and the sensational at Plattsburg.

[60]Ralph Barton Perry, "Impressions of a Plattsburg Recruit," in *The Free Man and the Soldier: Essays on the Reconciliation of Liberty and Discipline* (New York, 1916), pp. 74–75. For another professor's views, see F. J. Mather, Jr., "Rear-Rank Reflections," *Unpopular Review* 5 (January 1915): 15–25.

[61]Davis, "The Plattsburg Idea," pp. 8, 31.

[62]Alma Julia Johnston to Frank R. McCoy, September 5, 1915, McCoy MSS.

shades of the evening filled him with horror. Once I forcibly grasped his arm and said, 'Damn you, shake,' whereupon he became as immobile as an image and the lines of his face straightened. However, he survived and we still speak."[63]

The hike which occupied the last ten days of camp was the part everyone liked best. Roger Derby would never forget the "Battle of Rouse's Point" near the Canadian border (called "Souse's Point" by the TBMs because of the number of hard-drinking natives). Sitting in his Ford truck and waiting for orders, Derby had an excellent view of the businessmen, many of them with branches stuck in their hats as camouflage, attacking a position held by regular troops. "The usual method of advance of a TBM," he wrote, "was to duck his head and lope forward with a great deal of knee action, the branches weaving in the wind and making an ideal mark for the enemy. I recall one man advancing, almost bolt upright but with his head and shoulders ducked; the two branches on either side of his head waved and he looked like a bull moose coming through the under-brush." As Derby watched, he noticed a small dirt road that went around the west flank of the regulars' position and past a long red fence which ran west to east behind the regulars. He decided that if anything resembling an order to advance came his way he would charge his Ford up that dirt road. Derby cranked up the motor, and when he saw a dispatch rider waving in his direction he zoomed off. Slipping past the enemy, Derby recalled, "we parked the car in the bushes and dragged our machine gun up to a nicely concealed spot where we could sight down the trenches and open fire with blank cartridges. An officer arose in the trenches and shouted 'Get out of there!' 'Get out yourself,' I replied, 'You are all dead.' Then an umpire rode up on the other side of the fence and shouted 'Get to hell out of there with that machine gun. You're in Can-

[63]Wood to McCoy, October 1, 1915, Wood MSS. Also quoted in Hagedorn, *Leonard Wood*, 2:160–61.

ada.' "[64] The red fence happened to be the international boundary.

FOUR

Plattsburg was fun, but it was also hard work. The course of training followed the pattern of the student camps, except that it was intensified, with five weeks' work squeezed into four. The morning routine was the same: up at 5:45 with calisthenics and drill until lunchtime. Afternoons were given over to required instruction in one of the army's special arms—cavalry, signal corps, engineering, or artillery. The idea, Captain Dorey wrote, is to "start out at the very beginning to work them hard. . . . If you do this you will soon find . . . the men who expected simply a cheap vacation will find his [sic] business or family affairs are in such state as to require his withdrawing from camp."[65] Such a regimen enabled Dorey and his officers to extend the period of work "to an average of over nine hours per day per individual." According to Wood's official report, "the men covered the ground ordinarily covered by our recruits in 4 1/2 months and they received more hours of actual training than is received by the average militiaman in an enlistment of 3 years."[66]

More important, the intensive training brought real military results. Plattsburg was Wood's first opportunity to demonstrate on a large scale that civilians could be made into soldiers in relatively short periods of time. The student camps had perfected methods; now Wood and his officers had a group of trainees with enough intelligence, experience, and *élan* to test his theories.[67] With trainees who

[64]Derby, *Memoirs*, pp. 275–77.
[65]Halstead Dorey to Colonel D. A. Frederick, August 22, 1915, RG 98, "Records of the Plattsburg Barracks, 1916," National Archives.
[66]Wood, "Report on Military Instruction Camps," November 16, 1915, RG 94, AG2310060.
[67]The Plattsburgers were an experienced group, militarily. According to Wood's report to the adjutant general just prior to the opening of camp, "there are about 360 trainees who have had some kind of military service either as

had military experience acting as corporals and sergeants, the regular officers put the rookies through the schools of the soldier, squad, and company in record time. From the manual of arms (which Philip Roosevelt said was like learning to tango—you kept at it and suddenly you knew how) to the battalion-size skirmishing that took place on hike, the civilians worked hard to overcome their awkwardness. The results were more than Wood ever expected. Typical diary entries read: "men doing extremely well. . . . men as keen as can be. . . . Troops well handled. . . . Fine. Fine."[68]

This eagerness to work long hours showed that Plattsburg was a good deal more than Marie Antoinette playing milkmaid. "I have been very much surprised at the way in which the men have stood the work," Willard Straight reported. "The old fellows have been just as keen as the youngsters. . . . We have had very few lemons."[69] Straight was referring to "old fellows" past the military age, men like Bacon, Richard Harding Davis, and a sexagenarian from Boston named J. Winthrop Pickering, whose efforts gave inspiration to their juniors.[70] They "were as well disciplined as any bunch of men you ever saw," Wood told McCoy, "because they were living under a gentleman's agreement."[71] It was this seriousness of purpose which was the obverse side of Plattsburg's lightheartedness, a kind of camaraderie which infected both officers and civilians. Men who ran businesses inquired about the mess and the conduct of the quartermaster's office; the regular officers, flattered by such interest, responded with greater efforts.[72]

---

officers, non-commissioned officers or privates." This was more than one-fourth of the total enrollment. Wood to Adjutant General, August 7, 1915, RG 94, AG2310060.

[68]Wood Diary, August 13, 18, 30, September 5, 1915.

[69]Straight to Frank R. McCoy, August 21, 1915, McCoy MSS.

[70]See Pickering to Wood, September 21, 1915, Wood MSS. Also Pickering, "The Lesson of Plattsburg," *Boston Daily Advertiser,* September 21, 1915.

[71]Wood to McCoy, October 1, 1915, Wood MSS.

[72]See the interesting letter, Gordon Johnston to Henry T. Allen, December 30, 1915, Allen MSS. Johnston was trying to explain what it was like to deal with men of the Plattsburg type. Allen had been assigned to command a civilian camp at Fort Oglethorpe, Georgia, that winter.

"We 'fellows' were having our eyes opened wider every day," a Regular captain later commented.[73] Wood and Dorey paid tribute to the civilians at the end of camp by inviting suggestions and criticisms; and the resulting flood of comment revealed a grasp of military and organizational essentials.[74] Wood answered some of the letters personally and applied much of the advice to subsequent camps.

Even the Motor Machine Gun platoon managed to work up to military effectiveness. Discouraged at first by their late arrival and the requirement that they take basic instruction with the other rookies, Bolling's aristocrats were able to maintain morale by working together evenings and on Sundays. Captain William R. Smedberg, assigned to the group as a machine gun instructor, was especially helpful. Bolling told how Smedberg

> after instructing in the mechanism of the machine guns all the afternoon, when he had finally washed up and was starting to the officers' mess, [would] stop to explain some difficulty to one of the men who was working over a machine gun after hours. In a few minutes the Captain would have the gun all apart again explaining its intricate mechanism, his hands and clothes covered with grease, entirely oblivious to everything except the desire to impart instruction. When his pupils' thirst for information was temporarily satisfied, Captain Smedberg usually had to clean up again and get his mess sitting on a stool at the post exchange.[75]

[73]Merch B. Stewart, "The Military Training Camps," *Infantry Journal* 13 (November-December 1916): 249.

[74]See, for example, Robert Homans to Wood, September 7, 1915, Wood MSS; and Jasper Y. Brinton to Dorey, September 21, 1915. RG 98, "Records of the Plattsburg Barracks, 1916," National Archives. These and other letters, mostly from businessmen, reflect to a certain extent what a recent scholar has called "an attempt by the participants to create a model of stability and order. Camp supporters sought to reconstruct a responsible social order so as to preserve a familiar, but vanishing, social structure." See John Fitzpatrick, "The Plattsburg Training Camp for Business and Professional Men, 1915 – 1916: Genesis, Participation and Social Function" (unpublished MS, University of California, Spring 1968), p. 24. Undoubtedly, some of this kind of motivation existed, but it was essentially a subconscious motive. The letters of a vast majority of Plattsburgers reveal an overriding intellectual concern for preparedness as the reason for their own participation.

[75]Bolling to Wood, September 14, 1915, Wood MSS.

When the trainees went on hike, moreover, the machine gun troop found ways to demonstrate the superiority of motor transport over animal transport. During mock battles the armored trucks and cars acted independently, usually swinging wide around the "enemy's" flanks and interdicting his baggage train. They carried supplies themselves and on one occasion were able to transport a company of infantry twenty-one miles in forty-five minutes.[76] Wood was impressed. He stressed the obvious advantages of mechanization and told Bolling this was "the first armored car we have ever had out with our army as far as I know."[77]

The military progress of the civilians raised certain difficulties. One of Captain Dorey's old friends in the coast artillery complained that newspaper reports were giving the public a false impression of Plattsburg, that people believed rookies were being made into soldiers in four short weeks. This was impossible, and Dorey ought to institute some kind of censorship.[78] "There is no use of saying anything to you in a letter about the progress which is being made," Dorey replied, "because you couldn't believe it until you had seen it with your own eyes; but about the greatest progress of all has been made in convincing these men who are attending the camp that it takes a very long time and exceedingly hard work to even begin to get ready to learn anything about the soldier's business. There is absolutely no idea on the part of anyone here . . . that anyone is being made into even a finished recruit in the four weeks' duration of the camp."[79]

[76]Bolling, "Opportunity in Our National Defense," pp. 74–76.

[77]Wood to Bolling, September 17, 1915, Wood MSS. During the remainder of 1915 and 1916 several members of Bolling's troop attempted to organize local units and get the War Department to issue them equipment, either through the Regular Army or National Guard. The army, still wedded to horse transport, was slow to respond. In the fall of 1916, Wood wrote Roger Derby that "the War Department now is inclined to favor machine gun units carried by motor trucks or by automobiles. So you can see how rapidly the minds of the mighty change under the blows of the hammer. You will remember I told you last year that within a year they would want what you were putting up to them." Wood to Derby, September 15, 1916, Wood MSS.

[78]Captain John R. Procter to Dorey, August 18, 1915, RG 98, "Records of the Plattsburg Barracks, 1916," National Archives.

Here was a real problem for Wood and his officers: they were delighted with the military progress, but they did not want these achievements presented in a manner which gave support to those who opposed preparedness. During the first week of camp the general told the trainees that William Jennings Bryan's oft-quoted remark about a million men being able to spring to arms between sunrise and sunset was "a perfectly asinine statement."[80] Fearful that the public would draw exactly the wrong conclusions, Wood followed the advice of Clark and other civilian organizers and quietly killed plans to have the Plattsburgers march down New York's Fifth Avenue at the conclusion of camp.[81]

Indeed, in Wood's mind propaganda was synonymous with military training at Plattsburg. He wanted the men to learn the facts of military service and national defense, as well as to shoot a rifle and march in a straight line. America's state of unpreparedness was the theme, and the officer-instructors hammered it home. The lecturer on artillery pointed out that the Confederate generals Hill and Longstreet had only nine fewer field guns at Gettysburg than there were in the Continental United States at that very moment. A modern machine gun, the rookies learned, contained 183 parts, and it took twelve months to train a three-man crew to operate it under combat conditions. To allow a million men to spring to this kind of weapon overnight would be like pitting eleven grammar school students against the Yale football team.[82] The *New York Evening Sun* suggested that Wood was trying to make the trainees "ambassadors" of his own philosophy, men who would arouse others to the benefits of Switzerland's system of universal military training, who could testify that preparedness did not necessarily mean war, but rather the prevention of war.[83]

[79]Dorey to Procter, August 20, 1915, ibid.
[80]*New York Sun*, August 12, 1915.
[81]Theodore Roosevelt, Jr., to Wood, n.d. (ca. August 20, 1915), Wood MSS.
[82]*New York World,* August 15, 1915; *New York Evening Sun,* August 23, 1915.
[83]August 23, 1915.

The general liked to talk to the men after supper, as they sat around the campfire by the lake. He gave three or four of these evening lectures, delivered in his usual quiet, earnest tone. He publicized his program for making reserve officers out of college students, explained the difference between preparedness and militarism, and argued that "no one has a right to think that there is anything voluntary in the discharge of his [military] duty to the country."[84] Inevitably there were references to George Washington, Lord Roberts, Thomas Jefferson, Demosthenes, and "Lighthorse Harry" Lee. It was a successful effort. Newspaper editorials gave greater space to preparedness, and many adopted Wood's premises.[85] The two dozen or so magazine articles on Plattsburg which appeared (a majority of them written by Plattsburgers) were nearly all favorable, with several making an explicit appeal for universal military training.[86] Mayor Mitchel's first public statement on returning to New York was a paraphrase of Wood: "It would be a crime against the people of this country, amounting to nothing less than national suicide, to send into the field armies manned and officered by untrained volunteers."[87]

FIVE

The great danger in using Plattsburg as a propaganda vehicle was the possibility of stirring up opposition that might prove disastrous in the long run. Despite a visit from General John F. O'Ryan, New York's ranking National Guard officer, and endorsements from several state adjutant generals, the camp received a number of sharp attacks from members of the militia.[88] These citizen soldiers re-

[84]*New York Sun,* August 15, 1915.
[85]See "National Defense at Plattsburg," *Literary Digest* 51 (August 21, 1915): 336–37; and W. Menkel, "Plattsburg Response," *Review of Reviews* 52 (September 1915): 301–8. The Wood and Mitchel scrapbooks have a representative collection of newspaper opinion on Plattsburg.
[86]See, for example, Ralph W. Page, "What I Learned at Plattsburg," *World's Work* 31 (November 1915): 105–8.   [87]*New York Sun,* September 7, 1915.
[88]"National Defense at Plattsburg," p. 337; *New York Mail,* August 31, 1915; *New York World,* August 11, 1915.

sented the publicity given the "millionaires" and asked why their own service went unnoticed. Wood tried to blunt such criticism through personal correspondence with National Guard officers and by urging Plattsburg trainees to join local Guard units. Nevertheless, his strictures about "volunteers" and his talk about a "national reserve" had an ominous sound.[89]

The Wilson administration was a second potential adversary. Wood had little use for "the powers that be," as he liked to call them. His suspicions that spring and the rebuke which Secretary Garrison had administered the previous March in regard to the American Legion episode still rankled, and Wood was sorely disappointed in the General Staff, particularly General Scott, who he felt spent too much time away from his desk, pacifying Piutes in Utah and negotiating with Pancho Villa.[90] But Wood was willing to play by the rules, at least for the time being. He had talked with Colonel House a couple of times that summer, after the colonel had returned from his second European mission, and had learned of President Wilson's reluctant conversion to preparedness.[91] House promised to place Wood's ideas before the president, and Wood made an honest effort to keep Plattsburg a nonpartisan movement.

The general succeeded — up to a point. If most of those individuals who volunteered for training came from Republican backgrounds, there was a sprinkling of prominent Democrats like Mayor Mitchel and Dudley Field Malone, the collector of the Port of New York. A friend of the president, Malone wrote:

> I thought that if men like myself, closely identified with you and your administration, and of the Democratic party, should go to this camp at Plattsburg, it would at least be one of many steps to kill any idea that the opposition party and

[89]Wood to W. F. Sandler, August 16, 1915, Wood MSS; and *New York Times,* September 5, 6, 1915.

[90]See Scott to Wood, March 1, 1915, Wood MSS; and periodic entries in Wood's diary throughout the summer and autumn of 1915.

[91]Wood Diary, July 3, 1915; House to Wood, August 11, 1915, Wood MSS; and House to Woodrow Wilson, August 8, 1915, Wilson MSS.

> its returning prodigal, Mr. Roosevelt, alone are vitally in-
> terested in this great problem. . . . And if some of us show in
> this practical and not talkative interest, . . . I hope we
> may . . . help create a public opinion favorable to whatever
> proposals to Congress you may see fit to make in the future
> on the subject of defense.[92]

Wilson responded cordially and wished "good luck to . . . your military vacation."[93] Malone wrote back after a week in camp, reporting that "the spirit and purpose of all the men here . . . is without the slightest tinge of militarism" and that the prevailing philosophy in regard to the European war was simply to prepare defensively against any victor, Germany or the Allies.[94] It was as Malone said, for Wood insofar as possible made it a rule to avoid politics.[95] Whenever he or his officers dwelt on unpreparedness, it was within the context of America's historical tradition of unpreparedness and in comparison with the nations then at war. The general tried to avoid specific criticism of the administration. During the camp's closing ceremonies he again quoted Wilson's speech about "a citizenry trained to arms"; and when the liner *Arabic* was sunk on August 19, he pointedly omitted reference to the incident in that evening's lecture to the men — despite considerable speculation that he would talk about it.[96] "There is no outcry for war from this body," one trainee assured his mother. "The unanimous opinion seems to be: Wilson will do the right thing, and when he does the country will be behind him."[97]

But try as he might, Wood was no more able to main-

[92]Malone to Wilson, August 5, 1915, Wilson MSS.

[93]Wilson to Malone, August 7, 1915, ibid.

[94]Malone to Wilson, August 16, 1915, ibid.

[95]It was impossible to abolish politics in the trainees' private activities. One Democratically inclined recruit from Boston overheard what he thought was a militaristic conversation between Archie and Ted Roosevelt. The young Bostonian thereupon resigned from camp because "such things as this . . . caused me to sense this camp as a Roosevelt idea to create a spirit of blood-lust and land him in the president's chair with the wave of militarism." Edward J. Doherty to Joseph Tumulty, August 20, 1915, RG 94, AG2319130.

[96]*New York Herald*, September 5, 1915; *New York Evening World*, August 20, 1915.

[97]Quincy S. Mills to Mrs. Mills, August 22, 1915, Quincy Sharpe Mills MSS (microfilm copies), University of North Carolina Library, Chapel Hill.

tain complete neutrality than was the president. Mayor Mitchel and his tentmates made up the following ditty and sang it loudly while on march: "We're Captain Kelly's [*sic*] company/We're neutral to a man;/But if we have to lick the Dutch,/You bet your life we can."[98] People like Bacon and J. W. Ganson, a young American who had fought in the French army, gave out interviews of interventionist intent. And there were moments when the general's own enthusiasm got the better of him. One evening he proclaimed that critics of the camp were nothing but "fakers who do not care to place their own precious bodies in jeopardy."[99] Another time he made veiled references to Mexico, and once he told the men to work hard for defense legislation and to disregard "the ignorant masses" whose opinions on the subject were of no consequence.[100] General Scott later told Wood that the president resented this last speech and wanted none of his generals "rocking the boat."[101]

Herein lay the difference between Wood and Wilson in 1915. Only a recent convert to preparedness (and from diplomatic and political considerations as much as military), the president wanted to deliberate in quiet, hear all shades of expert opinion, then devise a program which would be sound in a military sense and still able to pass Congress.[102] Wood knew what he wanted and was willing to agitate the question. Secretary Garrison, something of an agitator himself, was caught between loyalty to Wilson and his essential sympathy with Wood's point of view.[103] It made for a volatile situation.

The spark which set off the explosion was named Theodore Roosevelt. Wood had invited his fellow Rough Rider to Plattsburg to see what was going on. He also issued invitations to President Wilson, former President Taft,

[98]*New York Evening Sun*, August 18, 1915.
[99]*New York Times*, August 20, 1915.
[100]*New York Sun*, August 12, 1915.
[101]Hugh L. Scott to Wood, September 1, 1915, Wood MSS; and notes of interview with Scott, April 4, 1930, Hagedorn MSS.
[102]Link, *Woodrow Wilson and the Progressive Era*, p. 177.
[103]See Garrison, "Reasonable Preparation," *Independent* 83 (August 16, 1915): 226–29.

Elihu Root, Samuel Gompers, Secretary Garrison, and assorted notables. Wilson and the others sent regrets,[104] not Roosevelt. Nothing could have held him back. His sons were at camp and he was proud of them. He promised to be present for the regimental review on August 25, just prior to the hike which would end the training session.

Roosevelt sent a wire to Plattsburg on the eve of his arrival, saying that he wished to speak to the men, preferably when they were off duty and in civilian clothes. President Drinker of Lehigh, visiting the camp that day, feared the worst. He warned Wood that a few indiscreet remarks might wreck all they had worked for. Wood assured him that Roosevelt would observe protocol.[105] That same evening, as he was leaving Oyster Bay, the former president wrote one of his sons that "Archie is fit to be Captain in a volunteer regiment now; and if this infernal skunk in the White House can be kicked into war a Captain Archie shall be."[106]

Roosevelt reached camp early on August 25, very warlike in his Rough Rider campaign hat and military leggings. Wood took one look and asked to see a copy of Roosevelt's speech. Together they went over it and eliminated most of the passages derogatory to President Wilson. Then they spent the day watching the TBMs work out a battle maneuver against the regular troops.[107]

After supper the former president had his opportunity to speak. It was a beautiful August evening, with the sun's rays brightly, then dimly, illuminating the Green Mountains far to the east. Some four thousand persons, in-

[104]*New York Sun*, August 14, 1915.

[105]Drinker to Wood, August 28, 1915, Wood MSS. Dudley Field Malone was also suspicious when he heard Roosevelt was coming. He urged the president to come to Plattsburg so as to thwart any partisan use of the camp by Roosevelt. Wilson replied: "What I want to say about preparedness I must say to Congress and I don't think any partisan use that can be made of this camp at Plattsburg will really do anyone any harm except those who try to turn it to those purposes." Wilson to Malone, August 19, 1915, Wilson MSS; see also Drinker, *Autobiography of Henry S. Drinker* (privately printed, 1931), pp. 46–53.

[106]Roosevelt to Kermit Roosevelt (mailed August 28, but written August 24, 1915), in Elting E. Morison, ed., *The Letters of Theodore Roosevelt*, 8 vols. (Cambridge, Mass., 1951–1954), 8:963.

[107]Notes of interview with Grenville Clark, April 15, 1930, Hagedorn MSS.

cluding visitors, listened intently to him. He praised the camp and those in it for "fulfilling the prime duty of free men." There should be many more such camps, open to everyone, not just to men who could pay their own way; Roosevelt was certain that "every man worth his salt" would attend. Then he lashed out at those persons who sought to "Chinafy" America and denounced all hyphenates, "professional pacifists, poltroons, and college sissies who organize peace-at-any-price societies." There was applause when the Rough Rider urged that we "shape our conduct as a nation in accordance with the highest rules of international morality." Roosevelt broke off abruptly, flashed his smile, and said he would accept applause from no one unless each person clapping felt a "burning sense of shame" at the fate of Belgium. The cheering intensified.

Roosevelt was warming up now, and he came to a passage which Wood's blue pencil had missed.[108] None in the audience could mistake the reference to President Wilson when Roosevelt said that "to treat elocution as a substitute for action, to rely on high-sounding words unbacked by deeds, is proof of a mind that dwells only in the realm of shadow and shame." This was strong language, and Roosevelt compounded it near the end of his speech when he again departed from the prepared text. It was dark by this time, when Captain Van Horn's little wire-haired terrier came wandering into the firelight looking for his master. Bewildered by the crowd, the puppy ran back and forth, finally bumping into the speaker and rolling on his back, legs in the air. "That's a very nice dog," said Roosevelt, as the audience laughed, "and I like him. His present attitude is strictly one of neutrality."[109]

The words uttered at Plattsburg did not seem half as

[108]It is possible that Roosevelt did not read this controversial passage. As Elting Morison points out, Roosevelt's secretary at Oyster Bay gave the unexpurgated version of his speech to the press, and many newspapers confused this with what Roosevelt actually said at Plattsburg. It seems likely, however, that he did make these snide references to Wilson, because the most detailed accounts quote this part of the speech along with Roosevelt's "off-the-cuff" remarks. See Morison, ed., *Letters of Theodore Roosevelt,* 8:965 n.

[109]*New York Times,* August 26, 1915; *New York Herald,* August 26, 1915; *New York Tribune,* August 26, 1915.

strong as some of the blasts Roosevelt had leveled at Wilson in recent months. So Wood counted himself fortunate as he and Captain Dorey drove their visitor to the railroad station later that evening. Unfortunately the train was slow in pulling out. Dorey and Wood were waving good-bye when they saw a cluster of reporters swarm around. Within seconds Roosevelt had let loose and, in the general's words, "went hard for the powers that be."[110] His most damaging statement was that the country "should stand by the President [only] . . . so long as the President stands by the country." Other remarks followed. Next morning the colonel's speech and "interview" made headlines all over the United States.[111]

Reaction was almost instantaneous. Henry Breckinridge first heard the reports in Washington at 5:00 A.M. He dressed quickly and rushed to Secretary Garrison's house three blocks away, where he and the secretary discussed the matter over breakfast. Breckinridge, whose opinion of Wood was a low one, urged that Garrison send an immediate reprimand without consulting President Wilson. Not only would he save the president from further embarrassment, he would be strengthening his own position.[112] Garrison hesitated, but at a press conference that morning he was pressed further by the antipreparedness editor, Oswald Garrison Villard.[113] Shortly after noon the following telegram arrived in Plattsburg:[114]

I have just seen the reports in the newspapers of the speech made by ex-President Roosevelt at the Plattsburg camp. It is difficult to conceive of anything which could have a more detrimental effect upon the real value of the experiment than such an incident. This camp, held under government

[110]Wood Diary, August 27, 1915. Notes of interview with Halstead Dorey, January 4, 1930, Hagedorn MSS.

[111]There were even repercussions in Germany, where the Berlin press made sarcastic comments about "the country club of New York" and "Terrible Teddy, eater up of Germans." See *Berliner Tageblatt*, August 31, 1915, clipping in the Wood Scrapbooks.

[112]Breckinridge, "Memoir," pp. 198–99.

[113]Villard, *Fighting Years* (New York, 1939), pp. 284–87.

[114]Garrison to Wood, August 26, 1915, Wood MSS.

auspices, was successfully demonstrating many things of great moment. Its virtues consisted in the fact that it conveyed its own impressive lesson in its practical and successful operation and results. No opportunity should have been furnished to anyone to present to the men any matter excepting that which they were to receive. Anything else could only have the effect of distracting attention to the real nature of the experiment, diverting consideration from issues which excite controversy, antagonism, and ill-feeling, and thereby impairing, if not destroying, what otherwise would have been so effective. There must not be any opportunity given at Plattsburg or any other similar camp for any such unfortunate circumstances.

Lindley M. Garrison
Secretary of War

Wood made no attempt to explain. "Your telegram received," he replied, "and the policies laid down will be rigidly adhered to."[115] But Roosevelt was not about to let the matter drop. "I am, of course, solely responsible for the whole speech," he told the press. "If the Administration had displayed one-tenth of . . . the energy in holding Germany and Mexico to account for the murder of American men, women, and children that it is now displaying . . . to prevent our people from being taught the need for preparation to prevent the repetition of such murders, . . . it would be rendering a service to the people of this country."[116] Garrison made a jocular reply, Roosevelt snapped back, and the reverberations were heard in the newspapers for several days.

It was an unfortunate incident. The standard reaction was to deplore Roosevelt's breach of propriety (the "Big Noise," Willard Straight called him) and to regret that Wood was singled out for reprimand.[117] Ironically, Wood

[115]Wood to Garrison, August 26, 1915, Wood MSS.

[116]*New York Tribune*, August 28, 1915.

[117]"He [Roosevelt] seems to have the unfortunate habit of deterring a great many people from supporting a perfectly good cause, for there are many who would be willing to stand for a better scheme of national preparedness who will be frightened off lest through the leadership of someone like TR we might become involved in European calculations," Straight to Henry P. Fletcher, September 16,

held no resentment whatsoever toward Roosevelt. But toward "the powers that be" his venom increased tenfold. "The Secretary hit me . . . below the belt," he told Captain McCoy, "but I am out to do what I can for national preparedness and no amount of nipping at my heels is going to stop it."[118] Although Secretary Garrison seemed willing enough to let the incident drop, cooperation between these two high-strung individuals would henceforth be impossible.[119] As for President Wilson, whatever suspicions he had harbored previously about the army's senior general were now confirmed.[120] According to Colonel House, it was this episode at Plattsburg which determined Wilson not to give Wood a field command if and when the United States went to war.[121] These personality clashes also were to have their effect on the military legislation planned for Congress that coming winter.

SIX

Fortunately for Wood and the future of the training camp movement, Theodore Roosevelt did not make the only important speech at Plattsburg that summer. About a week after the Roosevelt incident, near the town of Champlain, New York, another speech was delivered, with virtually no publicity—by Grenville Clark.

As was customary, Clark had remained in the background during the first weeks of camp.[122] He had told

---

1915, Straight MSS; see also Henry S. Drinker to Theodore Roosevelt, August 27, 1915, "I deeply deplore the fact that after all General Wood's splendidly tactful work in building up these camps . . . you should have brought down on him . . . this reproof, and I deplore that you have thus given the fool peace-at-any-price people . . . a handle to again antagonize General Wood's wise, patriotic, and effective moves for national defense." Roosevelt MSS.

[118]Wood to Roosevelt, August 29 and September 17, 1915; Wood to Frank R. McCoy, October 1, 1915, Wood MSS.

[119]Hugh L. Scott to McCoy, September 7, 1915, and Woodrow Wilson to Scott, September 3, 1915, Scott MSS.

[120]Wilson to Scott, September 3, 1915, ibid.

[121]Notes of interview with Edward M. House, December 27, 1928, Hagedorn MSS.

[122]Clark described the following scene in diary notes prepared for his wife: "As

Wood at the end of July that there ought to be some permanent reserve scheme into which the businessmen's movement could fit. "Where we come in is to act under your directions," he had said.[123] So Clark spent much of his time at Plattsburg talking to prominent individuals, listening to their ideas, suggesting his own. By September 1, 1915, he and his friends were ready. Calling the entire training body together and excluding the regular officers and men, Mitchel and Bacon chaired a meeting similar to the one held at Gettysburg two years earlier. This First Training Regiment, as they called themselves, pledged to encourage "a system of military training camps throughout the nation" and to assist in providing "a reasonable amount of military training for the citizens of the United States." Eight men were then chosen, one from each company, who in turn resolved "to increase their number to 35 . . . with due regard for representation from all sections of the country" and in "cooperation with representatives of other similar camps, shall prepare and submit a permanent plan of organization."[124]

Clark's speech introducing the resolutions was described by Willard Straight as expressing "better than anything I know the spirit of most of the men at Plattsburg."[125] Clark told the men how the enterprise had begun, how "we did not spring to arms in a single day," how it had taken a good deal of work. He explained how spirit had been the most important consideration and that "if the newspapers have told Americans extraordinary stories of our doings here it has been none of our doing." Clark spoke of the

---

I was walking down another company street today someone set up a yell — 'the man who thought of it all!' A number of people set up a yell but I have endeavored to keep absolutely in the background which is no trouble, everyone being too busy to bother about anything but their work." Notes for Mrs. Grenville Clark, August 1915, Clark MSS.

[123]Clark to Wood, July 30, 1915, Clark MSS. (Noted in Clark's hand, "not sent but told orally.")

[124]The eight company representatives were William M. Bullitt, Philip A. Carroll, Grenville Clark, J. W. Farley, Robert M. McElroy, John Purroy Mitchel, George Wharton Pepper, and William M. Rutter.

[125]Straight to Frank R. McCoy, September 27, 1915, McCoy MSS.

sacrifices each man had made to come to Plattsburg and the need to preserve this spirit in a permanent organization. Plattsburg "was not conceived as an emergency measure" but in the hope of fitting into "a permanent, sane and sound and reasonable military system for the United States." It "was not conceived merely as a means of obtaining security against external enemies, but in strengthening the nation internally against internal forces making for weakness and lack of national unity." Just as the Plattsburgers "felt the need ourselves of the training . . . we felt that such training for the general body of our citizens, if reasonably carried out, could be nothing but an immense benefit to them individually and to the nation." They must show that "such military training can be worked out under our institutions without the slightest danger of militarism or its evil results" and that "far from being undemocratic such a system may well be the very salvation of our democracy."

Clark also warned that "this camp was conceived as something entirely apart from and above all politics or partisan propaganda." The Plattsburg movement "must never become a talking organization. Other societies may be doing a useful work in pointing out by talk the seriousness of the United States in a military way, but if talk alone could secure . . . military security we should have been prepared long ago." Clark proposed work along other lines—"along lines of action and not of agitation." Plattsburgers "must continue our own training; we must encourage others to take the training, until by the very force of actual demonstration and not of words the country as a whole is convinced of the necessity of our idea." And if such a policy was to be effective, the movement must "loyally support and cooperate with the national administration in power, irrespective of personal opinion, and under any and all conceivable circumstances." Clark proposed that their immediate object should be to assist the proper authorities in working out an expanded training camp program where "no citizen need be forced to pay as much as we have

for the privilege of fitting himself to serve his country."
Other forms of action could be decided upon by committees.[126]

Thus was a second phase of the training camp movement initiated. Whether it could follow the pattern set
forth in Clark's speech was something only time could tell.
Much depended on subsequent organization by the civilians. Much also depended on continued cooperation between the civilians and General Wood. Their goals and
methods would not always be the same.

[126]"Remarks of Grenville Clark at Organization Meeting of Businessmen's . . . First Training Regiment," September 1, 1915, copies in the McCoy and
Clark MSS. For a good account of this meeting, see George Edward Buxton's
article in the *Providence Evening Journal,* October 15, 1915.

IV.

The Military Training Camps Association

Grenville Clark was determined that Plattsburg should not be a "flash in the pan."[1] He and the other men who organized the First Training Regiment in September 1915 realized that the accomplishments of the Business Men's Camp were more potential than immediate. The Plattsburgers had acquired the fundamentals of military training and had generated much enthusiasm. But this was not enough. General Wood told the trainees that they must act as missionaries for national defense in their home communities. What did Wood mean? How were these missionary activities to be coordinated? Secretary Garrison's reprimand of Wood over the Roosevelt affair had cast a shadow on the future of the training camp movement. Was it possible for the civilians to smooth over the disagreement between the sensitive secretary and the prickly general? Could the training camp organizers establish their own relationship with the War Department and secure a place for their program in the defense legislation planned for Congress that winter? Then, too, there were the questions of how the Plattsburg idea could be extended beyond its Philadelphia-Boston-New York axis and what kind of connection could be established between the Business Men's movement and the students' Society of the National Reserve Corps of the United States.

More than anyone else, it was Clark who provided the

answers to these questions. Throughout the autumn and early winter of 1915 – 1916 the young New York attorney devoted nearly all his time to training camp mat- ters — traveling back and forth to Washington, correspond- ing with representatives in all sections of the country, coordinating plans with Wood's staff on Governor's Island, giving definition to the "Plattsburg idea." The result of his labors was the Military Training Camps Association of the United States, formally organized on February 4, 1916.

O N E

The first step in this enlargement process took place almost automatically. On September 8, 1915, two days after the business men's course ended, a second camp opened at Plattsburg, with six hundred men just as hard-working as their predecessors in attendance. Most recruits were of the same sort as those who had trained in August: William Cooper Procter of Cincinnati (the soap manufacturer) and former Governor Charles R. Sligh of Michigan being per- haps the two best known individuals in camp.[2] Again the New York Bar Association was well represented.[3] General Scott came up from Washington to review the trainees after two weeks, and Henry L. Stimson and Mayor Mitchel made a weekend visit at the beginning of October while the men were on hike. As in August, General Wood and his officers were impressed with the military performance.[4] Nothing as spectacular as a visit from Theodore Roosevelt punctuated the proceedings.

[1]Clark to John W. Farley, December 24, 1915, Clark MSS.

[2]See the *Letters of William C. Procter* (Cincinnati, Ohio, 1957), pp. 59-62.

[3]Both Tompkins McIlvaine and Archibald G. Thacher, New York lawyers and future presidents of the Military Training Camps Association, were at the Septem- ber camp. Thacher, Harvard '97, was a good friend of Grenville Clark, and his Plattsburg papers are a part of the Clark MSS.

[4]See Wood Diary, September 8-October 10, 1915. When this second camp ended, Wood gave his officers a much needed vacation — a kind of "busman's holiday" during which they visited and inspected a Canadian officer training camp near Montreal. See Robert O. Van Horn to Halstead Dorey, n.d. (ca. October 20, 1915), RG 98, "Records of the Plattsburg Barracks, 1916."

Meanwhile, three other camps on the Plattsburg model were in operation. Beginning on August 20 and 28, respectively, camps for older men at the Presidio in San Francisco and at American Lake, Washington, occupied facilities used earlier in the summer by the college students. The combined enrollment was 210. And at Fort Sheridan, Illinois, near Chicago, a training course for 552 "Tired Business Men" was held from September 20 to October 17.[5]

None of the three was a natural offspring of Plattsburg, although the San Francisco camp seems to have been something close to that. Clark had tried during July to enlist several of his California acquaintances, most notably Benjamin H. Dibblee, a San Francisco banker and former Harvard football captain (1899). Because of the short notice and the expense of traveling to Plattsburg, Dibblee decided to forget about 1915 and concentrate on forming an organization for the next summer. It was at this time, late July, however, that Theodore Roosevelt visited the West Coast and delivered a series of red-blooded speeches at the Pacific Exposition in San Francisco.[6] Out of Roosevelt's patriotic urgings evolved the idea of a separate Plattsburg camp for California, a project which William Randolph Hearst's *San Francisco Examiner* endorsed with especial vigor.[7] Sympathetic at first, Dibblee and many other Republican businessmen shied away when the *Examiner's* influence became predominant.[8] The results were unimpressive in comparison with Plattsburg. Fewer than seventy-five men took the course at the Presidio, although, as one trainee later reported, over 80 percent were "college men and representative of the best young elements on the Pacific coast."[9] One positive feature was the thorough training

[5]Perry, *Plattsburg Movement*, pp. 29–31.

[6]D. L. Roscoe to Frank R. McCoy, July 26, 1915, McCoy MSS. Roosevelt at this time was hoping to raise a Rough Rider-like cavalry division in case of war and as a result was particularly bellicose.

[7]James G. Harbord to Wood, August 1, 1915, Wood MSS; also see the Wood Scrapbooks for articles from the *Examiner*.

[8]Benjamin F. Dibblee to Ralph Barton Perry, June 2, 1920, Perry MSS, Harvard University Archives.

[9]William H. Rutter to Clark, December 29, 1915, Clark MSS. B. F. Cator, vice

program supervised by Major James G. Harbord, a friend and disciple of General Wood.[10] Harbord reported his results to Governor's Island.[11]

While the camp at American Lake resembled the one at San Francisco in its relative mediocrity, the Fort Sheridan venture made a valiant effort to match Plattsburg. That a Chicago camp was held at all resulted mainly from the perseverance of an Illinois congressman, Martin B. Madden, who badgered reluctant officers at Fort Sheridan and made a special trip to Washington before obtaining authorization.[12] Unfortunately, the sixty-year-old Madden was called away from Chicago by an illness in the family and could not actively participate in a recruitment campaign. For a time in early September it looked as if the whole enterprise might fail. Then a young friend of Madden, a structural engineer named Wharton Clay, hit on the idea of holding noonday luncheons at a downtown hotel and contacting a few men who had attended the Plattsburg camp earlier that summer. These luncheons brought publicity, particularly when Clay invited Colonel Robert R. McCormick of the *Chicago Tribune* to speak. "We met morning, noon and night," Clay remembered, "and the papers began to take a very unusual interest in the camp; a few prominent men began to sign up, but not nearly as spontaneously as it sounds, and up to a very few days before the camp was [to] open, we had only about 250 men signed up. We had to run the names of the same applicants every other day, in order to show that the camp was a real thing, and the willingness of the papers to do this and continue to

---

president of the U. S. Fidelity and Guaranty Company, was the chief civilian organizer of the Presidio undertaking.

[10]See Harbord's official report, September 15, 1915, RG 94, AG2315058.

[11]Harbord to Wood, July 31, August 1, August 27, 1915, Wood MSS; see also Harbord to William Howard Taft, August 25, 1915, William Howard Taft MSS, Library of Congress; and Paul B. Malone to Wood, September 25, 1915, Wood MSS.

[12]*New York Times*, August 13, 1915. General Wood also helped by telephoning General Tasker Bliss to say that "it would give a black eye to the movement" not to have a camp for the Chicagoans. See Bliss to Wood, August 25, 1915, Bliss MSS, Library of Congress.

cooperate when they knew it was an uphill job was absolutely remarkable."[13]

By methods which may have been unorthodox in comparison to Plattsburg, the Fort Sheridanites managed to raise their number to over five hundred by the time training began on September 20. The utilities tycoon Samuel Insull saw to it that some seventy-five to one hundred of his employees were given time off to attend camp.[14] Other business firms sponsored smaller groups, and forty-two members of Chicago's Hamilton Club contributed expenses for forty-two recruits unable to pay their own way.[15] The upshot was a far more plebeian representation at Fort Sheridan than at Plattsburg. Honore Jaxon, head of a local carpenters' union, and also the Negro colonel of an Illinois National Guard regiment were able to dig trenches alongside representatives of Chicago society.[16] This "democratization" of attendance, due in large part to publicity, foreshadowed what was to take place in all training camps during 1916.

Military training was hampered by the lateness of the season and the fact that Fort Sheridan was too close to the city for extended maneuvers.[17] Nonetheless, the rookies did manage to absorb a rigorous body of fundamental and special instruction, climaxed by entrainment of the entire cadet corps north to the Great Lakes Naval Training Station, where the men marched in review, fought mock battles against regular troops (as well as students from the Culver Military Academy), and then hiked back to Fort Sheridan with full pack. "There seemed to be a general determination by all in camp," the officer in command reported, "to serve faithfully to the very last day and not to

[13]Clay to Ralph Barton Perry, April 22, 1920, Perry MSS.
[14]Ibid.
[15]See Clay's article, "The Lesson of the Training Camp," *The Hamiltonian* (Autumn 1915), a copy of which is in the Perry MSS.
[16]*Chicago Tribune*, August 25 and September 18, 1915; see also Richard H. Little to Wood, August 26, 1915, Wood MSS.
[17]Rumor had it that the trainees were to march into Chicago, bivouac on the streets for a night, then march back to Fort Sheridan, but the army thought better of the idea; see *Chicago Tribune*, October 4, 1915.

lose a single hour of the day's exercises. This spirit is all the more commendable as the work was hard and often painfully distressing, especially during days of digging entrenchments. . . . I feel proud to have seen so many loyal citizens leaving their daily toil in order to serve as a private soldier without pay."[18]

Toward the middle of the training course the men at Sheridan emulated the Plattsburgers and formed their own regimental association: Wharton Clay was elected secretary, and the mayor of Evanston, Harry B. Pearsons, became chairman.[19] One might have expected the Fort Sheridan Training Camp Association to cooperate with its New York counterpart, but the opposite occurred. When a Plattsburg emissary visited Chicago in mid-October with an invitation to merge with the larger organization, the Sheridanites turned him down. The Chicagoans had misconstrued all the stories about Eastern "aristocrats" and, as Clay recalled, were afraid the Plattsburgers "would overwhelm us."[20] The New Yorkers drew back after this refusal, so that for the remainder of the year the Fort Sheridan Association went its separate way—forming subcommittees, negotiating with the Central Department for a winter instruction course, planning for 1916.[21] Similarly, the smaller training camp groups on the Pacific Coast began to work out programs without connection with either Plattsburg or Fort Sheridan.[22] Nationwide coordination did not occur until 1916.

[18]See "Report on the Military Training Camp . . . Fort Sheridan, Illinois," by Colonel William J. Nicholson, November 17, 1915, RG 94, AG2330927.

[19]See Clay to Wood, November 29, 1915, Wood MSS.

[20]Clay to Ralph Barton Perry, April 22, 1920, Perry MSS. See also George F. Porter to Clark, December 23, 1915, Clark MSS; and Porter to Halstead Dorey, September 10, 1915, RG 98, "Records of the Plattsburg Barracks, 1916." Porter, a Chicago banker who went to Plattsburg, was the New Yorkers' emissary.

[21]See Clay to Colonel D. A. Frederick, January 12, 1916, RG 94, AG 2315058.

[22]Benjamin Dibblee went to New York in November, met with Wood and Clark, and worked out plans for organizing a movement for 1916. But Dibblee did not represent the group that had trained at the Presidio. See Dibblee to Ralph Barton Perry, May 28, 1920, Perry MSS. At this time, also, veterans of the American Lake Camp, working through the Tacoma branch of the Employers Association of Washington, persuaded the Western Department to offer a series of businessmen's lectures during the winter. See H. W. Sawyer to Hugh L. Scott, October 8, 1915, and John D. Barrette to Sawyer, November 4, 1915, RG 94, AG2315058.

T W O

Meanwhile, more far-reaching developments were taking place in New York. In mid-September 1915, while the Second Business Men's Camp was in progress at Plattsburg, the Committee of Eight, which included Clark, Mayor Mitchel, and George Wharton Pepper, strove to increase its number to thirty-five.[23] General Wood continued to show interest by sending Mitchel a list of some fifty names from the first camp whose reputations he deemed "most excellent."[24] By "sitting up till one o'clock" several nights in a row, by trying to find active men from several sections of the country, the civilians managed to get "the strongest committee possible."[25] The organizers sent an invitation to Plattsburg where, on September 28, the men of the second camp formed the "Third Battalion of the First Training Regiment" and elected an additional Committee of Eighteen. The Joint Organization Committee of fifty-three (combining the committees of thirty-five and eighteen) then met in New York on Friday, October 15. Pepper presided. Forty-four members were present, a number coming from distant points in the South and West. Out of their deliberations emerged a permanent organization consisting of four committees: Executive Committee (nine members who "shall determine all matters of policy and co-ordinate the activities of the other committees"); Finance Committee (twelve members); Enrollment Committee (thirty members who "shall have charge of all matters pertaining to the enrollment for future camps"); and Committee on Regimental Affairs (thirty-five members who "shall have general charge of all matters pertaining to the Regiment").[26]

The October 15 meeting also discussed future plans

[23]The eight men were Clark, Pepper, Mitchel, John W. Farley of Massachusetts, George F. Porter of Chicago, Arthur M. Morse of Missouri, William Marshall Bullitt of Louisville, and James Bruce of Maryland. Robert Bacon was an *ex officio* member of this organizing committee.

[24]Wood to Mitchel, September 14, 1915, Wood MSS.

[25]Clark to Wood, September 19, 1915, ibid.

[26]Military Training Camps, Organization Committee, First Training Regiment, "Bulletin No. 2," October 25, 1915, printed bulletin in Wood MSS; also a copy in Clark MSS.

and policies. There was unanimity as to securing "fifteen or twenty thousand properly qualified men for enrollment in such camps as the army authorities may provide for the coming year." The Plattsburgers reiterated their pledge of September not to agitate for special favors from Congress, but stipulated that "the Executive Committee should hold itself in readiness to confer about the terms of such legislation in case conference is asked by those who have such legislation to propose." A conciliatory position was taken toward the National Guard. Rather than make public statements which could arouse controversy, the organizers urged that each member of the Regiment "make it his business to get into personal contact with the leading Guardsmen in his locality, explain our true position, disclaim all intention of competing for army commissions with officers of the Guard, and offer hearty co-operation in every practicable way to increase enlistments in the Guard and otherwise to promote its interests." It was also decided that, while the Enrollment Committee could not act until the War Department announced training camp plans for 1916, the Finance Committee and the Committee on Regimental Affairs should form working subcommittees and begin functioning. Before adjourning, the Plattsburgers again expressed "the motive which should continue to animate them — which is the eager desire to discharge the duty resting upon every citizen in a democracy, to fit himself as well as he can for national defense and to put himself at the disposal of the government for such service as, whatever his age or capacity, he may be adjudged capable of rendering."[27]

The Committee on Regimental Affairs kept active during the next few months. Composed of men mostly from larger cities, the Committee formed local subdivisions, which in turn engaged in a variety of regimental pursuits. Most popular was the formation of special Plattsburg drill units. An early example was the Buffalo Cavalry Association, organized by Anson Conger Goodyear, a local busi-

[27]Ibid.

nessman and Plattsburger, and instructed by William J. Donovan, an attorney who was also captain of the Buffalo cavalry troop of the New York National Guard.[28] Beginning on November 1, 1915, the fifty-odd volunteers (known as "Goodyear's Gorillas" and "Konger's Kangaroos") took weekly instruction in equitation and mounted drill at the Troop I Armory. The course, approved by both General Wood and General O'Ryan, continued until the following June.[29] In Detroit, Frederick A. Alger, the son of President McKinley's secretary of war and an old friend of Wood, was instrumental in organizing a businessmen's training class. More than two hundred enthusiasts signed up for the weekly instruction which began at the Detroit Armory in early January 1916.[30] Similarly, there was a course for sixty-five Bostonians at the Charlestown Armory; twenty-three Plattsburgers from the Baltimore area formed an artillery battery in the Maryland National Guard; Wood's friend Basil Miles had organized the seventy-man Washington Rifle Association in October; and in the Pittsburgh area a contingent from Raynal Bolling's Machine Gun Troop continued to meet and hold maneuvers.[31] In each locality Plattsburgers were able to obtain professional cooperation from either the army or National Guard.[32]

New York remained active. The officers on Governor's Island devoted nearly all their spare time to civilian lectures, conducting weekly drill at the 69th Regiment Armory, organizing a correspondence course in military tactics which included over 1,700 Plattsburgers by mid-winter. In addition to efforts by the veterans of 1915, there was a training corps for two hundred newspapermen which met

[28]Donovan to Wood, October 6, 1915, Wood MSS. This was the same William J. ("Wild Bill") Donovan who later headed the Office of Strategic Services in World War II.

[29]"Autobiography of Anson Conger Goodyear," manuscript memoir in the Anson Conger Goodyear MSS, Buffalo Historical Society, Buffalo, New York.

[30]Frederick A. Alger to Wood, December 6 and 10, 1915, Wood MSS.

[31]*Bulletin of the First Training Regiment* (January 1916), pp. 38–43.

[32]For the activities in Philadelphia, see J. Franklin McFadden to Gordon Johnston, November 11, 1915, RG 98, "Records of the Plattsburg Barracks, 1916."

at the 71st Regiment Armory, as well as drill classes twice a week for inspectors and captains of the New York Police Department. The brunt of this work fell to Captain Dorey, Wood's aide-de-camp. "Both the days and nights have been rather busy here," he wrote facetiously, "and I don't see much chance of it letting up until I become a manchu, when I will cease coffee cooling and go back to the restful job of commanding four or five squads of old soldiers."[33]

New York also served as a convenient social center. Beginning in early December at the Harvard Club, the Committee on Regimental Affairs launched a series of monthly dinner meetings which were always well attended.[34] These gatherings, later extended to Boston and Philadelphia and made a part of the winter correspondence course, enabled the more active Plattsburgers to keep in touch. General Wood and Captain Dorey usually took part in the proceedings.[35] Then, too, there were smaller meetings, company reunions being the most colorful. An example was the dinner in honor of Captain W. L. Reed, given at the India House on Hanover Square, November 29, 1915, by the members of Company E, Second Battalion. This was Willard Straight's company. The meal included "Curry of Lobster Shrimp, Mushrooms with Rice, and Broiled English Mutton Chop," after which the former soldiers (in "regular evening dress" without "arms, canteens, or packs") regaled each other with speeches and songs. "First comes Lieutenant Straight," one verse ran, "the proudest of them all;/He's up in the morning before the first call,/And if you are sick or feeling rather frail,/It's McKinney, do your duty—put the millionaire in jail."[36] Company rosters were compiled and distributed at these reunions, thus accentuating the "Old Grad" atmosphere.[37]

[33]Halstead Dorey to Reginald H. Kelley, January 26, 1916, RG 98, "Records of the Plattsburg Barracks, 1916."

[34]See Langdon P. Marvin to Wood, October 21 and November 9, 1915, Wood MSS.

[35]Wood Diary, December 6, 1915, and January 3, 1916.

[36]Menu in the Clark MSS.

[37]See "Come and Get It," the printed roster of Company E, First Training Regiment, a copy of which is in the Straight MSS. Straight, an accomplished artist,

A more important regimental activity was publication of the *Bulletin of the First Training Regiment,* the first number of which appeared in December 1915. Edited by Plattsburger William Menkel (also an editor of *Review of Reviews*), the olive-colored *Bulletin* acted as both newsletter and forum for the 2,000-odd training camp men scattered around the country. Monthly issues contained articles by Frederick L. Huidekoper, General Wood, Grenville Clark, Mayor Mitchel, and others; there were anecdotes of 1915, news of local training activities, reports of Executive Committee meetings, discussion of future policy. Whenever Regimental officers wanted to poll the membership on some question, the *Bulletin* served this purpose. Starting with the January 1916 number, the *Bulletin* was also the medium for sending problems and solutions to men who were taking the military correspondence course at Governor's Island.[38] As a kind of companion piece, the Regimental Committee also published a *Roster of the First Training Regiment* — with the name, address, and company of trainees at both Plattsburg camps listed.[39] These two publications, the *Bulletin* and *Roster,* helped insure a strong nucleus for 1916.

THREE

The larger questions of Regimental policy were being decided at 31 Nassau Street in Manhattan. Meeting in a room across the hall from Grenville Clark's law offices, Clark, Robert Bacon, Mayor Mitchel, and others during September 1915 determined the makeup and direction of the mid-October organizational meeting. In making their plans, however, Clark and his friends encountered opposition from an unexpected source — General Wood. "We have

---

designed a coat-of-arms for his company, and, as president of the Company E Association, he was chiefly responsible for this regimental roster. There are a number of other rosters in Clark MSS.

[38]*Bulletin of the First Training Regiment,* Vol. 1, nos. 1–6 (December 1915-May 1916), copies in the Clark MSS, New York Public Library, and the Sterling Library at Yale University.

[39]*Roster of the First Training Regiment* (New York, 1916), Clark MSS.

discussed this matter very fully at various informal meetings . . . of our Organization Committee," Clark carefully informed the general on September 21, "and it was the general consensus of opinion that the wise and prudent course was to send a small delegation to see the Secretary of War and the Mayor, Mr. Geo. Wharton Pepper and I were selected to do so." Their thought was "that the camp movement had become or was about to become so important that we could hardly with safety go ahead with organization plans . . . without taking notice of the existence of the Secretary of War." Clark well remembered Secretary Garrison's unfair reprimand of Wood in August and promised that "we will all be 'from Missouri' on the question of his sincere interest . . . but we felt that a visit merely to see how the land lies can do no harm and may prevent a certain amount of antagonism, which would hurt what we are all trying for, viz. a continuance of the camps in a larger way and on a permanent scheme." Clark added that Willard Straight had called on Garrison about ten days before and had found the secretary very friendly. According to Straight, Garrison "intimated that he wanted to see them [Plattsburg representatives] before drafting his report . . . to the President and suggested the possibility of making a recommendation for an extension of the camps and getting an appropriation to reduce the expenses to the men somewhat."[40]

Clark's position was sound. The Plattsburgers knew that the War Department was drawing up a comprehensive plan for military reorganization and that President Wilson was expected to give it his support. Some discussion with Garrison was imperative. But, for reasons that are not altogether clear, Wood told the civilians to hold back. "I think the best thing to do is to go a little slowly," he informed Clark, "get the organization built up among yourselves and your committees arranged and not attempt too much just now in the way of work outside. We have unlimited authority at the

[40]Clark to Wood, September 21, 1915, Wood MSS. For Straight's visit to Garrison, see also Straight to Frank R. McCoy, September 27, 1915, McCoy MSS.

present to carry on these camps and the main thing . . . is to build up the attendance for next year by every possible and proper means. I think if you, as an organization, start in too actively now it may arouse the opposition of the militia."[41] Suspicious of the Wilson administration and unwilling to give the civilians free rein, Wood wanted to wait.[42]

For the next few weeks the Plattsburgers followed Wood's advice and kept at their organizational work. Then, just a few days after the Regimental meeting on October 15, an outline of Garrison's defense program was leaked to the newspapers.[43] While the plan contemplated substantial increases in the Regular Army, as expected, it provided also for a 400,000 man reserve force—a Continental Army. Replacing the National Guard as the country's first line of defense, this Continental Army would be made up of civilian volunteers who had passed through federal training camps on the Plattsburg model. Clark and his friends were jubilant. "*Fine* scheme—wonderfully much better than ever had hoped for," DeLancey Jay wrote. "What is our aim now? Has the Plattsburg Idea done its work? . . . If the scheme goes through, it might fairly be said that the task of 'Mr. Clark and his associates' . . . is finished; and you three original conspirators can tell your children how without rising above the rank of private you raised an army of a million men!"[44] Clark replied that he and Ted Roosevelt had anticipated Garrison's proposals and had written a memorandum which they showed to Wood ("who thought it good"). What they might do next, Clark thought, was officer training. On this point the Continental Army plan was vague. It "made no difference how the reserve was obtained; it must have officers & we are the boys to supply

[41]Wood to Clark, September 30, 1915, Wood MSS.

[42]When Bernard Baruch brought word of Washington's plans for military reorganization, Wood wrote in his diary, "I cannot convince myself that they seriously intend doing anything. It looks like an attempt to fool the people with more shifty measures." Wood Diary, September 6, 1915.

[43]For a detailed analysis of the War Department plan, see *New York Times,* November 6, 1915.

[44]Jay to Clark, October 18, 1915, Clark MSS.

them. . . . Talk of officering 400,000 men by militia officers and men from military schools is *bunk*."[45]

With these thoughts uppermost, Clark, accompanied by Philip Carroll and Willard Straight, went to Washington to meet with Garrison and Assistant Secretary Breckinridge. Though he found the secretary of war "surprisingly nebulous as to details of working out his plan," Clark thought the conference was highly satisfactory. He told Garrison of their desire to have the camps standardized and integrated into War Department policy. He asked that Plattsburgers have a chance to qualify as officers in the new reserve and that the camps themselves be part of a larger plan for training officers. Garrison was cooperative but could not promise anything because of congressional uncertainty. He did agree to appoint an officer board which at a later date would consult with the Plattsburg Executive Committee. At Clark's suggestion, the secretary named Captain Dorey as one of the three officers. Garrison wrote the orders immediately. Clark was pleased. "This gives us a big chance to write the officers' training camp scheme into the big policy," he wrote Jay, "and also to steer [the] general reserve plan into practical lines." The appointment of Dorey "will form connecting link with Wood wh[ich] is very essential."[46]

The Plattsburgers returned to New York, and Clark went over to Governor's Island to tell Wood the news. He found the general in a waspish mood. Why did the secretary want to appoint one of his subordinates to make a report on the training camps when he, as originator of the camps, had been making similar reports for the last three years? Dorey's appointment was an insult. "I thought this a pretty narrow view of the matter," Clark wrote, "and in the course of the discussion found that I told General Wood so very plainly." The interview ended abruptly.[47]

The general's attitude placed Clark in a difficult posi-

[45]Clark to Jay, October 23, 1915, Jay Box, ibid.

[46]Clark to Jay, October 27, 1915, ibid; see also "Memo. for the Sec'y of War re: 'Plattsburg' Military Training Camps," ibid.

[47]Clark to Franklin D. Roosevelt, November 11, 1915, ibid.

tion. Without Wood's backing the Plattsburg movement would collapse, and Clark knew it. He could understand Wood's anger and bitterness. Like most Plattsburgers, he admired Wood tremendously. But Clark was enough of a practical judge to see where the general's anger might lead. For the time being, therefore, Clark remained in the background, making tactful suggestions through intermediaries and hoping against hope that Wood and Garrison could effect a reconciliation.[48]

Unfortunately, the general's temper only worsened. Two visits to Washington during November 1915 convinced him that the Continental Army scheme was unworkable and that the War Department was too cowardly to advocate effective preparedness, namely, universal military training.[49] And when Wood publicly criticized Garrison's program in early December, he received a scathing five-page reprimand, his worst yet.[50] To Clark it was all "a very absurd and unfortunate situation." He told a Harvard classmate that "it looks as if the people responsible for a military policy were in a state of chaos, individually and collectively. . . . [It] seems to us preposterous that the Secretary of War and the most prominent figure in the army should have to deal at arm's length and not be able to cooperate cordially when . . . the fullest cooperation of ev-

[48]See DeLancey K. Jay to Wood, November 13, 1915, and Wood to Jay, November 15, 1915, Wood MSS. Jay was hoping to get Wood's endorsement of a plan whereby Plattsburgers would take reserve officer examinations which were open to men in the service. Wood told Jay to hold off for the time being. A carbon of Jay's letter to Wood is in the Clark MSS with the penciled phrase "I tried to introduce a little soft soap" in Jay's hand, and the words "Your letter very diplomatic!" in Clark's hand.

[49]See (Nov. 10) "all in confusion. No relations with Sec. and Scott. Left high and dry. Talk with Scott, Bliss, and General Enoch H. Crowder. Crowder seems to be doing the bill. Scott nothing. Bliss playing safe. . . . (Nov. 29) . . . Long and strong talk with Scott this morning. Evident that General Staff is dead, and Scott entirely neglected in all important matters. Insisted that G. S. should prepare a full plan and put the responsibility for any curtailment of necessary plan. Afraid I hurt Scott's feelings." Wood Diary, November 10, 29, 1915.

[50]Garrison to Wood, December 14, 1915, Wood MSS. Years later Garrison told Ray Stannard Baker (Woodrow Wilson's biographer) that he would have court-martialed Wood for insubordination if he, Garrison, had not resigned from the War Department in early 1916. See notes of an interview with Lindley M. Garrison, November 30, 1928, Baker MSS.

eryone interested in this proposition is required. . . . We should like to see them teamed up and pulling together, so that we can all stand by both of them at once."[51]

Clark's immediate reaction to Wood's hostility was to try to win support from the students' National Reserve Corps. He thought it "possibly in the cards that Wood stupidly would throw us over unless we fix it with the college presidents and the people who have influence over him."[52] Accordingly, Clark sought out Henry S. Drinker (with whom he had already talked several times during the summer) and with Drinker's approval proposed a merger at the annual meeting of the Advisory Board of College Presidents in mid-November.[53] Clark's argument was that "the emphasis from now on must be on the student end of the military training camps and that the business men can better direct the major part of their energies to cooperating and assisting in that movement." Although the older men intended to keep up their military activities, they had the money and organization to increase student participation far beyond what it had been in 1913, 1914, and 1915. Clark talked of raising $25,000, "sending a circular . . . to every student throughout the country," organizing "enrollment committees in every college," and launching "a systematic campaign of meetings and speeches to explain the movement."[54] Wood attended the meeting and "seemed to get the idea that we wanted to swallow up the students and . . . were trying to take the thing out of his hands."[55] Fortunately for Clark, Drinker and his fellow university presidents thought otherwise.

[51]Clark to Franklin D. Roosevelt, November 11, 1915, Clark MSS.

[52]Clark to John W. Farley, November 9, 1915, ibid.

[53]Drinker had been a bit fearful during the summer that the businessmen would overwhelm the students. Wood told him that, as far as he was concerned, the National Reserve Corps was definitely "the mother organization. . . . The business element, if we manage to wiggle through the present difficulties, will probably drop back to its previous attitude of indifference. . . . The real work has got to be done in the colleges and this we must stick to as our principal line of effort." Wood to Drinker, July 16, 1915, Wood MSS. When Drinker came to know Clark later that autumn, however, he became the Plattsburgers' most influential advocate.

[54]Clark to Drinker, November 15, 1915, Clark MSS.

[55]Clark to George F. Porter, December 6, 1915, ibid.

The next few weeks were spent in delicate maneuver. Clark had made a good friend in Drinker, who was willing to act as intermediary with both General Wood and the other educators. The Lehigh president made two trips to New York in late November and was in almost daily contact with Clark by mail and phone. Details of a new constitution were worked out, as was the composition of the governing committees. The first week in December found Drinker, Clark, Ted Roosevelt, and Philip Carroll visiting Princeton where they obtained the endorsement of John Grier Hibben, president of the Advisory Board. Presidents Hadley of Yale, Lowell of Harvard, and Schurman of Cornell also gave approval. Drinker mailed out copies of the proposed constitution to every student member of the Reserve Corps, and by December 16, 1915, a majority had ratified.[56] Even Wood, who was treated with the utmost tact, decided to go along. "Mr. Carroll had a long and very satisfactory talk with [the] General," Clark reported, "and I think everything is going to work out harmoniously."[57]

The next step was to sound out the Regiment. The January 1916 number of the *Bulletin* (which appeared in late December) contained a report by Clark about the proposed merger. He stated that the objective of the new association was to remain the same as the old — "To encourage reasonable military training for the citizens of the United States by promoting a national system of training camps and by other such means as may be deemed advisable." Clark emphasized that the Regiment would retain its organization regardless and that the amalgamation would not take place unless two-thirds of the Regiment approved. The Executive Committee urged acceptance.[58] Approval, which came by the middle of January, was practically unanimous.

[56]The step-by-step details of the merger can be found in the Drinker folder in the Clark MSS. There are some dozen or so letters from November 15 to mid-December.

[57]Clark to Drinker, November 30, 1915, ibid.

[58]*Bulletin of the First Training Regiment* (January 1916), pp. 35–36.

FOUR

There was a Regimental dinner at the Harvard Club on January 3, 1916, with approximately 800 Plattsburgers attending. General Wood spoke, giving his usual quotation from Demosthenes: "Go yourselves, every man of you, and stand in the ranks."[59] At this meeting and at a similar gathering in Boston two days later, the training camp men unanimously endorsed universal military training.[60] But these were spontaneous expressions, not official resolutions. Clark wondered whether it was good politics to advocate as an organization what nearly every Plattsburger advocated personally. Possibly the new Military Training Camps Association should take a controversial stand at its first formal meeting in early February.[61]

The expediency of calling for universal military training at such an early date was difficult to determine. Clark inclined toward caution. He and his friends had just begun to relax again after their near rupture with General Wood. Their organization and finances were still in the embryo stage, and it was not yet clear how Congress would react to Secretary Garrison's Continental Army plan. Thus, when Theodore Roosevelt had urged commitment in late November, Clark told the former president that "it may be a good combination if you go ahead to blaze the way and take an uncompromising stand, while the young fellows like the 'Plattsburgers' go ahead on the idea of practical education . . . then when we get over a million men . . . we can all strike openly and hard for universal service and put it through."[62] Nevertheless, the idea of a bold stand was almost irresistible. Clark toyed with the possibility of having Samuel Gompers, Elihu Root, Henry L. Stimson, and Roosevelt speak at a special Plattsburg dinner, after which the organization would commit itself. DeLancey Jay admit-

[59]Wood Diary, January 3, 1916; *Bulletin of the First Training Regiment* (February 1916), pp. 53–54.
[60]Clark to DeLancey Jay, January 7, 1916, Clark MSS.
[61]J. Lloyd Derby to Clark, n.d. (ca. January 1, 1916), ibid.
[62]Clark to Roosevelt, November 30, 1915, ibid.

ted that it would be "pretty dangerous for the Regiment" to appear as a "semi-political organization displaying pernicious activity against the Commander-in-Chief," but if such action "could accomplish any real advance toward this goal" the Regiment "should not hesitate to sacrifice itself."[63] Lloyd Derby's advice was that "logically, we should have some kind of written argument embodying our finding— we who have gone through the mill—and our faith."[64]

Clark decided in favor of moderation. Several Plattsburgers had objected to a universal training statement; Samuel Gompers, while interested and sympathetic, declined to speak.[65] "We shall avoid all propaganda not directly connected with our single purpose of getting men into the training camps," Clark wrote. "Of course, we expect by getting men into the camps ultimately to create a great body of public opinion, but we shall expect to do it by the education the men get by going through the camp."[66] According to Clark, each man who took training would create "a radius of influence that will gradually permeate the country. . . . We must build solidly, going from step to step, demonstrating success at each point before we undertake more."[67]

The next step for the Plattsburgers was to clear their recruitment plans with the War Department. By this time, mid-January 1916, Garrison's Continental Army program was experiencing trouble in Congress. Hearings before the House and Senate committees on military affairs had shown that most congressmen favored the National Guard over any new federal reserve. With the situation so unpromising, it was important that the Plattsburgers knew where they stood, particularly in view of the fact that they were already nearly halfway toward their goal of $100,000 for publicity purposes.[68] Since their meeting with Garrison

[63]Jay, memorandum (ca. January 1916), ibid.

[64]Derby to Clark, n.d. (ca. January 1916), ibid.

[65]Clark to Gompers, December 28, 1915; Gompers to Clark, January 7, 1916, ibid.

[66]Clark to S. Stanwood Menken, January 5, 1916, ibid.

[67]Clark to Walton Clark, Jr., January 7, 1916, ibid.

[68]See Grenville Clark to Walton Clark, Jr., Jan. 7, 1916, ibid. William Cooper

in November, they had been operating only on vague assurances. If the War Department approved, Clark and
Drinker had drawn up circulars and enrollment blanks
which they wanted to mail out. "We are not proposing
something in rivalry or opposition to the continental army
plan," Clark wrote to Assistant Secretary Breckinridge, "but
something which will help it out if it goes through and
provide a substitute if it does not."[69] A conference with
Breckinridge was arranged for January 15, 1916, with
Clark, Drinker, and Finance Committee chairman Tompkins McIlvaine present. As in November, the Plattsburgers
found the department cautious but sympathetic. Clark
summed up afterward: "If the Continental Army plan goes
through, we shall do our best to turn over the recruits that
we get to the Continental Army and will throw our
influence and recruiting organization behind the plan. If it
does not go through, we understand that we will have the
full support and active assistance of the War Department in
making the summer camps successful, on the theory that
the camps will then be the only thing standing for the
principle of a citizen force under exclusive Federal control."[70]

Clark wanted to launch a publicity campaign with full
fanfare at the inaugural meeting of the Military Training
Camps Association, set for February 4, 1916, in New York.
At the last moment Breckinridge urged him to hold back.
This was when President Wilson made his famous "swing
around the circle," wherein he spoke out eloquently in
favor of the Continental Army and "the greatest navy in
the world." The War Department wanted to see what the
president's Midwestern tour would bring. Breckinridge un-
derlined the fact that Garrison was seeking an exclusive
federal reserve; and "whether or not the starting out at this
date to make public any intentions with respect to the War
Department to hold these summer camps would have a

Procter and Percy H. Stewart had both pledged $5,000. Most Plattsburgers, in-
cluding Clark, gave sums of less than $100.

[69]Clark to Breckinridge, January 11, 1916, ibid.

[70]Ibid., January 20, 1916.

favorable or unfavorable effect on the essential principle of policy that he is urging, he alone must determine."[71] Clark grumbled, but withheld publicity.[72] As late as February 9, five days after the president returned to Washington, Garrison and Breckinridge told Drinker "not to say very much about our camps at present for reasons which seemed to be good."[73]

FIVE

With recruitment delayed, the Plattsburgers turned to lesser problems of organization. Curiously, this routine task took on new importance with the eleventh-hour additions of San Francisco and Fort Sheridan to the Military Training Camps Association (MTCA).

The central figure seems to have been Clark's good friend William M. Rutter, a Chicago businessman and member of the Executive Committee of the First Training Regiment. Rutter had written Clark early in December of his discovery that the chairman of the Fort Sheridan Training Camp Association "is an old boyhood friend of mine and [I] think there ought to be a very good chance of winning them around when the proper moment... arrives."[74] Busy with General Wood and the National Reserve Corps, Clark had let the matter rest. Later in the month, Rutter learned that a Yale man and a member of his "Club," Edwin D. Keith, had attended the Business Men's Camp at the Presidio and that Keith was authorized by the San Franciscans to join with the Plattsburg organization.[75] Clark was leery, since he had heard the stories from Dibblee and others about the *San Francisco Examiner's* "evil" influence.[76] Rutter was reassuring; and in early January, Clark sent Keith a formal merger proposal. If

[71]Breckinridge to Clark, January 29, 1916, ibid.
[72]Clark to Breckinridge, February 1, 1916, ibid.
[73]Drinker to Clark, February 9, 1916, ibid.
[74]Rutter to Clark, December 10, 1915, ibid.
[75]Ibid., December 24, 1915.
[76]Clark to Rutter, December 27, 1915, ibid.

they desired, the San Franciscans could even have dis-
proportionate representation on the new Governing Committee.[77] Keith accepted on January 17, 1916.[78]

The Fort Sheridanites joined because of Rutter and
Keith. Originally, Clark had intended to hold the inaugural
meeting of the MTCA in Chicago, but out of fear of
offending the Fort Sheridan Association he had changed
the site to New York. Keith, who had recently moved to
Illinois, was disappointed. He told Clark he had talked with
Harry Pearsons, head of the Chicago organization, and
found him ignorant of the New Yorkers' plans. The problem was one of misunderstanding, Keith argued, and if
Clark approached them tactfully the Fort Sheridanites
would be only too happy to join.[79] Rutter expressed similar
optimism a few days later, following a conversation with
Mayor Pearsons—his "old boyhood friend."[80] Clark was
convinced. "[It] is in the interest of all," he wrote to Pearsons on January 26, "that our efforts should not be scattered and disjointed." He apologized for previous mis-
conceptions and assured Pearsons that the Plattsburgers
were very anxious to have the Chicagoans cooperate. He
again offered more than proportionate membership on the
new Governing Committee.[81] The Fort Sheridan Association accepted Clark's invitation on February 1; and, after a
flurry of telegrams, Pearsons and two other Chicago representatives traveled by train to New York for the first meeting of the Governing Committee of the Military Training
Camps Association of the United States.[82]

Over one hundred persons attended the February 4
gathering at the Yale Club. The bylaws that were formally
adopted called for a permanent Governing Committee of
fifty, to include representatives of the Executive Com-

[77]Clark to Keith, January 3, 1916, ibid.
[78]Keith to Clark, January 17, 1916, ibid.
[79]Ibid., January 24, 1916.
[80]Rutter to Clark, January 29, 1916, ibid.
[81]Clark to Pearsons, January 26, 1916, ibid.
[82]Pearsons to Clark (telegram), February 1, 1916; Clark to Pearsons (telegrams), February 1 and 3, 1916, ibid.

mittees of the older organizations, together with members of the Advisory Board of College Presidents, and other members of the MTCA (not exceeding twenty) to be selected by the Governing Committee. The Governing Committee also appointed the following standing committees: an Executive Committee of nine, an Auditing Committee of three, a Finance Committee of twenty in each of the four military departments, and an Enrollment Committee of fifty in each department.[83] With exception of the Advisory Board of College Presidents, the MTCA was strictly a service organization — "A National Association composed of men who have completed one or more tours of duty in a Camp of Military Instruction, conducted by the Regular Army of the United States." Once again the Plattsburgers stated their "purpose of encouraging reasonable military training for the citizens of the United States, by promoting a national system of Federal Training Camps, and by such other means as may be advisable."[84]

Effective leadership of the Association was vested in the chairman and secretary of the Governing Committee, both of whom would be members *ex officio* of the Executive Committee. Drinker and Clark assumed these positions, respectively. Provision was made also for a salaried executive secretary and a treasurer. It was no coincidence that the two appointees were Clark's closest associates, Lloyd Derby and DeLancey Jay.[85]

SIX

Grenville Clark could look back with satisfaction on the accomplishments of the past six months. Not only had the training camp movement grown, it had retained the sup-

[83]The first Executive Committee of the MTCA consisted of Philip A. Carroll (New York), John W. Farley (Boston), Anson Conger Goodyear (Buffalo), Edwin D. Keith (San Francisco), Harry P. Pearsons (Chicago), William Cooper Procter (Cincinnati), George F. Tyler (Philadelphia), and D. A. Reed (Pittsburgh).

[84]"Minutes of First Meeting of Governing Committee of Military Training Camps Association of the United States at the Yale Club, New York City on February 4, 1916," Clark MSS. See also Perry, *Plattsburg Movement*, pp. 67-69.

[85]See Clark to Jay, December 23, 1915, Clark MSS.

port of Wood, established a nationwide organization, and gained the confidence of the War Department. Clark was not the least bit pessimistic as he contemplated a recruitment campaign for the summer of 1916.[86]

But suddenly, Clark's complacency was shattered, and the Plattsburg movement was placed in a position even more tenuous than that of the previous autumn. On February 10, 1916, Garrison and Breckinridge resigned from the War Department.

[86]See Clark to Harry P. Pearsons, February 8, 1916, ibid.

V.

The National Defense Act of 1916

The resignation of Garrison and Breckinridge from the War Department constituted a major crisis for the Plattsburg movement. Most observers interpreted the action as a protest against President Wilson's abandonment of Garrison's program to the antipreparedness forces in Congress, led by James Hay of Virginia, chairman of the House Committee on Military Affairs. "Hay voices the real sentiments of the powers that be," Wood growled on February 11, 1916, "and Garrison has just found it out. I told him long ago that Hay was speaking with the confidence of one with a strong backing. It looks to me pretty ugly.... The President can crush Hay if he wants to, but he doesn't want to."[1] And Wood continued to take this negative attitude in the following months during which Congress debated and eventually passed the National Defense Act. The fact that such legislation exalted the National Guard over a federal reserve blinded the general to other possibilities. "A more rotten thing has never been presented to Congress," he wrote in early May. "If this thing goes through you are going to have a militia pork barrel and an organization which will make the pension list look like a dried up lemon. This is not military preparedness. This is debauchery of public funds."[2]

The question was whether the Plattsburgers should follow their general and refuse to compromise or continue to work within the system and try to salvage what they could.

The organizers of the Military Training Camps Association chose the latter course. The day after Garrison's resignation Clark and Philip Carroll went to Washington to testify before Hay's committee, the first of many such trips by Clark and his associates. By the end of February, Lloyd Derby was keeping in daily contact with senators and congressmen on the military affairs committees. Every ten days or so, Clark and Drinker would join Derby for conferences with legislators and War Department officials. The Lehigh president said: "Clark, I think we ought to stay down at Washington all winter and put this through." The lobbying effort continued through the spring, and they "saw every senator but three or four."[3]

The result was that these "three musketeers" (as they called themselves) managed to secure the passage of Section 54 of the new National Defense Act.[4] This section authorized federal training camps for civilians and provided for the cost of uniforms, food, and transportation. As a consequence, the 16,000 men who took Plattsburg training in the summer of 1916 were the first to do so under federal statute. Even General Wood came to appreciate what the MTCA leaders had done.

ONE

The Defense Act had an interesting background.[5] As early as March 1915, Garrison had ordered the General Staff to

[1]Wood to Frank R. McCoy, February 11, 1916, McCoy MSS.

[2]Wood to Frederick A. Alger, May 1, 1916, Wood MSS.

[3]As quoted in minutes of meeting of the Governing Committee of the Military Training Camps Association, November 24, 1916, Clark MSS.

[4]Clark to Drinker, May 9, 1916, Clark MSS.

[5]Nearly every major study of the Wilson administration touches on the National Defense Act of 1916. The best published accounts are Arthur S. Link, *Woodrow Wilson and the Progressive Era, 1910-1917* (New York, 1954), pp. 179-89; Link, *Wilson*, 5 vols. (Princeton, N.J., 1947-   ), 4:18-52, 330-34; and George C. Herring, Jr., "James Hay and the Preparedness Controversy, 1915-1916," *Journal of Southern History* 30 (November 1964): 383-404. The most comprehensive and scholarly treatment is in James William Pohl, "The General Staff and American Defense Policy: The Formative Period, 1898-1917" (Ph.D. diss., University of Texas, 1967), pp. 272-361.

draw up a comprehensive plan for military reorganization. The secretary was anticipating President Wilson's conversion to preparedness (which came in mid-July) and hoped to have ready a program that would be an improvement over previous policy statements and at the same time stand a reasonable chance of passing Congress. Progress was swift. When the president made his decision on July 21, 1915, Garrison, Breckinridge, Generals Scott and Bliss, and selected staff officers had already held "five sessions on the results of the work of . . . the War College Division, five hours at a time."[6]

Wilson's support of preparedness was crucial, and it came only after considerable soul-searching. The *Lusitania* sinking in May and subsequent negotiations with Germany had raised the danger of war. The aroused state of public opinion made it impossible to ignore defense needs. So Wilson took up the War Department proposals — but with his own sense of priorities, as diplomatist and politician, as well as commander-in-chief.[7]

The essentials of Garrison's program became apparent in the middle of August, at the same time that Mayor Mitchel, Robert Bacon, and other rookies were beginning their second week at Plattsburg. In an article in the *Independent,* entitled "Reasonable Preparation," the secretary argued that "the one great lesson of all our wars is that they must be carried to a conclusion by citizen soldiers and these soldiers must be *trained.*" He went on to propose a national reserve force, or Continental Army, of some 400,000 to 500,000 civilian volunteers, trained in summer camps similar to those instituted for college students by General Wood in 1913. Garrison did not mention the militia. It was obvious that this proposed federal reserve would take over as the country's first line of defense after the Regular Army. Nor did the secretary advocate any great increases in the professional establishment. Rather, he warned of the consequences of invasion, and urged that "the wise anti-

---

[6]Hugh L. Scott to Frank R. McCoy, July 21, 1915, Scott MSS.
[7]Link, *Wilson,* 4:18.

militarist . . . be the most earnest advocate of reasonable preparation."[8]

Garrison's statement was a conscious "boiling down" of what his professional advisers desired. As the General Staff's "Statement of a Proper Military Policy for the United States" (published later that autumn) expressed it, they would have preferred a combination of Regular Army and federal reserves comprising nearly 1,500,000 men. But such a request would have been politically unattainable.[9] The decision to supersede the militia was almost unanimous.[10] These soldiers had read their Upton and had locked their minds against the practicality of federal control over state troops. The constitutional barrier was insurmountable; of this the General Staff was certain. General Scott told the secretary that "it is not material where the line is drawn, for under the [constitutional] view most favorable to Federal power over the Militia, we are still lacking in the authority to control the training of troops."[11] Some disagreement did arise over personnel for the proposed Continental Army. Furloughed regulars, militia veterans, and graduates of military and land-grant schools were to contribute substantial numbers, particularly in the officer categories, but this would not be enough. Even an expanded "Plattsburg" effort was likely to fall short. As for the possibility of conscripting the required men, nine of the eighteen officers in the War College Division were in favor of drafting civilians into the Continental Army from the beginning; seventeen endorsed conscription when voluntary recruitment proved inadequate.[12] None of these opinions appeared in print, however, not even in the "Statement of a Proper Military Policy." Some grumbling occurred as a result, especially among friends of General

[8]Lindley M. Garrison, "Reasonable Preparation," *Independent* 83 (August 16, 1915): 229.

[9]*War Department Annual Reports, 1915* (Washington, D.C., 1916), 1:114–30.

[10]Notes of War College Division meeting, June 29, 1915, WCD 9053–46, National Archives, Record Group 165.

[11]Scott to Garrison, July 31, 1915, Scott MSS.

[12]Notes of War College Division meeting, June 29, 1915, WCD 9053–46, RG 165.

Wood, who argued that it was foolish to advocate a military force which experts knew could not be recruited.[13]

Garrison was not naive. He later admitted before Congress the possible necessity for conscription.[14] But he could see that public opinion was not yet ready to support compulsory service. A federal reserve was the most he could hope for, and even that would require persuasion. His article in the *Independent* would begin the educational process. He urged President Wilson to speak out.[15]

Garrison received his answer on August 24, 1915, the day before Theodore Roosevelt made his incendiary speech at Plattsburg. That afternoon Wilson called Henry Breckinridge to the White House. The chief executive was in a bad mood, for the *Baltimore Sun* had just published a story concerning plans which the War College purportedly had drawn up for possible war with Germany. Wilson did not know of such plans; and if they did exist, he deplored that news should leak out and agitate the popular mind. Nor was he pleased with Garrison's recent article. He wanted a "plain business-like statement" from the secretary, not a lawyer's brief. The country, Wilson believed, was sufficiently aroused to the need for defense that it could trust the administration to formulate a program without indulging in propaganda.

The president then told Breckinridge of a conference with James Hay. The Virginia Democrat had promised to report out a bill for military reorganization if it originated with the president, but not if it came from Garrison. Hay said that the secretary had antagonized the Senate and House committees with his brusqueness and his unwillingness to consult or listen to advice. Garrison acted too much like a judge, and Wilson complained also of the resentment which Garrison's inflexible opinions had provoked among the members of the Cabinet. He hoped that Breckinridge

[13]See Colonel William H. Johnston to Wood, November 24, 1915, Wood MSS.

[14]"To Increase the Efficiency of the Military Establishment of the United States," *Hearings before the Committee on Military Affairs, House of Representatives*, 64th Cong., 1st sess. (Washington, D.C., 1916), p. 68.

[15]Garrison to Wilson, August 19, 1916, Wilson MSS.

would do whatever he could to try to curb such excesses.

The assistant secretary replied with equal candor, cautioning the president against accepting Hay's point of view. Because of their mutual hostility toward General Wood, Breckinridge at one time had been friendly with Hay. But after three years in the administration, he had come to see the congressman as "a narrow-minded venomous man, having no real interest in the Army, but a real antipathy for it." Hay did not get along with Garrison because the secretary refused to play politics and had opposed extra appropriations for the cavalry remount station at Front Royal, Virginia, a part of Hay's constituency. As far as Breckinridge knew, Garrison had maintained a perfectly cordial relationship with George E. Chamberlain of Oregon, chairman of the Senate Committee on Military Affairs. It was dangerous for the president to follow Hay's lead; unless the congressman were coerced, nothing productive was likely to come out of his committee. Wilson softened and inquired about the other members of the military committees. They were not strong for preparedness, Breckinridge admitted, but their position was the result of ignorance rather than hostility. Congress needed to be guided. The president repeated his injunction against stirring up public opinion. He said that the country did not want war and would oppose conscription. A defense program had to adapt to such circumstances. Breckinridge did not debate further.[16]

This conversation revealed the difference between Wilson and Garrison. In terms of policy it was not immediately apparent, for the chief executive eventually did support the Continental Army scheme—and with considerable eloquence. But Wilson could remain detached about military policy. It was not one of those public questions which engaged his lofty and sometimes stubborn sense of right and wrong. He was able to measure defense requirements against a hierarchy of objectives, not the least of which was maintenance of his own political leadership. He did not

[16]Breckinridge Diary, August 24, 1915.

want Garrison rocking the boat any more than he did the generals. To do so might drive an important segment of the Democratic party into opposition — James Hay, William Jennings Bryan, Warren Worth Bailey, Claude Kitchin, and other rural progressives who were suspicious of preparedness propaganda. Wilson had to maintain flexibility. For the next two months, therefore, congressional leaders went in and out of the White House, listening to the president's quiet arguments. It was not until November 4, 1915, in a speech before the Manhattan Club in New York, that Wilson formally presented the administration's program. Until that time he did not make public his conversion to preparedness.[17]

The president's attitude placed Garrison in a difficult position. The secretary was not detached. While Wilson conversed with politicians, Garrison chafed and worried as he and his advisers went over each item in the "Statement of a Proper Military Policy." Two months of enforced silence and the knowledge that the president did not have full confidence in him made Garrison jumpy and apt to overreact. His reprimand of General Wood following the Roosevelt affair at Plattsburg was a case in point. So acutely aware was Garrison of the need to guide public opinion that he could not understand Wilson's willingness to consider politics. Even before the president's Manhattan Club speech the lines of conflict were drawn — Garrison, unwilling to compromise on what he believed was already an irreducible program; and Wilson, supporting his secretary of war in principle but without Garrison's sense of urgency.[18]

TWO

It was with high-sounding words that Wilson launched the preparedness campaign in New York on November 4,

[17]Link, *Wilson*, 4:21.

[18]On the early conflicts between Wilson and Garrison, see Pohl, "The General Staff and American Defense Policy," pp. 287–93.

1915. "We have it in mind," he said, "to be prepared, not for war, but only for defense; and with the thought constantly in our minds that the principles we hold most dear can be achieved by the slow processes of history only in the kindly and wholesome atmosphere of peace, and not by the use of hostile force." He proposed a moderately increased Regular Army, a strengthened National Guard, and a 400,000-man Continental Army as the proper means for securing such principles.[19] Wilson was hoping to unite all shades of opinion under a nonpartisan banner.

The speech brought a roar of outrage from pacifists and other opponents of militarism. The well-known radical Emma Goldman spoke of Wilson's betrayal and concluded that there was no longer any difference between Theodore Roosevelt, "the born bully who uses a club," and Wilson, "the history professor who uses the smooth polished university mask." Men like Robert M. La Follette and William Jennings Bryan charged that the president was being duped, that it was profiteers and munition-makers who were the real proponents of preparedness.[20] This was the time, also, when Henry Ford chartered his famous "peace ship," *Oscar II*, which sailed to Europe in a bizarre attempt to get the soldiers "out of the trenches by Christmas."[21]

This surge of opinion gave heart to antipreparedness advocates in Congress. Claude Kitchin of North Carolina, the new House majority leader and spokesman for a bloc of some thirty to fifty progressive Democrats, told Wilson on November 8, 1915, that he could not support the War Department program.[22] An opposition quickly coalesced, composed of National Guard partisans, congressmen who could see no possible danger of invasion, Southerners fearful of Negro enlistment in the Continental Army, and

[19]Link, *Wilson*, 4:21.

[20]For a good summary of the reaction to Wilson's speech, see Arthur A. Ekirch, Jr., *The Civilian and the Military* (New York, 1956), pp. 163–65.

[21]Burnett Hershey, *The Odyssey of Henry Ford and the Great Peace Ship* (New York, 1967).

[22]Link, *Wilson*, 4:26–29; Herring, "James Hay," pp. 390–91; and Alex Mathews Arnett, *Claude Kitchin and the Wilson War Policies* (Boston, 1937), pp. 68–86.

personal enemies of Secretary Garrison. When Congress convened in early December, Kitchin and Hay were able to pack the House Military Affairs Committee so that seven out of eleven members represented Southern districts.[23] Even though the president made preparedness the keynote of his annual message on December 7, his party responded with a noticeable lack of enthusiasm. Vigorous leadership at this juncture might have reversed the momentum, and Wilson did begin to twist arms and confer with Republican leaders. But on December 18, 1915, the president married Edith Bolling Galt of Washington and went off on an extended honeymoon. It was, as Arthur S. Link has observed, one of the few instances in his public career that Wilson seemed confused and ineffective.[24]

The War Department was disappointed. The hostile reaction seemed to justify everything that Garrison had said about prior publicity. Conferences with the National Guard Association in early November and promises from Hay ("I will make every effort to put it through") had raised false hopes.[25] Now, the politicians seemed to be bending with the breeze. "Hay came down here in November," General Scott complained, "and told the Secretary of War to have no misgivings at all, that he was going to pass the bill right through. He came down last week and said that he did not know whether anything would get through; and he had no more than gotten out of the office before Senator Chamberlain came along and said the same thing. . . . They are very lukewarm, and desirous of doing as little as possible. So nobody here knows what is coming out of the box."[26]

Committee hearings began early in January 1916; and since both Hay and Chamberlain gave notice that they were preparing their own reorganization bills, the chief of staff did not joke about something unknown "coming out of the

[23]Herring, "James Hay," p. 392.

[24]Link, *Wilson*, 4:35–36.

[25]*Richmond Times-Dispatch*, October 25, 1915, cited in Herring, "James Hay," p. 390.

[26]Scott to E. St. J. Greble, December 27, 1915, Scott MSS.

box." In fact, Chamberlain, an outspoken and energetic Democrat, was more in tune with War Department proposals than Scott suspected.[27] Past differences with Garrison and an unwillingness to split his party led him to draw up separate legislation, but when this bill finally emerged from committee in March 1916 it included a federal reserve, 261,000 strong, along lines similar to Garrison's Continental Army. Nearly every feature of the Senate bill was of greater advantage than that reported out by Hay's committee.

The House hearings constituted the army's real test. Hay's defense of legislative prerogative and suspicion of professional soldiers gave Garrison and his advisers little cause for optimism. Even worse, it soon became apparent that Hay was being advised by General Wood's old antagonist, Fred C. Ainsworth, and that a prime object of Hay and his friends was to reduce the power of the General Staff.[28] On the question of the Continental Army versus the National Guard, the Virginia congressman took the view that the Organized Militia was by itself capable of providing the country with an effective reserve. By increasing federal pay, Hay believed that the government had a lever for raising militia standards. The Regular Army could take a larger part in training personnel and issuing equipment, and if the War Department were given authority to qualify state officers for equivalent federal commissions, charges of political corruption could be lessened. The constitutional question of militia service outside the United States could be solved by requiring Guardsmen to swear an oath that they would answer, as units, calls for federal service anywhere.[29]

Garrison's testimony before the House Committee (January 6 and 8, 1916), though powerful, was vulnerable

[27]According to one officer on the General Staff in 1915–1916, Chamberlain was "extremely frank, and when he got a drink or two under his belt . . . he became double frank." Moseley, "One Soldier's Journey," 1:130–31, Moseley MSS.

[28]On Ainsworth's involvement, see "Woodrow Wilson and Preparedness," an unpublished essay by James Hay in the Hay MSS, Library of Congress.

[29]Weigley, *History of the United States Army*, p. 345.

to Hay's logic. For reasons that were more political than military, the secretary said he would favor a "militia pay" measure, but that the nation's first line of reserve should fall to the Continental Army. The testimony of Generals Scott, Bliss, and Crowder, and that of Assistant Secretary Breckinridge echoed this premise. Garrison denied that anyone was trying to undercut the National Guard; it was just constitutionally impossible to make a federal force out of that organization. When asked who would enlist in the Continental Army, the secretary admitted that many Guardsmen whose interest was in federal service would probably fill the ranks. But he maintained that the two forces were not necessarily incompatible and that the Continental Army might follow the Plattsburg example and attract a different type of man. The inevitable question arose as to how the War Department expected to induce some 400,000 persons to volunteer for a federal reserve, when the Regular Army and militia were finding it difficult to recruit even less than that number. Garrison offered a few details, mostly variations on General Wood's short enlistment theories, but was not entirely convincing. Then he remarked candidly that if the necessary volunteers were not forthcoming, the government might have to recommend conscription.[30] Scott and Breckinridge also alluded to the possibility of compulsory service, as did Wood in his appearance before the committee later in the month.[31]

The upshot of such argument was to harden opposition within the Congress. It seemed neither logical nor economical to advocate two reserve systems (Wood's advice regarding the militia was to "make it a straight Federal force without any relationship whatever to the state"); and when faced with a choice most politicians were likely to favor an organization which already existed and whose members could vote.[32] Repeated salvos of Uptonian dogma could not convince the committee that the National Guard was in-

[30]*House Hearings*, pp. 1–79.
[31]Ibid., pp. 83, 126–27, 738.
[32]Ibid., p. 676.

herently rotten. Nor did it help for War Department representatives to become arrogant and deliver judgments as
though they were the last word in expert opinion. Breckinridge showed tendencies in this direction, and there were
times when he seemed more intent on making debate
points than on providing information. Once, when queried
as to who originated the Continental Army plan, the assistant secretary sarcastically informed everyone that it had
been Thomas Jefferson.[33] Breckinridge was asked on another occasion what hopes the War Department had for
recruiting the Continental Army, and he replied: "No more
and no less hope, Mr. Chairman, than anyone who believes
that an adequate military system in this country can be
based on the voluntary principle."[34] Testimony such as this
did not win converts.

Garrison and his advisers found themselves in a difficult
position. As the hundred-odd witnesses, including pacifists
and National Guard officers, appeared before Hay's committee during January and early February, it became clear
that only two or three committee members were inclined to
support the Continental Army plan. Since such a force was
deemed the bare minimum for effective preparedness, the
War Department was understandably bitter. General Bliss
may have hit close to the truth when he complained: "Congress is afraid of any proposition for training citizen reserves under the voluntary principle. They do not believe
that citizens will volunteer in sufficient numbers. And that
will bring them face to face with the issue of compulsory
training. And that they do not want. So they fall back on
the militia as a sop to public sentiment."[35] The only hope
for Garrison's program lay in enlisting President Wilson's
unequivocal support. This the secretary tried to bring
about.

Wilson had first learned the details of Hay's militia
scheme on January 11, after returning from his wedding

[33]Ibid., p. 128. See also Breckinridge, "Memoir," pp. 218–19.
[34]*House Hearings*, p. 127.
[35]Tasker H. Bliss to Thomas R. Barry, February 8, 1916, Bliss MSS.

trip. The next day Garrison warned him that "there can be no honest or worthy solution which does not result in national forces under the exclusive control of the national government." Hay's plan, he told Wilson, compelled a choice "between reliance upon a system of state troops, forever subject to constitutional limitations" and "reliance upon national forces, raised, officered, trained, and controlled by national authority." To accept the National Guard as a federal force would be to "delude the people into believing the subject had been settled" and would "set back the whole cause of legitimate, honest national defense in an entirely unjustifiable way."[36] The secretary was delivering an ultimatum.[37]

The president tried to soothe Garrison, saying that he accepted the premise of a federal reserve, but admitting that he was "not irrevocably or dogmatically committed to any one plan of providing the nation with such a reserve."[38] At the same time he told Hay that, in his opinion, the constitutional barriers to a federalized militia were insurmountable.[39] Then Wilson on January 27 began an eight-day speaking tour in which he explained and defended the administration's preparedness program before the public. Everywhere he went — New York, Pittsburgh, Cleveland, Chicago, Milwaukee, Kansas City, St. Louis — vast and cheering throngs seemed to accept his arguments without reservations. Satisfied, the president returned to Washington to await the upsurge which would topple congressional opposition.

But Wilson, it turned out, had waited too long. The huzzas which he received from Midwestern audiences came mostly from city folk, where preparedness sentiment was high. That he had convinced the nation's farmers was unlikely.[40] Hay informed him on February 5 that congression-

[36]Garrison to Wilson, January 12, 1916, Wilson MSS.

[37]"Yours is the ultimate responsibility; yours is the final determination as to the manner in which the situation shall be faced and treated." Garrison to Wilson, January 14, 1916, ibid.

[38]Wilson to Garrison, January 17, 1916, ibid.

[39]Wilson to James Hay, January 18, 1916, Hay MSS.

al Democrats unalterably opposed the Continental Army and that his own militia pay proposal was the only way to salvage party unity. Hay was certain that the bill could be written so as to assure both federal control and constitutionality.[41] Three days later he reported that Garrison had thoroughly antagonized the House committee.[42] The president had virtually no choice. He attempted to persuade Garrison of the necessity for compromise, but the secretary would have none of it. Bowing to the inevitable and convinced that national security was being sacrificed to politics, Garrison resigned from the administration on February 10, 1916. Henry Breckinridge loyally followed suit.[43]

THREE

These legislative and War Department preliminaries had the close attention of Plattsburg leaders. Clark and his friends sympathized fully with Garrison's position vis-à-vis the Continental Army and National Guard.[44] Privately, they could even grumble about the hypocrisy of supporting both organizations: "The plain truth of the thing is that everybody interested in getting a sound system [Clark wrote] is preparing to knife the National Guard at the first opportunity."[45] Publicly, the Plattsburgers remained cautious. Relying on their two visits to the War Department in October and January, they hoped to get the training camps incorporated into military reorganization without having to make any special plea before Congress. Clark talked about sending someone to watch things in Washington and had asked advice from a fellow Plattsburger, Congressman Thomas W. Miller of Delaware.[46] Miller, too,

---

[40]Link, *Woodrow Wilson and the Progressive Era,* pp. 186–87.

[41]Hay to Wilson, February 5, 1916, Hay MSS.

[42]Hay to Wilson, February 8, 1916, ibid.

[43]Garrison to Wilson, February 10, 1916; and Breckinridge to Wilson, February 10, 1916, Breckinridge MSS.

[44]Clark to DeLancey Jay, October 27, 1915, Clark MSS.

[45]Clark to Redmond Stewart, October 30, 1915, ibid.

[46]Clark to George F. Porter, December 6, 1915; and Clark to Thomas W. Miller, December 17, 1915, ibid.

counseled caution, and so the MTCA left its fate in the hands of the War Department.[47]

Garrison's resignation altered the situation drastically. Realizing that the training camps no longer had any assured status, Clark and Philip Carroll appeared before Hay's committee on February 11, the last day of the House hearings. "We are not here to advocate any general military plan," said Clark, who did most of the talking. He reiterated the MTCA's pledge to "steer clear of political activities and, as distinguished from other societies for national defense, avoid legislative propaganda and devote ourselves exclusively to . . . encouraging reasonable military training for young men." Clark assured the congressmen that the MTCA had no desire whatever to compete with the National Guard and made clear that "this movement was purely a citizens' movement, suggested by citizens to General Wood, who received it cordially but did not suggest it." What the Plattsburgers wanted was legislative recognition. If the camps were to become democratic in fact as well as in spirit, persons of every social class should be able to attend. Clark therefore urged that the federal government assume the expenses of each trainee during the course of instruction. This would exclude travel costs, and the MTCA itself would provide for recruitment.[48] Clark made an effective witness. Congressman Julius Kahn, Republican from California and a strong advocate of preparedness, asked the right questions; and even Chairman Hay seemed sympathetic. Whether or not the Plattsburgers could transform this sympathy into effective legislation was the big question.

Clark spent the next ten days in New York contemplating strategy. "Important developments pending in

---

[47]Miller to Clark, December 20, 1915, ibid. As it was, the Plattsburg camps were fairly well represented at the House hearings. Henry S. Drinker (as president of the American Institute of Mining Engineers), Richard Derby (representing the New York State Medical Association), General Wood, and Assistant Secretary Breckinridge all gave strong testimony in favor of training camps. When the hearings began to indicate congressional rejection of the Continental Army plan, Clark contemplated an appearance before the appropriations committee in mid-March, but nothing previous to that time. See Clark to Miller, January 28 and February 1, 1916, Clark MSS.

[48]*House Hearings,* copies in Clark MSS.

Washington regarding camps," he wired Drinker on February 14, "with excellent prospects for appropriation if handled with utmost care. Hope you can arrange time for conference to canvass whole situation with General Wood and me tomorrow."[49] Since Congressman Kahn had promised to do what he could in the way of adding a training camp section to Hay's committee report, Clark kept up a barrage of encouraging letters.[50] He sent Lloyd Derby to Washington not only to confer with Kahn, but also to feel out the situation in Senator Chamberlain's committee. Through his friend Senator Henry A. DuPont of Delaware, Derby arranged interviews with members of the Senate committee for Monday, February 24.[51]

Accompanied by Drinker, Clark made progress in this second visit to Capitol Hill. His conversations with the senators emphasized what was to become a standard Plattsburg argument regarding the relationship of the MTCA to the National Guard. According to Clark, the two organizations attracted different classes of men: individuals went to Plattsburg but would not join the Guard because, as businessmen, they were unable to devote the regular one night a week to drill, but could take off thirty days for summer camp; because they might object to the use of militia in labor disputes; because they believed strongly in the principle of a federal reserve; and because they might live too far from the nearest Guard unit to attend meetings on a regular basis. "The best men in the training camps," Clark promised, "can be formed into regiments . . . under exclusive Federal control, side by side with the National Guard." They will "mutually assist one another."[52] Drinker and Clark were delighted to learn that Senator Chamberlain had included in his bill provision for a federal reserve force of volunteers, trained and organized according to congressional districts. They talked with Judge Advocate

[49]Clark to Drinker (telegram), February 14, 1916, Clark MSS.
[50]Clark to Kahn, February 17, 18, 1916; Kahn to Clark, February 16, 19, 1916, ibid.
[51]Clark to Drinker, February 18, 1916, ibid.
[52]Clark to Members of the Senate Committee on Military Affairs, February 22, 1916, RG 94, AG2384423.

General Enoch H. Crowder and General William H. Carter of the General Staff, both of whom were helping Chamberlain draft his bill, and both men received their suggestions cordially.[53]

The Plattsburgers also received assurances from the House committee. "Mr. Kahn of California and Mr. [Daniel R.] Anthony [Jr.] of Kansas and Mr. [Richard] Olney [II] of Massachusetts," Clark reported, "have interested themselves in getting a provision in the House Bill authorizing the Secretary of War to hold camps at his discretion. I have seen the provision and in fact made some suggestions about it. They told us yesterday that Mr. Hay . . . was favorably impressed, but I will not believe it until I see it."[54] Derby remained in Washington for the next week, encouraging Kahn at every opportunity.[55] Then, on March 2, 1916, the House committee unanimously approved the training camp provision.[56] According to Section 83 of H.R. 12766 (formally reported by Hay on March 6), the secretary of war was authorized to maintain "camps for the military instruction and training of such citizens as may be selected for such instruction and training, upon their application and under such terms of enlistment and regulations" as he might prescribe; and "to furnish, at the expense of the United States, subsistence and medical supplies" to persons attending such camps.[57] Exultant, Kahn predicted that Section 83 would become the "entering wedge for a real army of the people."[58]

Notwithstanding this accomplishment in the House, the MTCA still had far to go. Getting the camps into the Hay bill had been a close thing, and Clark was not at all happy

[53]See Lloyd Derby to Clark, February 29, 1916, Clark MSS.

[54]Clark to Harry P. Pearsons, February 25, 1916, ibid.

[55]"I am drawn to the wisdom of omitting any specific [enlistment] obligation at present, since on general principles it is never wise to make unnecessary commitments at the experimental stage. The Secretary [of War] can, under this agreement, feel his way and adopt the best proposition that seems advisable when the issue is squarely raised." Derby to Clark, February 29, 1916, Clark MSS.

[56]Richard Olney II to Clark (telegram), March 2, 1916, Clark MSS; Drinker to Wood, March 3, 1916, Wood MSS.

[57]As quoted in Perry, *Plattsburg Movement,* pp. 97–98.

[58]Kahn to Clark, March 3, 1916, Clark MSS.

with the way House members seemed so subservient to the National Guard. Like Wood and most professional soldiers, Clark looked upon Hay's militia pay scheme as both unconstitutional and militarily unworkable.[59] He had hopes that if the Senate committee reported out an exclusive federal reserve, some favorable compromise might be worked out. "The House Committee seems to have swallowed whole the self-interested arguments of the high National Guard officers," Clark lamented to one senator. "It seems to us so obvious that no successful citizen soldiery can be organized without the support of either organized labor or the thinking part of the community that we wonder how anyone can seriously contemplate" reliance on the old militia system. "Possibly that result is now inevitable, but at least let us have an alternative plan which both the laboring classes of the nation and educated men who have thought the matter out will take part in."[60] With Derby keeping watch in Washington, Clark consulted with former Secretaries of War Stimson and Root in New York.[61] Stimson, who was in touch with the General Staff officers working on the Senate bill, told the Plattsburgers not to worry.[62] Drinker worried just the same: "I am intensely interested in the success of our legislation in Washington and really look on it just now as the most important business I have in the world," he wrote from Lehigh. "I want you *to count on me*."[63]

There was really no reason for concern. Senator Chamberlain introduced his own bill (S. 4840) on March 4, 1916, in which Sections 56 and 58 authorized a federal volunteer force separate from the Regular Army and National

[59]For Wood's opinion of the Hay bill, see Wood to John Purroy Mitchel, February 28, 1916, Mitchel MSS. For other adverse opinions, see Douglas A. MacArthur to Wood, March 20, 1916, Wood MSS; George Van Horne Moseley to Henry L. Stimson, March 3, 1916, Moseley MSS; Hugh L. Scott to Stimson, April 6, 1916, Scott MSS; and William H. Johnston to Wood, March 17, 1916, Wood MSS.

[60]Clark to Senator John W. Weeks [Massachusetts], February 28, 1916, Clark MSS.

[61]Clark to Stimson, March 2, 1916, Henry L. Stimson MSS, Sterling Library, Yale University; Clark to Weeks, February 28, 1916, Clark MSS.

[62]Stimson to Frank R. McCoy, February 28, 1916, McCoy MSS; and George Van Horne Moseley to Stimson, March 3, 1916, Moseley MSS.

[63]Drinker to Clark, March 1, 1916, Clark MSS.

Guard.[64] "This is to be purely a federal force, not to be used except in case of actual or threatened hostilities," Chamberlain later explained. "Under the limitations imposed these volunteers will form a valuable asset to our national defense plans, and will replace and provide for the public-spirited citizens who heretofore have manifested their willingness to serve the nation by participation in the so-called students' camps and business men's camps of the past four years. The volunteer force so created will have a maximum strength of about 261,000 officers and enlisted men."[65] Even though the Senate bill contained no specific provision for training camps (as did the Hay bill), the Plattsburgers preferred it because of its advocacy of the federal principle. Clark and Drinker visited Washington again on March 7 and promised General Crowder that "we will do all we can to get your Section 58 . . . adopted in both Houses. . . . If this measure becomes law, we will also do our best to make the volunteer system succeed, putting our recruitment organization at the disposal of the War Department."[66] As Clark subsequently explained to Thomas Miller, the establishment of a federal reserve was a prerequisite to the ultimate Plattsburg object of universal military training. Such an object would be impossible under a state militia system. "My own view," Clark wrote, "is that the training camp idea is simply a means to an end, namely, to get sane principles established, and I believe that if this Volunteer Bill is passed, we will practically have done our job."[67]

FOUR

Before either the Chamberlain or Hay bill came up for debate, two events occurred which complicated the situation. The first was the notorious raid on March 9, 1916, in

[64]U.S., Congress, Senate, *Congressional Record*, 64th Cong., 1st sess., 1916, pp. 3519–20.

[65]Ibid., p. 4877.

[66]Clark to Enoch H. Crowder, March 8, 1916, Clark MSS.

[67]Clark to Miller, March 11, 1916, ibid.

which Pancho Villa's nondescript cavalry swept across the border and shot up the sleepy frontier community of Columbus, New Mexico, killing seventeen Americans. Rumors were rife, as the shock waves rumbled through Washington. The so-called Punitive Expedition under Brigadier General John J. Pershing was hastily formed in Texas and on March 15 sent over the border. The previous day someone in the War Department had given out a report that, because of the sudden movement of troops, none of the civilian training camps scheduled for the spring and summer could be held. The Plattsburgers protested immediately, and General Scott issued a retraction.[68] Nevertheless, the border crisis made the training camp situation extremely fluid.[69] Just what effect Villa's raid would have on the military bills, no one could tell.

The second event was the confirmation of Newton D. Baker as the new secretary of war. Since the amiable former mayor of Cleveland was reputed to be something of a pacifist, the appointment seemed to signal another retreat on the part of the administration. Such was the interpretation of General Wood, who refused to make any overtures whatsoever to the new incumbent. Clark took a different attitude. After talking with Colonel House on March 13, he and Drinker obtained an interview with Baker for the sixteenth.[70] The recent rumor about the training camps' being cancelled and the fact that the MTCA had raised most of their $100,000 recruitment fund made such a meeting imperative. To their surprise, the Plattsburgers found the secretary cordial and entirely sympathetic. The administration would give full approval to the series of camps being planned for the summer. Clark then urged

[68]Henry S. Drinker to Hugh L. Scott, March 14, 1915; Scott to Drinker, March 15, 1916, Scott MSS.

[69]As it was, the training camp scheduled for Fort Oglethorpe, Georgia, in March had to be postponed until April because of troop movements. When President Wilson mobilized the entire National Guard in June, this also caused postponement and cancellation of several camps.

[70]See Clark to Drinker, March 13, 1916, Clark MSS; "File Delivered to Col. House, March 1916," memorandum in Clark's handwriting, ibid.; Drinker to Baker, March 17, 1916, RG 94, AG2638725.

that the board of officers appointed by Garrison to draw up
military regulations which would apply nationally to all
civilian camps be continued. Baker agreed. For the committee, Clark mentioned Wood's aides, Johnston and Dorey. Baker told General Bliss to appoint them. Clark asked
for a formal letter so as to encourage recruitment. Baker
requested his visitor to draft one, and he would sign it.
Clark asked for expenses and equipment for fifteen thousand or more trainees. The secretary promised to do his
best.

It was an extraordinary meeting, and Clark was elated
as he went out to Governor's Island the next day to tell
Wood. On hearing what happened, however, the general
exploded at Clark for interfering with his business. After
many heated words, Clark also lost his temper. "I've done
you a great service," he shouted while leaving the general's
office. "But I'm through. No one can help you!" Striding
toward the ferry a few minutes later, Clark heard footsteps
behind him and then Wood's voice. "Come back here." The
fit of anger had subsided. With a contrition that revealed
some of the tragedy in his personality, Wood asked the
younger man's forgiveness. "You've done a helpful thing,"
he confessed, "and I am grateful."[71]

Clark followed up his interview with Baker with a letter
urging the secretary to support Section 58 of the Senate bill
over Section 83 of the House bill. "The absolutely essential
point for us," he reiterated, "is that the training camps shall
obtain some reasonable legislative recognition and appropriation."[72]

The next move was not by the War Department, but by
the House of Representatives, where on March 17 debate
began on the Hay bill. Described by Hay as "a peace proposition and not . . . a war proposition," H.R. 12766 did not
arouse much controversy.[73] Next to such questions as the

[71]Notes of interview with Grenville Clark (1930–1931), Hagedorn MSS; see
also Clark to Hagedorn, January 23, 1931, ibid.
[72]Clark to Baker, March 18, 1916, Clark MSS.
[73]U.S., Congress, House, *Congressional Record*, 64th Cong., 1st sess., 1916, p.
4307.

size of the Regular Army and the composition of the National Guard, Section 83 went relatively unnoticed. Congressman Miller spoke in support of Plattsburg interests early in the debate and read into the record Secretary Baker's letter to Clark of March 16. His ten-minute disquisition repeated familiar arguments ("I was making practically the same speech you would have made," he told Clark), emphasizing the need for appropriations if the camps were to become democratic and the fact that no conflict was intended between the MTCA and the National Guard. Miller reproduced a letter from General O'Ryan in support of the latter point.[74] Richard Olney II of Massachusetts endorsed Miller's remarks and suggested that "the continental-army plan having fallen to pieces, why not encourage . . . summer military training camps all over the country" as a substitute.[75] No one spoke in opposition.

As discussion of the Hay bill continued, the essentially pacific mood of the House became obvious. Efforts to substitute a Continental Army proposal for the militia were beaten down easily, as was an amendment to prohibit the use of the National Guard as strike breakers.[76] The most serious challenge by the preparedness forces, an amendment by Kahn to raise the maximum strength of the Regular Army in Hay's bill from 140,000 to 220,000 men, failed by a vote of 213 to 191.[77] In reply to Clark's importunities, Kahn admitted, "I am almost afraid to offer any amendments on the floor." Because the Senate bill had much better provisions, the California Republican thought it best not to push it but to wait until the bills reached the House-Senate conference.[78] Accordingly, the Hay bill passed the House, substantially as written, by a vote of 403 to 2 on March 23, 1916.[79]

The scene shifted to the Senate, where discussion of

[74]Ibid., pp. 4326–67; Thomas W. Miller to Clark, March 18, 1916, Clark MSS.
[75]*Congressional Record*, p. 4325.
[76]Herring, "James Hay," p. 400–401.
[77]*Congressional Record*, p. 4729.
[78]Kahn to Clark, March 21, 1916, Clark MSS; see also Colonel William H. Johnston to Wood, March 22, 1916, Wood MSS.
[79]*Congressional Record*, p. 4731.

Senator Chamberlain's bill began on March 29. Here the preparedness sentiment was a good deal stronger, especially after the torpedoing of the French packet ship *Sussex* on March 24 brought the country into a new crisis with Germany. The authoritative *Army-Navy Journal* on March 25 predicted a clash between the powerful National Guard Association lobby and the Military Training Camps Association over the Volunteer Army provisions (Section 56) of the Senate bill.[80] The Plattsburgers knew of the militia's hostility and did not intend to sit back passively.[81]

After some preliminary sparring, the crisis came on April 4 when a motion was made to strike Section 56 from the Senate bill. The MTCA mobilized. The Executive Committee drew up a circular letter and sent it to the members of the First Training Regiment and to all men enrolled for the 1916 camps. The letter described the legislative situation and called for support. Telegrams began to pour into the Senate from all over the country. "The Executive Committee of the Military Training Camps Association," Clark wired Chamberlain, "has watched with concern the effort to kill the Federal volunteer provision. We have no axes to grind, no pay or favors to ask. All we want is a chance to serve the country in an effective manner."[82] Hundreds of telegrams were printed in the *Congressional Record,* and many were read on the Senate floor.[83] The results were impressive. Despite mutterings about "canned telegrams," the cumulative effect was such that on April 6 the motion to strike out Section 56 was defeated by a vote of 36 to 34.[84]

The debate over Section 56 set the tone for the final

[80]*Army-Navy Journal* 53 (March 25, 1916): 951.

[81]"The sentiment for basing our reserve system on the state militia has, in my opinion, been grossly exaggerated. There are comparatively few intelligent men in the country who believe in it, and I have not found that it has much support even in the militia itself. Whatever the House may do, all of us men who have been working on this training camp movement earnestly hope that the Senate will not be deceived into enacting anything like the Hay bill." Clark to Senator William E. Borah, March 18, 1916, Clark MSS.

[82]*Congressional Record,* p. 5487.

[83]Ibid., pp. 5487–91, 5561–64.

[84]Ibid., p. 5587; see also Wood to Henry Cabot Lodge, April 8, 1916, Wood MSS.

vote on the Chamberlain bill on April 18. In the April number of the *Bulletin of the First Training Regiment,* Clark had baldly characterized the Volunteer Army sections as "a national system of 'Plattsburg Camps.' "[85] It was in this context that the senators approached the issue, as a contest between the Plattsburg idea and the militia system. Opponents of a federal reserve ridiculed the military effectiveness of a Plattsburg camp, calling it a "frolic" and a "camping expedition" and saying that the men who went to Plattsburg in 1915 were not serious.[86] "A grand army of enthusiasm that is going to meet once a year for thirty days" was one senator's description.[87] Those who supported the Plattsburg position argued that the National Guard lobby was being selfish and that Plattsburgers were perfectly willing to accept an enlistment obligation.[88] According to Senator John W. Weeks of Massachusetts, the militia was telling Plattsburg men that "you must either come into the service as a National Guardsman or we do not want you at all."[89] In all probability, what saved Section 56 was the fact that both systems would be included. "Why . . . piddle around in a quarrel between the National Guard and the Plattsburg Camp?" one Southern senator asked. "Tweedledum and Tweedledee. What does it all amount to? If there is any virtue in either one, let us have both. If there is virtue in neither, let us have neither."[90] More preparedness-minded than their colleagues in the House, the senators opted for both alternatives. A final attempt to defeat Section 56 failed by a vote of 40 to 37 on April 18.[91] The Chamberlain bill as a whole passed by a 2-to-1 majority.[92]

F I V E

Throughout the Senate debates, which lasted more than three weeks, the MTCA seemed to violate its rule of not

[85]P. 101.   [86] *Congressional Record,* p. 5358.
[87]Ibid., p. 5571.   [88]Ibid., p. 5369.
[89]Ibid., p. 5358.   [90]Ibid., p. 5537.
[91]Ibid., p. 6372.   [92]Ibid., p. 6376.

engaging in politics. Using the *Bulletin* as his medium of communication, Clark tried to push the idea that the future of the Plattsburg movement was tied up with events in Washington.[93] Even after the barrage of telegrams saved Section 56 on April 6, he continued to urge Plattsburgers to write their congressmen.[94] Although the resulting letters and wires were not fabricated as some senators charged, they were not the spontaneous outpouring of disinterested patriotism that Clark would have had everyone believe. How could such lobbying tactics be rationalized, given the Plattsburg philosophy? No doubt, the MTCA leaders could justify their intervention and still believe in their own non-partisanship. Since militia lobby *was* playing politics, the Plattsburgers had to defend themselves.[95] It was a matter of necessity. Clark's attitude was ambiguous. He intensely disliked the Militia Pay bill—"an incubus that we are likely never to get rid of. . . . All the intelligence of the country is against it, including all the Secretaries of War, without regard for party, for the last ten years."[96] At the same time, he knew that the militia provisions had more than enough votes to pass. Justifying his tactics with the argument that "we were threatened with the annihilation of the training camps" if Section 56 failed and "nothing equivalent was substituted for it," Clark agitated for a plan that would have to be compromised in the long run. "I think," he wrote on April 18, "that we have probably gained the

[93]"If our training camp idea stands for anything, it stands for the principle that the nation must organize and control absolutely its military forces without interference from the states. . . . Many . . . believe that the establishment of the principle of Federal control is more difficult and at present more important than the question of universal training. It would be of comparatively small value (even if it were possible) to establish universal training under 48 different sets of laws in 48 states, while if it is once definitely settled that our military forces are to be under the sole control of the nation, the question of how to raise these forces in an equitable and effective way under a universal system will be relatively simple." Report by Clark in *Bulletin of the First Training Regiment* (March 1916), p. 102.

[94]"To members of the First Training Regiment and men enrolled for 1916," n.d. (ca. April 10, 1916), Clark MSS.

[95]See Martha Derthick, *The National Guard in Politics* (Cambridge, Mass., 1962), pp. 34–40.

[96]Clark to George A. Batchelder, April 10, 1916, Clark MSS.

substance of what we want, namely, legislative authority for the camps."[97] It was an effective combination of idealism and expedience.

One of the last Plattsburg efforts prior to passage of the Senate bill was the joint meeting of the Governing Committee and Finance Committee of the Military Training Camps Association at the New Willard Hotel in Washington on April 14. This was the first formal meeting of the Governing Committee since February, and Clark gave an accounting of the recent legislative doings. Once again the MTCA resolved in favor of "reasonable military training" for civilians, saying that "no effective or sufficient citizen reserve can be created either under a volunteer or universal system of training unless such reserve is under the direct and exclusive control of the Federal Government." Sentiments were voiced about the need for training camps as an alternative to the militia and about the necessity for appropriations if the camps were to become democratic.[98]

Later that evening the Plattsburgers gave a formal dinner at the New Willard with congressmen, General Staff officers, and War Department representatives as guests. Clark and Drinker had been trying for two weeks to get Secretary Baker to attend, and Baker did come at the last minute.[99] After listening to Clark's speech and the resolutions passed earlier in the evening, the secretary endorsed the Plattsburg program and promised the full support of his department.[100] This was what the MTCA wanted. General Wood stayed in New York and disapproved, but the Plattsburgers went ahead. "I see that Section 56 passed the Senate yesterday," Clark wrote to Drinker on April 19, "and that General Wood has been summoned to Washington to see the Secretary of War about the camps. So the pot

[97]Clark to Edward A. Sumner, April 18, 1916, ibid.

[98]"Minutes of a Joint Meeting of the Governing Committee (Eastern Department) and Finance Committee of the Military Training Camps Association of the United States at the New Willard Hotel, Washington D.C., April 14, 1916," ibid.

[99]Clark to Drinker, April 10, 12, 1916, Clark MSS; Clark to Scott, April 10, 12, 1916, Scott MSS; Scott to Wood, April 15, 1916, Scott MSS.

[100]"Minutes of a Joint Meeting . . . ," April 14, 1916, Clark MSS.

is boiling, and I only hope that something satisfactory will come out of it."[101]

Once the Senate and House bills went to conference, the Plattsburgers could afford to relax a little. Clark, who had devoted full time to work on MTCA matters the past few weeks, went back to practicing law for a few days. Drinker returned to Lehigh. Only Lloyd Derby remained in Washington where he could keep in touch with Kahn and Senator DuPont, both of whom were conferees.[102] Though he was "pretty sure that something effective will be done for the camps," Clark continued to encourage the writing of letters to Congress. "Mr. Kahn is very friendly and doing his best for us," he told one Plattsburger. "The Senators are all friendly, but the real obstacle comes with Messrs. Hay and [Samuel H.] Dent [of Alabama], who though not openly hostile cannot be much depended on."[103] It did not seem wise to do anything more than write letters.[104] "I strongly suggest," Thomas W. Miller wrote from Washington, "that you follow your inclination not to agitate the matter in Congress because your good work in connection with Section 56 in the Senate has not made any friends for you in the House."[105]

And so the Plattsburgers remained on the sidelines until the results of the House-Senate conference became known on May 5. The MTCA was busy recruiting for the summer at this time, and Clark noted that Secretary Baker "has submitted an estimate to the House Committee of

[101]Clark to Drinker, April 19, 1916, Clark MSS; Wood to Frank R. McCoy, April 24, 1916, Wood MSS.

[102]Clark to Drinker, April 19, 1916, Clark MSS. The conferees were Senators Chamberlain, DuPont, and Hitchcock (of Nevada), and Congressmen Kahn, Hay, and Dent (of Alabama).

[103]Clark to George A. Batchelder, April 22, 1916, ibid.

[104]"I am a trifle afraid of doing any active work there just at this juncture, and I hope and believe that left to themselves the conference committee will report a favorable provision for the camps. If things look to be going wrong of course we have got to act, but as long as things seem to be in pretty good shape and going our way, I rather feel inclined to let well enough alone. If your judgment is otherwise, let me know. It is awfully hard to tell what do do. I should certainly be chagrined to see our efforts fail and legislative provision for the camps thrown out at the last moment." Clark to Drinker, April 21, 1916, ibid.

[105]Miller to Clark, April 27, 1916, ibid.

$450,000 to pay the expenses of the camps, that is, ammunition, ranges, tentage, etc. This is absolutely distinct from the pending legislation or from . . . paying the expenses of the men, but it indicates a friendly spirit on the part of the Secretary of War."[106] Baker's friendliness was to be of even greater benefit later on. The Plattsburgers also busied themselves getting ready for the massive Preparedness Day Parade in New York on May 13, where some 500,000 patriotic citizens demonstrated ther faith. The Plattsburg contingents were to march "at the head of each division of the parade, carrying small banners," the only group to carry banners in the entire procession.[107]

MTCA attentions returned to Washington when the House-Senate conference reported a deadlock on May 5. The House conferees would not accept Section 56 of the Chamberlain bill, and the senators refused any substitute.[108] Once again the Executive Committee sent out telegrams and circulars calling on Plattsburgers to make their voices heard in Congress.[109] This time the effort failed; the House of Representatives on May 8 beat back a motion to substitute Section 56 for Section 83 of the Hay bill by a decisive 256-to-109 margin.[110] "I guess this means definitely for this year that the training camps are not to be used for developing an organized force," Clark observed. "This has been obvious to me for some time because it was clear that Hay was hostile and that it was impossible to overcome his opposition." He still hoped that in a second conference the senators might get a favorable compromise. Derby was going back to the Capitol, and "it may be [that] the time is coming around where the three musketeers had better make another assault on Congress."[111]

As it turned out, Clark and Drinker did not have to make another assault. The Senate on May 9 refused to

---

[106]Clark to Edwin D. Keith, May 1, 1916, ibid.
[107]Clark to Henry S. Drinker, May 9, 1916, ibid.
[108]*Congressional Record,* p. 7494.
[109]Clark to Mitchel (enclosure), May 5, 1916, Mitchel MSS.
[110]*Congressional Record,* p. 7600.
[111]Clark to Drinker, May 9, 1916, Clark MSS.

accept the Hay bill and asked for a new conference. With Derby doing his usual capable job of observation, it became apparent that the best tactic for the Plattsburgers was to jettison Section 56 in hope of strengthening the training camp sections of the House bill. "I am told that Mr. Hay opposes the proposed provision for mere expenses," Mayor Mitchel wired the president on May 10. "The effect of this will be to exclude thousands of men willing and ready to offer their services to the government but who cannot stand the expense. . . . I trust that this may be remedied. . . . [It] would be absolutely in line with your speech . . . where you said that opportunity should be furnished for every man who wished to take fundamental military training."[112] Wilson did talk to Hay and later reported that the Virginian had been eager to help.[113] The MTCA Executive Committee also sent Hay a telegram, which, according to Clark, "was very impertinent and I think somewhat insulting. The imprudent clause was not my suggestion, but I acquiesced in it in a moment of haste."[114] Fortunately, Philip Carroll and DeLancey Jay sent a second telegram which smoothed any ruffled feathers.

This time the Senate and House conferees were able to reconcile their differences. The conference report, accepted by the Senate on May 17 and the House on May 20 and finally signed into law by President Wilson on June 3, 1916, contained a compromise between Section 83 and Section 56 of the House and Senate bills.[115] In return for giving up a separate federal reserve, the Senate conferees persuaded Hay to accept provisions for uniforms and transportation for men attending federal training camps.[116] "This is the

[112]Mitchel to Wilson (telegram), May 10, 1916, Mitchel MSS.
[113]Wilson to Mitchel, May 17, 1916, ibid.
[114]Clark to Drinker, May 13, 1916, Clark MSS.
[115]*Congressional Record,*pp. 8406, 8546, 8577.
[116]The text of Section 54 of the National Defense Act reads as follows: "TRAINING CAMPS. The Secretary of War is hereby authorized to maintain, upon military reservations or elsewhere, camps for the military instruction and training of such citizens as may be selected for such instruction and training, upon their application and under such terms of enlistment and regulations as may be prescribed by the Secretary of War; to use, for the purpose of maintaining said camps and imparting

result which I think we want," Clark wrote when he heard of the agreement. "I think we are in a stronger position without receiving pay."[117] The Plattsburgers had reason to feel pleased, for it was through Secretary Baker that they were able to safeguard their interests. "Derby saw him twice in Washington and was much impressed," Clark told Drinker. "It was really through his influence on Hay that the camp provision was agreed to in the Conference Committee. He appears to have been impressed by the dinner in Washington on April 14, and I am awfully glad we had that dinner. I am sure we can rely on his support to a finish."[118] And so with Woodrow Wilson's signature on June 3, the Plattsburg movement for the first time found itself in a position of statutory legitimacy.

SIX

There was an epilogue to the MTCA's role in the military legislation of 1916, that of securing sufficient money for the training camps in the Army Appropriation bill that sum-

---

military instruction and training thereat, such arms, ammunition, accouterments, equipments, tentage, field equipage, and transportation belonging to the United States as he may deem necessary; to furnish, at the expense of the United States, uniforms, subsistence, transportation by the most usual and direct route within such limits as to territory as the Secretary of War may prescribe, and medical supplies to persons receiving instruction at said camps during the period of their attendance thereat, to authorize such expenditures, from proper Army appropriations, as he may deem necessary for water, fuel, light, temporary structures, not including quarters for officers nor barracks for men, screenings and damages resulting from field exercises, and other expenses incidental to the maintenance of said camps, and the theoretical winter instruction at said camps, for cash and at cost price plus ten per centum, quartermaster and ordnance property, the amount of such property to be sold to any one person to be limited to that which is required for his proper equipment. All monies arising from such sales shall remain available throughout the fiscal year following that in which the sales are made, for the purpose of that appropriation from which the property was sold was authorized to be supplied at the time of the sale. The Secretary of War is authorized further to prescribe the courses of theoretical and practical instruction to be pursued by persons attending the camps authorized by this section; prescribe rules and regulations for the government thereof; and to employ thereat officers and enlisted men of the Regular Army in such numbers and upon such duties as he may designate." See Perry, *Plattsburg Movement*, pp. 100 – 101.
[117]Clark to Drinker, May 13, 1916, Clark MSS.
[118]Ibid., May 15, 1916.

mer. It was a confused and frustrating affair for the Plattsburgers, something out of *Alice in Wonderland.*

Once the training camp section of the Defense Act was
agreed upon, the MTCA wanted to announce to all en-
rollees that transportation to Plattsburg and other camps
that summer would be paid for by the government. Clark
reasoned that such a guarantee would increase trainees for
1916 by 15,000 or more, an argument he used in numerous letters and announcements during May and June.[119]
Unfortunately, another snarl occurred between the House
and the more preparedness-minded Senate over appropriations. Secretary Baker on May 27 recommended an
expenditure of upwards of $2,000,000 to cover the cost of
50,000 men, but Hay's committee promptly cut the figure
to $500,000, barely enough to provide for overhead
maintenance and virtually eliminating expenses for any
sizable body of trainees. The Senate Committee proposed a
sum of $4,300,000 to provide not only for the summer of
1916 but for winter instruction and camps the following
spring.[120] The Plattsburgers were furious with Hay. Clark
sent an urgent letter to Baker on May 28 and asked Derby
and Jay to go to Washington to investigate. "Hay promised
the Secretary to do something," Clark told Drinker, "but
then grossly misrepresented the Secretary's attitude to
Kahn, and the latest news I have is that Hay is standing
firm and doing his best to block the whole thing."[121]

The result was another assault on Washington—
telegrams to the president, visits to the War Department, letters to congressmen.[122] "We are not getting discouraged," Clark told one General Staff officer, "but we are
getting mad. . . . [We will] make as much of a row over the
matter as we conveniently can."[123] A Plattsburg delegation,

[119]See Clark to Baker (telegram), May 27, 1916, and May 28, 31, 1916 RG 94,
AG2384423. See also Clark to Frank B. Brandegee, June 2, 1916; to George Van
Horne Moseley, May 26, 1916, Clark MSS. There are several other letters and
bulletins of a similar type in the Clark MSS.

[120]Perry, *Plattsburg Movement*, p. 104.

[121]Clark to Drinker, June 2, 1916, Clark MSS.

[122]Executive Committee Military Training Camps Association to Wilson (telegram), May 31, 1916, RG 94, AG2384423.

headed by Clark and Drinker, even had an interview with President Wilson on the afternoon of June 20, the only occasion prior to America's entry into the war that an official MTCA representation talked with the president.[124]

Even though the Wilson administration did its best to help, it was not until late in the summer that an appropriation of $2,000,000 passed Congress. The call-up of practically the entire National Guard on June 18 to protect the Southwest border had complicated matters greatly. Then, in early August, Wilson was forced to veto the appropriation bill because Hay had attached a rider that would have hamstrung the General Staff. A second bill finally passed on August 27, 1916. Although the appropriation was retroactive — that is, men who attended the 1916 camps at their own expense could obtain reimbursement — it came too late in the year to have any positive effect on recruiting.[125] When James Hay resigned from the House of Representatives on October 1, 1916, to accept an appointment as federal judge, the Military Training Camps Association was as happy to see him go as the most hard-boiled professional officer in the United States Army.

SEVEN

The *Literary Digest* described the National Defense Act of 1916 as "at least a step in the right direction — as long a step as a Democratic Congress could be expected to take."[126] This was a fair analysis. The reformed military establishment was not capable of fighting the German Imperial Army, but none of its sponsors intended that it should. In main outline the new legislation authorized an increase in the Regular Army to 175,000 men over a period of five years and made the tactical organization of this force read-

---

[123]Clark to George Van Horne Moseley, June 2, 1916, Clark MSS.

[124]Joseph Tumulty to Drinker, June 16, 1916, ibid.

[125]As it was, slightly fewer than 17,000 men attended federal training camps during 1916, far fewer than the 35,000-50,000 predicted by Clark. The confusion over appropriations was partly responsible.

[126]*Literary Digest* 52 (May 4, 1916): 547.

ily expansible to 286,000 in time of war. The National Guard, as Hay had affirmed, constituted the first line of reserve, its strength to be increased gradually from 100,000 to 400,000 men. According to the new law, the militia was to come under federal supervision. Guard units were required to take part in forty-eight drill periods annually, plus fifteen days of field training; equipment and instructors were to be provided by the Regular Army; and discipline was to be the same as for the regulars. A new Militia Section of the General Staff had general powers of supervision, and the secretary of war could cut off funds to any state not complying with federal regulations. The law also reaffirmed a Guardsman's obligation to federal service outside the borders of the United States.[127]

While the framers of the Defense Act intended the National Guard to be the heart of any citizen reserve, there were other reserve features. Besides the training camps, the new legislation provided for a Regular Army enlisted reserve, composed of trained veterans and recruited through an elaborate system of bounties. Included also was an Officers' Reserve Corps (ORC) and a Reserve Officers' Training Corps (ROTC), the latter to be established in authorized colleges and universities and dovetailed with the summer training camps for students. Another Enlisted Reserve Corps would recruit specialists for the quartermaster, ordnance, signal, engineer, and medical services.[128]

Several provisions in the Defense Act dealing with the General Staff infuriated General Wood and his friends. Quite possibly the result of Hay's friendship with General Ainsworth, the act provided for a gradual enlargement of the General Staff to three general officers and fifty-two junior officers; however, it also stipulated that no more than half of these junior officers could be on duty in or near the District of Columbia. General Staff duties were limited to nonadministrative matters, thus raising the question of General Staff supremacy over the bureaus which

[127]U.S., *Statutes at Large*, vol. 39, pt. 2, pp. 197–213.
[128]Ibid., pp. 166–97.

Wood and Stimson supposedly had settled in 1912. Baker resolved the question by ruling that the authority of the General Staff was not impaired and was to continue as before. Nonetheless, the curtailment of its numbers badly hampered General Staff planning as war approached. There would be fewer than twenty-five officers on duty with the General Staff in March of 1917.[129]

Most professional soldiers were so blinded by the National Guard sections of the law that they could say nothing good about it. From February to June 1916, General Scott told all who would listen that Congress was enacting a "gold brick" and that the country would be better off if the president used his veto power.[130] General Bliss called the militia provisions a "broken reed," while Douglas MacArthur remarked "as to the utter worthlessness of the measure, . . . the direct result of the chaotic condition . . . which enabled Mr. Hay to work without serious opposition towards his own sinister ends."[131] "Totally inadequate" was Robert Bacon's comment.[132] Henry Breckinridge, in a pamphlet written after his resignation from the War Department, could not decide whether the Defense Act was a great comedy or a great tragedy.[133] Theodore Roosevelt characterized it as a piece of "flintlock legislation."[134] And, according to Leonard Wood, Hay's militia plan was "the most dangerous menace to the national defense that has been proposed since I have been a member of the Army."[135]

Amid such a chorus of condemnation, the Plattsburg attitude toward the Defense Act takes on perspective. Clark, Drinker, and the other MTCA officers were no more

[129]Ibid., pp. 167–69. Much of this analysis follows Weigley, *History of the United States Army*, pp. 348–50.

[130]Scott to Frederick Funston, February 6, 1916; to Buck Connor, February 5; to Leonard Wood, February 23; to H. L. Stimson, April 6, 1916; and many other letters in the Scott MSS.

[131]Bliss to John J. Pershing, February 8, 1916, Bliss MSS; MacArthur to Wood, March 20, 1916, Wood MSS.

[132]Bacon to Woodrow Wilson, May 26, 1916, Wilson MSS.

[133]Breckinridge, *Preparedness* (New York, 1916), p. 3.

[134]See Roosevelt to S. Stanwood Menken, December 23, 1916, Roosevelt MSS.

[135]Wood to Edward M. House, April 17, 1916, Wilson MSS.

happy about Hay's National Guard proposals than were their more militant friends. Nonetheless, while Wood sulked in his tents and refused even to talk to Secretary Baker until ordered to Washington on April 19, the Plattsburgers made an effort to work within the system. In doing so, they not only secured Section 54 of the Defense Act (which was no minor accomplishment) but also built up a reservoir of good will in the War Department and among important congressional leaders. Certainly the training camp movement was better off for having made the effort.

In fact, Section 54 was worded in such a way as to hold promise for the future. The failure to obtain a federal reserve notwithstanding, the clause "under such terms of enlistment and regulations as may be prescribed by the Secretary of War" opened the door to providing for such a force administratively. The Training Camps Association, because of its desire to stand for the principle of universal military obligation, persuaded Secretary Baker to set the enlistment contract in 1916 to cover only the thirty-day period of camp instruction.[136] The possibility remained, however, that a reserve force could be built out of Section 54. When war was declared in April 1917, it was this section which made possible the organization of the ninety-day Officers' Training Camps, beginning in May of that year, before passage of the Draft Act by Congress.[137]

Perhaps the most rewarding commentary on the MTCA's legislative activity took place later that summer when Clark went up to Plattsburg for two weeks of training. This was a time when nearly 7,000 civilians were taking military instruction at Plattsburg, a direct result of what the MTCA had done the previous winter and spring. Clark, who had made it a practice to deal with Wood through intermediaries whenever possible, was surprised to find the general acting so cordial. He "has quite come around,"

[136]See Henry S. Drinker to Newton D. Baker, June 29, 1916, RG 94, AG2384423.
[137]There is a good discussion of the effect of Section 54 in Perry, *Plattsburg Movement,* pp. 102–3.

Clark wrote to a friend, and it "nearly knocked me over." The two men had a "nice talk," and Wood admitted that he and his officers were "absolutely dependent upon the help of the Association."[138] For Clark, there could have been no sweeter praise.

[138]Clark to John W. Farley, August 15, 1916, Clark MSS.

VI.

The 1916 Camps

A young Princeton student named Edmund Wilson went up to Plattsburg in the summer of 1916. Not yet embarked on the literary pursuits which would make him one of America's foremost men of letters, Wilson enrolled for four weeks of military training for the simple reason that he could think of nothing better to do during his long college vacation. He found the training course "very boring," and his general military ineptitude showed that he could never become an officer and had no desire to be a soldier. Many years later he recalled that his performance on the rifle range was probably as poor as that of any rookie at Plattsburg.[1]

Wilson was only one of 16,134 civilians, young and old, who attended the twelve Regular Army Instruction Camps held that spring and summer. This was four times the number that had trained in 1915. Although the effect on young Wilson was apparently minor, the training camp movement as a whole became a powerful national force during 1916. Had it not been for the uncertainty and confusion created by mobilization of the National Guard on the Texas border in June (as well as the delay in passage of the 1916 Army Appropriation Act), it is likely that more than 50,000 trainees would have demonstrated their military faith at Plattsburg and other camps. Authorized by the National Defense Act and the product of hard work and cooperation between the War Department and the Military Training Camps Association, the 1916 camps gave increased publicity to preparedness and the idea that citizens had a universal military obligation. The camps also augmented the country's trained military personnel, as Plattsburgers by the hundreds flocked to join the new Officers' Reserve Corps (ORC) and Reserve Officers' Training Corps (ROTC).

The Plattsburg camps, still small in comparison to 1917 and 1918, were no longer a portent.

O N E

On March 17, 1916, the day after Secretary Baker gave Drinker and Clark assurances of War Department support, the MTCA Executive Committee in New York sent out form letters to every member of the First Training Regiment. Enclosed with each letter were five application blanks and five official circulars describing the camps to be held that spring and summer at Plattsburg and at Fort Oglethorpe, Georgia. "Carry them in your pocket and hand them to men interested," the letter urged. "Make a practice of enclosing them in your letters to men likely to be interested." Already "some men have turned in twenty or thirty names by these simple methods. . . . Let every man undertake a personal responsibility to get two or three recruits without fail within three weeks. This will guarantee success."[2]

This "endless chain," as DeLancey Jay described it, was only part of the intensive recruitment which the MTCA pushed during the winter and spring of 1916.[3] To obtain the thousands of volunteers that Clark was telling congressmen about, the Plattsburgers had to adopt an approach different from 1915.

Publicity was one major object. The stories and articles which had appeared about the Business Men's Camp the previous summer already had provided Plattsburg with a

[1]Wilson, *A Prelude* (New York, 1967), pp. 150–52.
[2]"To the Members of the First Training Regiment," March 17, 1916, Clark MSS.
[3]Military Training Camps Association, *Report of Executive Secretary for 1916* (New York, 1916), copy in Clark MSS.

national reputation. Since the autumn of 1915 Plattsburg-ers had been recruiting their friends.[4] But more needed to be done, and beginning in January 1916 the MTCA undertook to raise a publicity fund of some $100,000. Jay and Tompkins McIlvaine, chairman of the Finance Committee, were in charge. Although members of the First Training Regiment accounted for much of this sum in $10, $25, and $50 contributions, Jay also solicited from wealthy and older persons without Plattsburg connections.[5] By the middle of March a sufficient fund had been collected.[6] All told, 426 subscribers, mostly in the New York area, contributed $81,426.46 in amounts ranging from twenty-five cents to $5,000.[7]

One of the first things the MTCA did was to sponsor speaking tours for General Wood. Even though he disapproved of some of the MTCA's activities in Washington, Wood was more than willing to talk. As the founder of the training camp movement and chief spokesman for preparedness, he traveled back and forth across the eastern half of the United States between December 1, 1915, and June 3, 1916, making, according to his own count, 134 talks to approximately 130,000 persons. These were the usual short speeches delivered in college auditoriums and at club dinners, sometimes a diatribe against the Hay bill, sometimes an argument for universal military training, always an appeal for attendance at next summer's camps.[8] In

[4]In the Wood Scrapbooks for the autumn and winter of 1915–1916, there are numerous newspaper clippings concerning speeches made by Plattsburg veterans to their hometown audiences; Wood MSS.

[5]DeLancey Jay to Mrs. Whitelaw Reid, January 5, 1916; circular letters "To the Members of the New York Stock Exchange," February 8, 1916, and "To the Members of the New York Bar," February 22, 1916; Clark to O'Donnell Iselin, February 7, 1916; Clark to Archibald G. Thacher, January 18, February 7, 9, 1916; and Thacher to Clark, February 5, 29, 1916, Clark MSS.

[6]See Clark to Horace C. Stebbins, February 14, 1916, ibid.

[7]Military Training Camps Association, *Report of Treasurer for 1916* (New York, 1916), copy in ibid.

[8]Near the end of August 1916, Wood went over his diary for the previous year, listing his speaking engagements and the number of persons attending them; Wood Diary. He also noted that "there is an unending flow of correspondence on preparedness, military training camps, etc. Postage and package charges [at Gover-

addition to Wood's speeches, the MTCA bought full-page advertisements in national magazines and printed and distributed its own promotional literature.[9] "Give your vacation to your country and still have the best vacation you ever had" — such was the slogan in *Collier's* and the *Saturday Evening Post* on May 6, 1916.[10] The Plattsburgers even worked out an arrangement whereby the United Cigar Stores provided free poster space in their shops throughout the country.[11]

Because the army had no funds for recruitment, the MTCA took over practically all the work. In early January 1916, Lloyd Derby made a "momentous discovery" — a central catalog of students and alumni of nearly every American college.[12] The Enrollment Committee took this list and other lists of professional men and, using the government frank, printed and distributed "over three and a half million pieces of official Government literature besides 38,000 illustrated booklets and 10,000 photograph albums."[13] The Plattsburgers also adopted a "nucleus system," organizing local committees, interesting one or two leading persons in smaller towns and especially in the colleges. MTCA headquarters in New York would supply these individuals with propaganda material and keep in touch through visits and

nor's Island] run from fifty to eighty dollars per month and sometimes more." Wood Diary, November 29, 1916.

[9]The magazines were the *Saturday Evening Post, Collier's, Leslie's, Literary Digest,* and *Scientific American*. The *Outlook* gave free advertising. Altogether, the circulation ran to over four million readers; see DeLancey Jay to John Purroy Mitchel, April 26, 1915, Mitchel MSS. MTCA publications included *Attention!* (May 1916), a fifteen-page pamphlet with pictures and an article, "Life at Plattsburg in 1915," by M. L. Cornell; and *Views of First Training Regiment at Plattsburg, N.Y., 1915* (New York, 1916), a fifty-page booklet with excellent photographs. There was also a travel brochure: "Plattsburg, New York: U. S. Government Military Training Camp." Full of beautiful photographs, this brochure was put out by the Delaware and Hudson Railroad and endorsed by the MTCA. Samples of all this literature are in the Clark MSS.

[10]Quoted in Fitzpatrick, "The Plattsburg Camp for Business and Professional Men," p. 13.

[11]Jay to Mitchel, April 26, 1916, Mitchel MSS.

[12]Derby to DeLancey Jay, [January?], 1916, Clark MSS.

[13]Military Training Camps Association, *Report of Executive Secretary for 1916* (New York, 1916), copy in Clark MSS.

correspondence.[14] Some local branches set up their own programs: news services, lecture bureaus, special funds, and "Plattsburg scholarships" for deserving students who could not otherwise go to camp. Rochester, only sparsely represented in 1915, had sixty men enrolled for Plattsburg by mid-May. Montclair, New Jersey, boasted fifty recruits.[15]

Another method was to secure the patriotic cooperation of employers. President Wilson in a Memorial Day address in 1916 spoke of the growing advocacy of preparedness among businessmen and asked: "Will they give the young men in their employment freedom to volunteer for this thing [training camps]? It is all very well to say that some-body else must prepare; but are the business men of this country ready themselves . . . to sacrifice an interest in or-der that we may get ready?"[16] The answer was affirmative, for throughout the spring the MTCA published lists of over eight hundred major business concerns pledged "to permit a reasonable number of their employees to attend the Regular Army Instruction Camps, to be held during the year 1916, and will grant to such employees four weeks' leave of absence for this purpose, without prejudice to their advancement and without loss of salary."[17] The intent was to attract a broader sampling of American society than the much publicized elites of 1915.

The emphasis on publicity and employers' pledges un-derlined a fundamental shift in the Plattsburg movement during 1916 — toward numbers and "democratization." The Plattsburgers were sensitive to charges of aristocratic bias; they wanted to extend military training, to keep it from being a class affair. As such, the MTCA's purpose differed somewhat from that of General Wood.

Wood had encountered the problem of class con-

[14]Ibid.   [15]*Bulletin of the First Training Regiment* (May 1916).

[16]As quoted in Perry, *Plattsburg Movement*, p. 111. It was ironic that Wilson found it constitutionally impossible to permit federal employees four weeks off for training camps; see Attorney General Thomas W. Gregory to Woodrow Wilson, June 5, 1916, Wilson MSS.

[17]Perry, *Plattsburg Movement*, p. 111. See also *New York Times*, April 16 and 21, 1916.

sciousness the previous summer when he invited Samuel Gompers to visit Plattsburg. A recent convert to preparedness, the president of the American Federation of Labor was unable to visit the camp, but expressed concern that military training "based upon professional distinctions or any other distinction that has resulted from special opportunities available to a few, has a tendency to develop one of the evils of militarism, that is, military castes."[18] There followed an interesting correspondence between Gompers and Wood, in which the general tried to point out the necessity for educational standards in training reserve officers, and Gompers urged that "plans for national defense ought to take into consideration all of the people of the country in order to best utilize our resources."[19] The results were beneficial, since Wood agreed to try some of Gompers's ideas in the 1916 camps. The two men met several times during the autumn and winter of 1915 – 1916, working out broader qualifications for camp attendance.[20] Gompers, for his part, gave vocal support that spring to the MTCA campaign in Congress for training camp appropriations.[21]

There was still some disagreement between Wood and the MTCA when the latter began to press hard for enrollments in late March. Anson Conger Goodyear, chairman of the Buffalo branch of the MTCA, complained that many of the applications approved and forwarded by his committee were being rejected by Wood's officers. "I have today received a letter from the President of one of the larger corporations here," he wrote Clark, "stating that he wishes to go to Plattsburg, but doubts if he would be accepted as he has only had one year at Harvard. If he is . . . to be troubled with communications from Governor's Island,

[18]Gompers to Wood, September 15, 1915, Wood MSS.
[19]Gompers to Wood, October 6, 1915, ibid. See John Garry Clifford, "Leonard Wood, Samuel Gompers, and the Plattsburg Training Camps," *New York History* (April 1971), pp. 169–89.
[20]Wood to Frank R. McCoy, October 15, 1915, Wood MSS; and Wood Diary, January 3, 1916.
[21]See *Congressional Record*, p. 5531.

asking what his 'equivalent' [education] is, I do not want to enroll him at all." Goodyear asked if there was any "way in which the stupidity of our beloved friends can be stopped."[22]

Clark, who thought "an immense amount of harm is being done the movement by a tendency to make it a class affair," at first blamed the difficulty on Captain Dorey and other army officers "who can't see the forest for the trees."[23] Clark wrote a very correct letter to Wood:

It is argued that we are losing a great many desirable men who are timid about describing their educational qualifications, and defining the 'equivalent' of a college or high school education. Further than that it is also thought that the emphasis on educational qualifications is producing a wrong impression in the press and public mind as to the character of the camps and characterizes them to some extent as a class affair. Many of the men think, and I personally agree with them, that educational qualifications ought to be wholly dropped for the senior camps and that the blank and circulars ought to state that the camps are open to all citizens of the United States between twenty-one and forty-five, of good moral character. . . . Some of the men feel so strongly in the matter that they are disposed to be pretty lukewarm about pushing the recruiting work unless the qualifications are substantially modified.[24]

With this hint of blackmail, Clark was able to get a decision making it "clear that any man of good character and the equivalent of a high school education is welcome." Wood agreed to define "high school education" so as to include "any man who has made good in his occupation." Clark hoped that the new policy would "remove any impression that these camps are conducted primarily for college men or for any particular class." [25]

[22]Goodyear to Clark, March 28, 1916, Record Group 98, "Records of the Plattsburg Barracks, 1916."

[23]Clark to Goodyear, March 29, 1916, Clark MSS.

[24]Clark to Wood, March 29, 1916, RG 98, "Records of the Plattsburg Barracks, 1916."

[25]Clark to George A. Batchelder, March 30, 1916, Clark MSS.

Any possibility that Wood might open the camps completely was eliminated a few days later when one of Clark's Boston friends suggested that all educational requirements be dropped.[26] Wood rejected the idea because it would "largely eliminate the camp as a source of supply for officers, which is the principal reason for its existence at present."[27] Clark received copies of this correspondence, along with the penciled comment that Wood "has about as much capacity for sizing up a political or non-military situation as a porcupine."[28]

The result therefore was a compromise, perhaps the best policy under the circumstances. Looking at Plattsburg primarily as a vehicle for training reserve officers, Wood continued throughout the summer to move cautiously. "I think we had better go rather slowly in making changes," he advised General Scott in late June.

> We are getting all the men we can handle right now and they are of the right type. When we give too much consideration to numbers we shall lose in quality and efficiency of the camp. When we have a system of universal compulsory military training — which we must have in the near future — we shall have a condition under which we can segregate our men for training without difficulty. Just now, I am afraid if we put in a lot of men who are not up to the mark, we shall lower the standard of our camps to such an extent as to destroy public confidence in them.[29]

Although Clark and his friends saw the camps more as a demonstration for universal training than for making officers, they had to be content with "democratization" as interpreted by Wood. As it turned out, the delay in appropriations and the National Guard mobilization cut attendance; hence, the camps were of a size equally suitable for propaganda and military purposes.

[26]John A. Farley to Wood, April 3, 1916, ibid.
[27]Wood to Farley, April 4, 1916, ibid.
[28]Farley to Clark, April 5, 1916, ibid.
[29]Wood to Scott, June 29, 1916, Scott MSS.

T W O

The first training camp of the season at Fort Oglethorpe set the pattern for subsequent camps. Wood had selected this site, just below Chattanooga near the old Chickamauga battleground, in hope of stirring up preparedness sentiment in the South. A series of five camps was originally scheduled, beginning in April 1916, but because of the movement of troops to Texas, only the camps in May and June were held.

The army did most of the recruiting for Oglethorpe. Wood put his aide in charge, Captain Gordon Johnston, and the young officer proceeded on a "vigorous campaign of education and information."[30] Accompanied by Landon Thomas, a Plattsburg veteran and Harvard classmate of Ted Roosevelt, Johnston spent the better part of two months stumping the South, speaking to college groups, chambers of commerce, businessmen, politicians.[31] Wood made a tour in early February, visiting eight cities and making ten speeches to some 4,600 persons.[32] The response did not match the effort. "Enrollments so far have been unsatisfactory," Thomas noted in early March.[33]

When the training course began in early May, the first roll calls showed that Southern volunteers were far outnumbered by men from the northern cities, many of whom had been at Plattsburg in 1915. Wealthy Robert Bacon, the former secretary of state and soon-to-be Republican candidate for the United States Senate in New York, set out to remedy the situation. Obtaining a few days' leave from camp, Bacon managed to recruit seventy-five employees from the Tennessee Coal and Iron Company of Birmingham. A partner of J. P. Morgan and Company, he wired Judge Elbert H. Gary of United States Steel and asked for

[30]Johnston to Clark, January 4, 1916, Clark MSS.
[31]Interview with Landon Thomas, Augusta, Georgia, February 10, 1969. Thomas later became an officer during World War I and was aide-de-camp to General Wood from the autumn of 1917 to the summer of 1919.
[32]Wood Diary, February 4-12, 1916.
[33]Thomas to Colonel Henry T. Allen, March 14, 1916, Allen MSS.

volunteers, saying that if the company could not afford to pay expenses he, Bacon, would do so out of his own pocket.[34] Bacon got his recruits, and their attendance on the parade ground gave emphasis to the *Atlanta Journal*'s earlier remark that "millionaire and clerk are sweating side by side."[35]

Fort Oglethorpe attracted 335 rookies in May; 221 in June. The prospects were bright for even larger numbers in July and August, but the Mexican situation necessitated the withdrawal of all regular officers and troops at the end of June. General Wood provided a special fund to bring some of the Oglethorpe applicants north; and when Grenville Clark went to Plattsburg in early August he remarked about "the presence of a fine crowd of Southerners, a first-class lot of men."[36]

The one other camp in the South—at Fort Sam Houston, near San Antonio—also was affected by the border mobilization. Opening in mid-June with some 421 civilians in attendance, the camp looked like a Texas version of Plattsburg. Mayor Clinton G. Brown of San Antonio seemed to emulate Mayor Mitchel when he posed for photographers while setting up his bedding.[37] After two weeks of instruction, however, the influx of army and militia troops into the area resulted in the removal of all horses, field pieces, and other equipment.[38] Training came to a halt. Perhaps it did not matter, for an officer who had been at Plattsburg reported that the camp at Fort Sam Houston "did not *compare* in tone, morale, and spirit. . . . They will never get the same class of men as a whole up north."[39]

The problems in the Midwest were even more frustrating. Here the MTCA faced the delicate situation of coordinating the old Fort Sheridan organization with Plattsburg

[34]*Atlanta Journal,* May 11, 1916.

[35]Ibid., May 4, 1916.

[36]Wood to Henry T. Allen, July 7, 1916, Wood MSS; Clark to John R. Van Horne, August 10, 1916, Clark MSS.

[37]*San Antonio Express,* June 18, 1916.

[38]Ibid., June 28, 1916.

[39]Robert O. Van Horn to Wood, August 22, 1916, Wood MSS.

leadership from New York. The two groups did not always see eye to eye.[40] Moreover, the two officers in command of the Central Department that winter and spring showed little enthusiasm for civilian training.[41] After some prodding, the army reluctantly scheduled a series of camps beginning in July at Fort Benjamin Harrison, near Indianapolis. Recruiting bogged down, however; and it was decided to send DeLancey Jay out "to put some pep" into the region. Jay was not pleased by what he saw in his seven-day (June 4 – 10, 1916) tour of Chicago, Milwaukee, Omaha, Kansas City, and Pittsburgh. The usually taciturn New Yorker talked to local MTCA committees, business groups, university clubs, and became so disgusted that he peppered his diary with such comments as "unattractive crowd. . . . They seem to have small ideas . . . a lot of tightwads." Jay thought he had "started something" by organizing "four good committees in 4 large but hitherto absolutely dead cities." He concluded that "the Enrollment Committee for the Central Department is rotten. It might have been better for us to try to run the whole Middle West from New York, as the Chicago outfit is really useless."[42]

Jay's visit did seem to stir enrollment. Some eleven hundred applicants, including Grenville Clark, had signed up for Fort Benjamin Harrison by mid-June.[43] Then, on June 18, 1916, President Wilson called out the National Guard, and shortly thereafter all civilian training camps were cancelled in the Central Department. Those applicants who could afford the trip went to Plattsburg instead.[44]

[40]See George F. Porter to Grenville Clark, March 16, 1916, Clark MSS.

[41]Colonel D. A. Frederick and General Thomas R. Barry were the two department commanders.

[42]Memorandum-diary of DeLancey Jay, June 4– 10, 1916, Clark MSS. Jay's first impression of Chicago, written to his wife, was that it was "an *awful* hole — there is so far practically no knowledge whatever as to what the Plattsburg Idea is, & those that are interested in preparedness talk about the militia. The men I have seen seem like nice fellows but dreadful bores!" Jay to Mrs. D. K. Jay, June 6, 1916, Clark MSS.

[43]Perry, *Plattsburg Movement*, p. 115.

[44]Wharton Clay to Ralph Barton Perry, April 22, 1920, Perry MSS. See also notes of meeting of the Governing Committee of the Military Training Camps Association, November 24, 1916, Clark MSS.

The camps fared better in the Western Department. Wood's predecessor as chief of staff, Major General J. Franklin Bell, had taken over command of this department at the beginning of the year and developed cordial relations with local MTCA representatives.[45] The initiative for holding camps on the West Coast came from New York when the Executive Committee sent out two organizers in late February 1916. The two men—Harold Blanchard and Edwin D. Keith—talked with Bell (who was "not fully advised . . . but was heartily in favor of having at least one camp here"), Ben Dibblee, and other San Franciscans who had done military work the previous year. After several days in San Francisco, Keith went to Los Angeles and points south, while Blanchard traveled north to Oregon and Washington.[46] Their visit, coinciding as it did with Pancho Villa's raid into New Mexico on March 9, aroused preparedness advocates in the West.[47] Already that winter General Bell's officers had begun a series of weekly lectures for business and professional men at the Palace Hotel in San Francisco, a practice later imitated in San Diego, Oakland, Los Angeles, and other western cities. When Bell on March 1 announced three camps for the summer—at Monterey, American Lake (Washington), and Fort Douglas (Utah)—he allowed the civilians to set up a central recruiting office at Department headquarters in San Francisco and assigned Captain John B. Murphy to work full time as liaison officer. Assisted by Governor Hiram Johnson, President Wheeler of the University of California, and some fifty other notables, the MTCA committees obtained more than two thousand applicants for the Monterey camp, of which 1,090 showed up when camp opened the second week of July.[48]

"It is painful to discover that the masses are not respon-

[45]See Bell to Adjutant General (copy), April 13, 1916, Clark MSS.
[46]"Report of Mr. Blanchard and Mr. Keith on the California Training Camp Situation," memorandum in the Clark MSS. Keith stayed on in San Francisco.
[47]See Keith to Clark, March 15, 1916, ibid.
[48]A good discussion of the origins of the training camps in California can be found in Benjamin H. Dibblee to Ralph Barton Perry, May 28, 1920, Perry MSS.

ding as well as the classes," one Californian wrote to Clark, "but that, I think, is due more to the $60.00 [for expenses] than lack of patriotism."[49] "The class of men we have so far has been high," he judged, "and if we can get 2,000 men of this type . . . it will be a very fine camp."[50] The upper class orientation was much in evidence at Monterey, partly because preparedness opinion was most marked among the wealthy, partly because a train ride to and from Monterey was an expensive proposition for persons of humbler means.[51] Because of the vast distances involved, the western camps probably suffered more than those in the East from the delay in congressional appropriations.

The border mobilization also caused problems, and Bell saw many of his best officers and troops transferred to Texas. He held the camps nonetheless, using the Coast Artillery at Monterey. Few instructors had any experience in training civilians, with the result that discipline suffered and real military progress became almost impossible. One trainee who later went through the first officer training camp in 1917 regretted the lack of theoretical instruction in 1916. "Had there been some attempt at an introduction to the mysteries of military law and procedure," he wrote, "even a hasty skimming of the Manual of Courts Martial, the whole business would have had an entirely different air."[52] Part of the laxness was due to General Bell. "I wanted to make the first camp as easy as possible," he told one of the rookies, "so that it would encourage them possibly to get other men to come. I didn't want to make the discipline too hard for them, but I think I made a mistake; next year it will be very different."[53]

The fact that the camp was set up on the grounds of

[49]George A. Batchelder to Clark, April 4, 1916, Clark MSS.

[50]Batchelder to Clark, May 25, 1916, ibid.

[51]For the effect of appropriations on recruitment in California, see Batchelder to Clark, June 5, 1916, ibid.

[52]Silsby M. Spalding to Benjamin H. Dibblee, June 1, 1920 (copy), Perry MSS.

[53]As quoted by Mark W. Gerstle in the minutes of the Meeting of the Standing Committees of the Military Training Camps Association, New York City, November 24, 1916, Clark MSS.

the luxurious Del Monte Hotel added to the slack atmosphere. A captain recently assigned to Bell's staff from the Philippines was treated to dinner at the hotel his first night in camp by a few of the wealthier rookies. "I saw more Rolls Royces and other fine cars around there than I had ever seen collected before," he later recalled. "They were all the hot bloods of San Francisco."[54] This officer had seen service as a National Guard instructor on the East Coast, so Bell detailed him to command a different training company each day and make sure that discipline was at least up to militia standards. One of his first companies was especially lax and had even arranged for a champagne lunch to be brought over in picnic baskets by their wives and girl friends. Drill that afternoon became so ragged that the captain called a halt. "You fellows came down here," he said, "because you were enthusiastic to do something in this time of emergency and you are paying your own expenses. This morning you . . . hardly marched at all . . . and it has been quite delightful to sit under the trees. Now you are so exhausted from this war service you can't do a damn thing. I'm going to go out there and drill you again, and if you can't drill I am going to march you in and report you as wholly ineffective."[55] Drill them the captain did, and before long the unit was responding with snap and polish. The men at Monterey soon hung the nickname "Dynamite" on this officer, whose full name was George Catlett Marshall, Jr.

Captain Marshall became adjutant later that summer at the Fort Douglas training camp, near Salt Lake City.[56] This was a good camp, and the 578 rookies worked hard. President Wilson's veto of the Army Appropriation bill on Au-

---

[54]Quoted in Forrest C. Pogue, *George C. Marshall: Education of a General, 1880–1939* (New York, 1963), p. 136.

[55]Ibid., pp. 137–38.

[56]It was after the Fort Douglas camp that Marshall's superior, Lieutenant Colonel Johnson Hagood, wrote one of the most extraordinary responses ever found in an officer's efficiency report. In answer to the form question of whether he would wish to have Marshall again serve under his command, Hagood wrote: "Yes, but I would prefer to serve *under his command.*" See ibid., p. 138.

gust 18, 1916, threatened to hold down attendance, but Senator Reed Smoot of Utah arranged with both the army and the railroads to defer transportation expenses until another bill could pass.[57] The Oregon Short Line was especially cooperative, sending over a hundred employees to camp and donating a large section of railroad trackage for engineering work. Salt Lake City voted $2,500 in municipal funds to help with equipment and recruiting.[58]

Weather was excellent, the terrain ideal. The trainees were out on hike near beautiful Butlerville Mesa when General Bell made an inspection the second week in September. Like Wood, Bell used the occasion to lecture the young men on the virtues of preparedness. His strictures about William Jennings Bryan and the foolish notion of "a million men springing to arms overnight" had a familiar ring.[59] The Fort Douglas camp made effective propaganda in the mountain states, one of the direct results being the introduction of ROTC at the University of Utah in early 1917.[60]

THREE

"Went to Harvard Club," Wood wrote in his diary, "and made a short talk; great crowd. Loving cup from Training Committee. 1800 men present. Largest crowd ever in Club rooms for a talk."[61] As in 1915, the general's appearance gave a boost to recruiting; and the results showed that the center of the training camp movement in 1916 was still Plattsburg. Altogether, 12,198 persons attended six different camps in northern New York, from June to October. Senior camps for men between the ages of twenty-four and forty-five lasted four weeks; junior camps for college stu-

[57]*Deseret Evening News,* August 18, 19, and 21, 1916.

[58]Remarks of "Mr. Armstrong of Utah" in the minutes of the Meeting of the Standing Committees of the Military Training Camps Association, New York City, November 24, 1916, Clark MSS.

[59]*Deseret Evening News,* September 15, 1916.

[60]Ralph V. Chamberlain, *The University of Utah: A History of the First Hundred Years, 1850–1950* (Salt Lake City, 1960), pp. 349–50.

[61]May 1, 1916.

dents were for five weeks at a time. There was also a special camp on Long Island during July for boys aged fifteen to eighteen.[62]

DeLancey Jay later estimated that 85 percent of the men trained at Plattsburg in 1915 returned the following summer.[63] And many of the better-known veterans seemed to congregate in the August senior camp: Mayor Mitchel, Willard Straight, the Roosevelt boys, Hamilton Fish, Jr., Elihu Root, Jr., George Wharton Pepper. Joining them as rookies were Bishop J. D. Perry of Rhode Island, Henry L. Stimson, and Henry Breckinridge. Bishop Charles H. Brent, the Philippines missionary and an old friend of Wood, acted as unofficial camp chaplain. The bishop became enraptured. His first Sunday at Plattsburg he held Episcopal services "in the open overlooking the lake," and dedicated the sermon to "Christ, the Supreme Commander."[64] Suffering from heart trouble, Brent told a friend, "I feel rather shabby in that I am not taking the training."[65] Wood caught the enthusiasm and was proud of the fact that one of his sons and young Ted Roosevelt were in the same company. "Mr. Stimson is out as an acting lieutenant with one of the cavalry troops and is having the time of his life," he reported to Frank McCoy. "There are many distinguished men who are carrying their fifty odd pounds gracefully."[66] It looked like 1915 all over again.

The Plattsburg camps of 1915 and 1916 nonetheless were different. The border mobilization created almost insurmountable difficulties. As commander of the army's Eastern Department, Wood had the task of preparing approximately three-fourths of the nation's militia for movement to Texas, and this forced him to remain near Governor's Island where nearly the entire month of June was given over to paperwork, finding officers and equipment

[62]Military Training Camps Association, *Report of Chairman and Secretary of the Governing Committee* (New York, 1916), copy in Clark MSS.

[63]Jay to Ralph Barton Perry, March 19, 1920, Perry MSS.

[64]Brent Diary, August 13, 1916, Charles H. Brent MSS, Library of Congress.

[65]Brent to Samuel S. Drury, August 17, 1916, ibid.

[66]Wood to McCoy, September 4, 1916, Wood MSS.

for units, inspections, arranging railroad and shipping schedules. Plattsburg was neglected. Orders from Washington caused some of Wood's best regular troops to be withdrawn from the department. Transfer of the Thirtieth Infantry in early May was an especial hardship, for this regiment, stationed at Plattsburg since the previous summer, had been groomed for the training and physical care of civilian recruits.[67] Replacements had to be rushed up from Panama or detailed from the Coast Artillery and plow horses were pressed into service from nearby farms; as a result, the instruction in the June and July camps was not what the general would have liked.

To make matters worse, there were a series of cloudbursts in northern New York in mid-June. "Our first camp," one rookie complained, "was a big clay mud hole and with the odor of a first class pig pen attached. They had to move us, as we were getting sick."[68] Another Plattsburger told how the latrines overflowed into the stream where clothing was washed; he also criticized army cooking—"the soup was burned, the fish raw for two-thirds of its diameter, the rice pudding too hard to chew."[69] There were several others, more understanding of the army's predicament, who still thought that the officers were too lax in matters of discipline. One trainee commented that "the men who were trying 'to play the game' rather resented

---

[67]There was suspicion on the part of Wood and his staff that the withdrawal of the Thirtieth Infantry—suddenly and without warning, when there were other regiments that might have been selected—was politically motivated. "The death of the Plattsburg camps would not be a paralyzing blow to the powers that be," Wood wrote, "but it would be a paralyzing blow to the best influence we could put behind the army and the movement for preparedness." Wood to McCoy, July 5, 1916, quoted in Hagedorn, *Leonard Wood*, 2:194; see also notes of an interview with Halstead Dorey (ca. 1930), Hagedorn MSS.

[68]O'Donnell Iselin to Clark, July (?), 1916, Clark MSS.

[69]Memorandum of Sinclair Kennedy, November 21, 1916, ibid. Another rookie wrote: "The rain . . . followed us pretty persistently through the three weeks . . . in Plattsburg. There was but one period of 24 hours, I believe, during which the rain did not fall. The situation would have been bearable if the camp had not been pitched on a field of pure clay, which was soon puddled into a mire. . . . The mud emitted a peculiarly offensive smell, due, it was said, to the fact that the field had been used as a hog run; and no one who has not experienced our situation could well imagine the relief we felt when we received our orders, after a week of this, to move camp to the site which had been used last year." Manuscript essay, Clive Day MSS, Sterling Library, Yale University.

tardiness and absence of men who were obviously not 'playing the game.' "[70] In return, officers were rather defensive and apt to put the blame on changed conditions and increased numbers. Even Captain Dorey, who visited Plattsburg in June, excused the poor performance by saying that the class of men did not seem "up to last year's."[71]

The situation did improve. Once the National Guard mobilization was well underway, Wood had time to offer Plattsburg the supervision only he could give. By the end of July there were more than seven thousand trainees and regular troops taking part in war maneuvers near Plattsburg, a performance which Wood regarded as superior to that shown by the militia.[72] Grenville Clark was there at the time. "The camp was successful on the whole," he wrote. "The average of the personnel was not quite up to last year but still very good. The optional work was cut out in the afternoon and the men drilled considerably harder. In consequence, in spite of slightly less enthusiasm than last year, the military results were better and some of the companies were really splendid. The heat during the hike was excessive and took out a good many of the weaker ones who could not stand it, but I don't think this did any harm."[73]

Another result brought about by the large number of rookies and the shortage of regular officers was the use of veteran Plattsburgers as "noncoms" and drill instructors.

[70]Frank M. Sawtell to Major Joseph S. Herron, July 7, 1916, RG 98, "Records of the Plattsburg Barracks, 1916." See also William H. Coon to Herron, July 7, 1916; George W. T. Skinner to Captain Joseph H. Baer, July 7, 1916, ibid. There are a number of Plattsburger critiques in the barracks records. The officers asked the civilians to make comments.

[71]Dorey to Wood, June 11, 1916, Wood MSS.

[72]"We have a far more efficient command in these 6,500 men who have had a month of intensive training here than any equal number of men on the border outside the regular service. When I say this I say it literally . . . because they have learned the basic principles. We have only had to send away three men for failure of discipline and during eight days of hard marching under a *full* pack we have had only 60 to 70 men who have had to give up the game. Most of these from physical defects such as flat feet and weak hearts. . . . This shows you what you can do if you have the right sort of people. . . . We are putting over the sentiment for universal training and perhaps that is the most important thing we can do." Wood to Henry T. Allen, August 6, 1916, Allen MSS.

[73]Clark to John R. Van Horne, August 10, 1916, Clark MSS.

Beginning with the August camp, Wood made a rule that graduates of one training camp would enter their second camp at the same rank at which they left their first.[74] Thus did Mayor Mitchel and Archie Roosevelt, both of whom had won stripes in 1915, progress to first lieutenants by the time their regiment went on hike in late August.[75] These would-be officers had few illusions about their promotions. "The captain has 'broken' several noncoms," one Plattsburg sergeant wrote home, "and I have a notion the only reason I've lasted this long is that he hasn't gotten around to me yet." A week later he was lamenting that "if there is any harder labor than trying to teach a bonehead rookie — and there are a lot of them — how to shoot under a broiling sun, I will have to be shown."[76] These men knew they could not compare with their professional counterparts, but they realized that, if war came, men like themselves would have to make soldiers out of democracy's raw masses — because there were not enough regular officers.[77]

A related development was the way in which Plattsburgers were able to pass examinations for the Officers' Reserve Corps. When Wood had become reconciled to James Hay's version of the National Guard, he pushed hard for the ROTC and ORC sections of the new National Defense Act. Because the latter envisioned civilians, ages twenty-five to forty-three, qualifying for reserve commissions from second lieutenants to majors, he pressed the War Department to speed up the bureaucratic process and convene an examining board during July and August when most of the older men would be at Plattsburg. He urged General Scott to see that the examiners gave consideration to a candidate's cultural background, his superior education, his Plattsburg record and recommendations. Wood did not want the army prejudiced in favor of enlisted men

---

[74]Wood to General Montgomery M. Macomb, August 26, 1916, Wood MSS.

[75]*New York Times,* August 30, 1916.

[76]Quincy Sharpe Mills to Mrs. Mills (mother), August 17 and 23, 1916, Mills MSS.

[77]For an excellent example of this attitude on the part of Plattsburgers, see the novel by Allen French, *At Plattsburg* (New York, 1917).

(also eligible for ORC commissions) who could memorize textbook regulations but lacked qualities of leadership.[78] The MTCA supported Wood's efforts.[79]

The General Staff incorporated some of these suggestions, and by late August the ORC examinations were ready. Almost six hundred civilians took these first exams at Plattsburg. Many had stayed over after the July camp for such a purpose; practically all were veterans of more than one training camp.[80] The results were very satisfactory. Aided by a special refresher course given by Wood's staff officers, more than three hundred Plattsburgers qualified for reserve commissions during August and September — with twice that number expected to follow. Not only did this constitute "practical returns," Wood exulted to McCoy, but it was "the most hopeful and inspiring thing imaginable, and it does a lot to remove the impressions which one gets from contact with the great crowd of money chasers — the crowd who believes that anything is better than war — the crowd, in short, who have [*sic*] laid the foundation for a series of wars."[81]

FOUR

Since 1916 was an election year, politics played a part in the summer camps. In April the Democratic governor of New Jersey had discovered that the MTCA, not the army, was recruiting men for Plattsburg. In it, he discerned a Republican plot for "making political converts under the guise of preparedness."[82] One of the governor's associates was more explicit: "the work is being done under the aus-

[78]Wood to Hugh L. Scott, August 8, 10, and 12, 1916; Scott to Wood, August 10, 1916, Wood MSS.

[79]See Clark to Newton D. Baker, August 12, 1916, RG 94, AG2450169.

[80]*New York Times*, August 28, 1916. Grenville Clark, after considerable soul-searching, decided against taking the reserve exam. "Really, ought not our consciences to be clear about having done our share," he wrote to Jay, "and isn't it up to the younger men without families and responsibilities?" Clark to Jay, August 25, 1916, Clark MSS.

[81]Wood to Frank R. McCoy, October 6, 1916, Wood MSS.

[82]Governor James F. Fielder to Joseph Tumulty, April 4, 1916, Woodrow Wilson MSS.

pices . . . of an organization located at No. 31 Nassau Street, of which Elihu Root's office boy [Grenville Clark] is president and a brother to Col. Roosevelt's son-in-law [Lloyd Derby] is treasurer & office manager. Every minute of the time the organization, aided by Wood's staff, is working over time proselytizing from the Democratic Party and lining up anti-Administration sentiment."[83]

A more serious situation occurred at the first Plattsburg camp, during late June and early July. General Scott advised Henry S. Drinker that "the administration is receiving many letters from parents and from members of the first camp in regard to political activities there." According to Scott, Secretary Baker had peremptorily transferred Colonel Edwin F. Glenn from Plattsburg to Texas because Glenn had been making partisan speeches in favor of universal military training.[84] Drinker got in touch with Derby and Jay, both at Plattsburg for the July camp, and determined that the rumors were without foundation and that under the grueling training schedule everybody was too busy to engage in politics.[85] Drinker reassured Scott.[86]

How much truth was there to the rumors? General Wood certainly had political ambitions. Since December 1915 he had been listening to the presidential siren. Theodore Roosevelt had given him encouragement; and a group of enthusiastic political amateurs led by the sculptor Gutzon Borglum made quiet plans to capture the Republican nomination for Wood in June 1916. The general had been present at a well-publicized luncheon on March 31, along with Robert Bacon, Roosevelt, Henry Cabot Lodge, and Elihu Root. It marked the first meeting between Roosevelt and Root since the Republican Convention of 1912 and seemed to signal united backing for Roosevelt (or, if not

[83]George T. Fry to Tumulty, April 3, 1916, Wilson MSS.

[84]Scott to Drinker, July 13, 1916, Scott MSS.

[85]DeLancey Jay to Drinker, July 20, 1916 (copy), Scott MSS. One rookie wrote astutely, giving his own definition of politics: "The real function of the camps is political rather than military. They are designed to teach citizens the difficulty of building up an army, and to educate voters to such sacrifices of time and money as may be necessary for that purpose." Unpublished essay, Clive Day MSS.

[86]Drinker to Scott, July 24, 1916, Scott MSS.

Roosevelt, then for Wood) in the forthcoming campaign. A Wood boom did materialize that spring, prompting an administration spokesman to hint publicly of "a transfer to some other and more soldier-like department of the army where the military abilities of General Wood can be of some service to the government that pays him $8,000 a year for *military duty,* and not for political campaigning."[87] The general's hopes came to naught in early June when the Republicans at Chicago nominated Charles Evans Hughes. Disappointed at first ("very much disgusted about Convention," he wrote in his diary on June 12), Wood may have been indiscreet during his short visit to Plattsburg in the middle of the month. Duties in connection with the National Guard mobilization kept him from brooding; and by the time of his return to Plattsburg in mid-July his ambition was again under control.

Wood's aspirations notwithstanding, the question of how politically oriented the training camp movement was depended on the extent to which one considered preparedness a partisan issue. Wood believed that his agitation for military training was more patriotic than political. So did a Democrat like Mayor Mitchel.[88] It is interesting to note Grenville Clark's response when Drinker sent him copies of his correspondence with General Scott about politics at Plattsburg. "I will write to Derby and Jay," he said,

> and ask them to write a brief joint letter to say there are no political activities in camp. Of course there actually are not, I am certain, and I do not believe there were any in the June camp. Aside from other considerations nobody has time to

[87]As quoted in Hagedorn, *Leonard Wood,* 2:186.

[88]Mitchel had been criticized by Democrats for speeches attacking the Hay bill. He replied: "It would seem to me that my friendliness toward the President ought by this time to be too well known to him and the men immediately about him, to be open to question every time a newspaper quotes me as saying something that can be tortured by inference into a criticism. . . . Anyone who stood as I did last Friday on the Pier at 131st Street and saw members of the National Guard roping out a herd of utterly unbroken and unbranded western horses which had never known saddle or halter . . . must have felt some indignation against the kind of system that makes the country depend for its protection on this kind of military preparation." Mitchel to Dudley Field Malone, June (?), 1916, Mitchel MSS.

bother with politics in camp. So far as our Training Camps Association is concerned, *I consider that we have avoided politics with the greatest scrupulousness.* Of course we all must recognize that General Wood's activities are very distasteful to the Administration but I do not see what we can do about that even if we wanted to and I do not believe we would want to do anything because the General is doing a great work all the time.[89]

The Wilson administration remained suspicious of Plattsburg, but continued to support the principle of voluntary training for civilians under federal auspices.[90]

The MTCA flirted with politics more actively later in the summer. As in 1915, there were attempts to persuade prominent individuals to visit Plattsburg. President Wilson was asked.[91] So was the Republican candidate for president. "Charles Evans Hughes, Jr. came to see me yesterday," Clark reported to Drinker on July 19.

He was chosen at the June camp as a member of our Governing Committee. He is a very intelligent, active fellow and has a lot of good ideas. He said that his distinguished father was very much in favor of our work and also that he was in favor of a system of universal training, although apparently he has not made up his mind whether to make a campaign issue of it. Incidentally the question was mentioned of the possibility and advisability of Judge Hughes' paying a visit to camp. He said if we wanted him to, he would speak to his father about it. Personally he was rather doubtful whether it would be a good plan. I am myself more than doubtful. While it would be a great advertisement, it would lend color to the politics idea, especially if the President does not go.[92]

[89]Clark to Drinker, July 18, 1916, Clark MSS. Italics added.

[90]"Gordon Johnston . . . was also a student of mine [at Princeton], and a very headstrong one. His character is fine, but I have no means of judging his discretion. He has been right-hand man to General Wood in recent months and has been a little too much inclined to follow his chief's example in the way of political agitation." Woodrow Wilson to Newton D. Baker, July 3, 1916, Baker MSS.

[91]"I shall do what I can to get the President to go to Plattsburg for I agree with you that he should do so." Edward M. House to Mitchel, August 19, 1916, Mitchel MSS.

[92]Clark to Drinker, July 19, 1916, Clark MSS.

There was no question about the Plattsburg leaders preferring Hughes to Wilson.[93] They wanted Hughes to take a strong stand for preparedness, but the Republican leadership chose to run a moderate campaign.[94] "Hughes would get very much more enthusiastic support from all preparedness people, especially from the twenty thousand campers," Jay complained in early September, "if he could let it be known that he was really in favor of universal training even if he did not have the nerve to come out for it in public speeches."[95]

Then, in a surprise move, Clark informed Wood that the Republican hopeful was coming to Plattsburg for a visit. The general's diary for September 12, 1916, tells the story:

Met Charles E. Hughes at the 12:45 train and drove with him as far as the hotel. Called me up a few days ago and said he would like to come over as his son had been at the camp. Told him I should be delighted to have him come, but there should be no speeches. In this he entirely concurred. At four o'clock Mr. Hughes came out. We took him over the camp and he stayed for supper. He seems to fully appreciate the work going on. Had a long talk with him and strongly urged him to come out for universal service and training. Pointed out the necessity of having some definite issue and tried to impress upon him the keen interest throughout the country in this subject. Apparently he had never given it very serious attention. Lou [Mrs. Wood] was given a box and went to Hughes' meeting in the evening. I didn't go as it was purely a political meeting.[96]

[93]See Clark to George W. Wickersham, n.d. (ca. July 1916), ibid. This letter, which Clark never sent, proposed that Hughes strongly endorse the twin principles of a federal reserve and universal military training. The Plattsburgers "are for the most part disgusted with the present administration, on the ground that President Wilson has taken an unsound position on the two great issues referred to. His attitude on the Federal principle was shown by his desertion of Secretary Garrison at the critical moment & on universal obligation by his talk about 'universal voluntary' training which all the men who attend these camps regard as nonsense." Clark said a firm statement on military issues would "help his canvass immensely."

[94]Harbaugh, "Wilson, Roosevelt, and American Interventionism," pp. 219-21.

[95]Jay to Clark, September 6, 1916, Clark MSS.

[96]Clark to Wood, September 9, 1916, Wood MSS; Wood Diary, September 12, 1916.

Although the rumors said otherwise, this visit to Plattsburg was the extent of Republican "domination" of the training camp movement in 1916.[97] However much Wood and the Plattsburgers might have appeared partisan, their political involvement was a good deal less than friends of President Wilson suspected.[98]

FIVE

The way in which the MTCA conducted training camp strategy during the summer of 1916 underlined its non-partisanship. The object, as Clark, Jay, and Drinker saw it, was to further the cause of universal military training; and for the time being this meant staying away from controversy.

The mobilization of the National Guard on June 18 had raised important issues. Several MTCA officers were members of the Guard and left to join their regiments.[99] What attitude or policy should the MTCA as an organization adopt: Should Plattsburgers volunteer en masse for the border, or should they go to camp as if nothing had happened? If they did nothing, opponents would say "we told you so; these fellows were silk stockings and dudes and were just playing soldier, not meaning to come forward when their country called them."[100] As a result, the MTCA leaders debated the question during the last week in June and decided to form a Plattsburg Volunteer Force.[101]

[97]Wood, especially, suffered from charges of political agitation at Plattsburg; see Hagedorn, *Leonard Wood*, 2:183-203.

[98]See J. C. O'Laughlin to Leonard Wood, July 15, 1916, Wood MSS; Frank R. McCoy to Hugh L. Scott, August 3, 1916; and Scott to McCoy, August 8, 1916, Scott MSS.

[99]Landon Thomas joined the Georgia National Guard and went to Texas because he felt it was his duty to go. He had agitated so hard for preparedness, it would have been "shirking" for him not to go. Thomas interview. See also Thomas to Clark, December 23, 1916, Clark MSS. John R. Van Horne, a close friend of Clark and an original Plattsburger, went to Texas with the New York National Guard. He reported that there were at least eleven members of Company F, First Training Regiment, on the border, "I think we have every reason to believe that Plattsburg 1915 is well represented at the border." Van Horne to DeLancey Jay, September 9, 1916, Clark MSS.

[100]Peter Bowditch to Clark, July 3, 1916, ibid.

[101]Clark to John R. Van Horne, July 5, 1916, ibid.

The MTCA sent out circular letters to all persons enrolled in the 1916 camps, asking if they would be willing to
serve on the border if President Wilson called for volunteers. A Military Committee then set about forming a "paper organization" with such men as Wood, Dorey, Johnston, George Van Horne Moseley, and Frank R. McCoy
designated to command. It was, according to Clark, an
attempt

> to 'save the face' of the camps in view of the present situ-
> ation, while at the same time conducting them on the old
> line. . . . The idea is not for a regiment but for a large force
> of which the Plattsburg men would form only the frame-
> work. The way it would work out in practice would be that if
> there were a call for volunteers the men who had expressed
> a wish to go to Mexico, having previously been assigned to
> positions as junior officers and non-commissioned officers
> would be put into a separate mobilization and general re-
> cruiting would be conducted for the rank and file. The other
> men would pick up and go home having already made their
> position clear by signing the enrollment blank that they were
> not prepared for service in Mexico. . . . In this sense the idea
> of the Plattsburg volunteer force would not be out of line
> with the training of men to instruct others but would be a
> practical demonstration of what it could accomplish in this
> line. There was never any idea of having Plattsburg men go
> as a body or as men in the ranks.[102]

The volunteer force was a compromise, an MTCA attempt
to "save . . . face and at the same time not scare off all the
conservatives who would not want to get involved in going
to Mexico."[103] As it turned out, the president never called
for volunteers; and the spectacle of the Plattsburgers emu-
lating their spiritual predecessors, the Rough Riders, never
came to pass.

It was just as well that the Plattsburgers did not go to
Mexico, for this would have been an obstacle to their larger

[102]Clark to Robert Homans, July 5, 1916, Clark MSS; see also DeLancey Jay to
Wood, June 28, 1916, Wood MSS; "Notes on Plattsburg Volunteer Force" in Clark
MSS.
[103]Clark to John R. Van Horne, July 5, 1916, Clark MSS.

purpose, demonstrating for universal military training. The MTCA in June 1916 opposed the volunteer system. Clark and Drinker persuaded Secretary Baker over the course of the summer not to require an enlistment contract (first instituted in the September 1916 camp at Plattsburg) that covered more than the thirty-odd days of camp instruction. The MTCA did not want a reserve obligation attached to camp attendance, arguing that Plattsburg trainees would serve without hesitation in time of national peril but did not wish to be singled out for a duty which, they believed, was universal.[104] This was a subtle argument, on the surface seeming to endorse the Wilsonian policy of voluntary training, but in fact advocating a universal obligation.[105]

The logical extension of this Plattsburg philosophy was to poll the men at camp as to their position on universal training. To Clark, it was imperative to have thousands of training camp graduates individually pledged to serve the country. Then they could protest against any obligation that was not universal. "I can imagine appearing before the military committees," he told Jay, "and arguing for no obligation without being able to produce evidence that the men are in earnest. We could not succeed."[106] The upshot was a very careful procedure whereby the MTCA had representatives attend each of the camps at Plattsburg. "The idea," Clark wrote, "is to have a uniform set of resolutions, fitting in with the by-laws, which each camp will be asked to pass."[107] They would wait for the "psychological moment," usually when the trainees were on hike and sitting around the campfire at night. A speech would ex-

[104]See, especially, Drinker to Clark, September 15, 1916, Clark MSS. This letter summarizes the MTCA position on enlistment taken during the summer.

[105]There is often the hint, not openly expressed, that Clark opposed any enlistment obligation because it might scare away applicants. Clark wanted to use the large numbers at the 1916 camps to demonstrate for the principle of universal obligation, even if the persons in question were not as enthusiastic as the MTCA leaders. Clark to Benjamin Joy, July 8, 1916, Clark MSS. See also George V. H. Moseley to Clark, June 8, 1916, ibid.

[106]Clark to Jay, July 11, 1916, ibid.

[107]Clark to Kenneth P. Budd, June 16, 1916, ibid.

plain the organization and purpose of the Military Training Camp Association. New delegates would be chosen. Finally the MTCA representatives would ask for a unanimous endorsement of universal military training. According to Clark, who secured more than 6,000 pledges at the July camp, it was "all over in a few moments."[108]

These resolutions in favor of universal training again raised the problem of politics. When the head of the Association for National Service (a prominent preparedness group) approached the MTCA in July about a public campaign for universal military training, Clark was hesitant. To do so might involve the Plattsburg movement in politics, which they wanted to avoid.[109] Accordingly, the MTCA played safe. Clark kept political fences mended by inviting General Scott and Secretary Baker to Plattsburg in early August.[110] A congressional delegation headed by Richard Olney II of Massachusetts also paid a visit.[111] The response was gratifying, as Baker wrote General Wood that he "enjoyed the inspiration of the camp, its officers, its men, its spirit, and its meaning."[112] Olney told Clark that he was "more enthusiastic than ever over the idea of the summer military training camps."[113] These visits were a high point of the summer. Not only did they indicate the wisdom of avoiding partisanship, their success brought about a reconciliation between Wood and Clark.[114] Communication became easier between the two, and the general began to echo the Plattsburgers in their advocacy of larger numbers and more camps for 1917.[115]

Clark was in New York in late August when he received a telegram from Ted Roosevelt at Plattsburg, inquiring about future policy. "I think that times have changed,"

[108]Clark to John A. Farley, August 15, 1916, ibid.
[109]Clark to General S. B. M. Young, July 18, 1916, ibid.
[110]Clark to Newton D. Baker, July 12, 1916, ibid.
[111]Clark to Olney, July 18, 1916; Olney to Clark, July 19, 1916, ibid.
[112]Baker to Wood, August 3, 1916, Wood MSS. See also *New York Times,* August 3, 1916; and Wood Diary, August 2, 1916.
[113]Olney to Clark, August 10, 1916, Clark MSS.
[114]Clark to John A. Farley, August 15, 1916, ibid.
[115]See Clark to Wood, August 13 and August (?), 1916, Wood MSS.

Clark replied. "I think that the training camp movement as a sort of vague protest and attempt to arouse patriotism . . . in a general way has about reached its height. I think it has got to be given a definite objective." The movement had reached a crossroad. The MTCA might follow one path and concentrate on conducting the camps as a means of training reserve officers and "go no further." This did not appeal to Clark, although he thought the Plattsburgers should "develop the camps in that direction so far as possible." He preferred to push the camps as a propaganda vehicle for universal military training. With twenty thousand new members from the 1916 camps, Clark thought "we have the most powerful instrument to that end in the country." His idea was to keep the movement together by publishing a bigger and better magazine than the *Bulletin of the First Training Regiment* and "at the same time . . . go right ahead developing the camps in . . . a more systematic way." The two propositions should be linked together with the emphasis on universal military training. Because he thought that at least 90 percent of the men favored universal training, Clark did not feel that such a policy would "misrepresent them, but on the contrary, I think, would be in accordance with their views."

There seemed to be no great obstacle from a political standpoint. "If Hughes is elected," Clark noted, "we will be on the right side of the fence, as he is said personally to be in favor of universal training and we will be in a position to force his hand. If Wilson is elected, the game will be much harder but we might as well be in the open about it and do what we can." Clark did not think Secretary Baker would object, for he thought that the secretary actually favored universal training and was "certainly not hostile to it." President Wilson would never give his active support in any case, and it seemed unlikely that the Plattsburgers would arouse any more hostility from the president by backing universal training than by remaining silent. Now that the training camps were protected under law, Clark did not see how Wilson could abolish them. "Of course," he observed, "the universal training propaganda must be conducted ostensibly in a nonpartisan way, but I think there will be no difficulty about that."

Plattsburg strategy had to consider the difficulties to be faced that winter. There would probably be an attempt to impose a service obligation on the men who go to training camps—"the National Guard will see to that." Clark feared that any "drastic obligation would kill off the camps and the game would be up. We must be in a position to resist it." If the Plattsburgers were simply seeking to build up a strong volunteer reserve, the issue would be academic. But if the MTCA were avowedly committed to bringing a system of universal military training, they could logically say that it was unfair to impose any obligation on Plattsburgers until a universal obligation was imposed on all able-bodied male citizens. Clark thought this "a fair position, and I think we could get away with it." He urged Roosevelt to work hard to get the universal training pledge adopted at the August camp. "There wasn't the slightest difficulty about it at the July camp. It was simply read and everybody said 'aye' as a matter of course. I think we need to have the resolution passed if we are to adopt the universal training policy so as to be able to say that it has the backing of the men."[116]

If Clark was projecting a more aggressive and controversial strategy for the future, he could do so partly because caution and avoidance of politics had provided a sufficient base.

SIX

The success of the training camps in 1916 gave rise to much talk about the "Plattsburg Idea." Strictly defined, the phrase referred only to the federal training camps and the implicit goal of universal military training. In a larger sense, however, the "Plattsburg Idea" came to include all organized efforts to prepare civilians for service in time of war. During the summer of 1916 a voluntary National

[116]Clark to Theodore Roosevelt, Jr., August 21, 1916, Clark MSS.

Service School for young women was set up in Chevy Chase, Maryland, with courses in sanitation and first aid.[117] Training was also popular in Philadelphia, where A. J. Drexel Biddle, the eccentric sportsman and millionaire, introduced military drill into his famous Bible classes. By the spring of 1916 over ten thousand Philadelphians were taking weekend training.[118] It was this kind of active demonstration for preparedness that became a legitimate expression of the "Plattsburg Idea."

One of the offshoots of the idea in 1916 was the "Naval Plattsburgs." Franklin Delano Roosevelt, assistant secretary of the navy, was the intellectual godfather. Like his Republican cousins, Roosevelt had wanted very much to be at Plattsburg in 1915, but an emergency appendectomy prevented his attending. "I particularly want to find out what the course consists of," he lamented to Wood, "as I am very anxious to have the Navy Department follow the Army in this splendid & already successful work."[119] More aggressive than his chief at the department, Josephus Daniels, he wanted to build a naval reserve of 50,000 men, consisting of former officers and enlisted men, plus civilian volunteers who were familiar with navigation, ship's engines, radios, and other skills. The way to attract civilian interest, Roosevelt reasoned, was to follow the Plattsburg example and offer summer training cruises. Aided by President Wilson's push for a "Navy second to none" during the winter of 1915 – 1916, Roosevelt convinced Secretary Daniels that his plan had merit and would appeal to more than wealthy yachtsmen and fun-loving college boys. In the spring of 1916 the navy announced that nine ships of the Atlantic reserve fleet and two of the Pacific fleet would accept civilian volunteers for a four-week training cruise during August and September. The course of instruction was open to high school graduates between the ages of nineteen and

[117]*Army-Navy Journal* 53 (May 6, 1916): 1153.
[118]Wood Diary, April 26, 1916. "Report upon the Military Instruction Camp Drexel Biddle, Lansdowne, Penn., October 20-November 27, 1915," RG 94, AG2352720.
[119]Franklin D. Roosevelt to Wood, August 16, 1915, Wood MSS.

forty-five and would cost $30 per man. The purpose of the experiment, the navy said, was threefold: to qualify men as naval reservists; to foster public knowledge; and to help prepare a select group of trainees for commissions as reserve officers.[120]

"The John Paul Jones cruise," as Daniels jokingly referred to it, became Roosevelt's contribution to the preparedness movement. The assistant secretary worked hard publicizing it; more than once he and General Wood shared the same speaking platform, each pushing the other's program as well as his own.[121] With Grenville Clark and DeLancey Jay present to give advice, an informal committee of supporters met at the Harvard Club in June and laid plans for a recruitment campaign. The Naval Plattsburgers soon were occupying offices that adjoined MTCA headquarters.[122] When the old battleships designated for the cruise steamed out of Boston, New York, Philadelphia, Norfolk, and other ports on August 15, some 1,928 fledgling sailors were on board. It was not a large number, but, as Roosevelt later put it, they "represented the highest type of professional and young business men of the country, and almost without exception they left the cruise in excellent health, the best of spirits, ardent friends of the Navy, and advocates for preparedness."[123]

While the training fleet took part in war games off southern New England, delegates from each ship met aboard the U.S.S. *Rhode Island* on September 1, 1916, and, like the Plattsburgers before them, the naval rookies decided to organize formally and pledged to work for further training cruises. Another meeting in October created the

[120]"A Plattsburg of the Sea," *Outlook* 113 (May 10, 1916): 51. See also Franklin D. Roosevelt, "The Naval Plattsburg," *Outlook* 113 (June 28, 1916): 495–501; Frank Freidel, *Franklin D. Roosevelt: The Apprenticeship* (Boston, 1952), pp. 256–58; H. Howland, "Amateur Sea Dogs," *Independent* 88 (October 2, 1916): 18–20; E. B. Marshall, "Life of a Naval Volunteer," *Scientific American* 115 (September 23, 1916): 278–79.

[121]Wood Diary, May 19, June 9, 1916; additional details of Roosevelt's campaign for the "Naval Plattsburgs" can be found in Record Group 10, Box 16, Franklin D. Roosevelt Library, Hyde Park, New York.

[122]William Greenough to Perry, May 26, 1920, Perry MSS.

[123]Franklin D. Roosevelt to Perry, May 5, 1920, ibid.

Naval Training Association with William Greenough of New York as executive chairman. That winter the Navy Department established civilian correspondence courses and made preparations for using twelve battleships in the next summer's cruises. By the time the United States declared war on Germany in April 1917 over ten thousand applications had been processed.[124]

For all their apparent success, the "Naval Plattsburgs" had considerably less effect than their army counterparts. Roosevelt's hopes notwithstanding, it was essentially well-to-do yachtsmen and speedboat owners who took advantage of the cruises. In the popular mind, naval preparedness seemed more a matter of building ships than training men; and, as a propaganda source, the Naval Training Association ranked far behind the powerful Navy League of the United States. There was some talk of amalgamation with the MTCA in the autumn of 1916, but the navy men balked at the commitment to universal military training. "We found them not particularly sympathetic to the fundamental ideas we had in mind," Clark recalled. "The point was that they did not see the big idea that we were after, but were thinking just of some naval training."[125]

Another area in which the "Plattsburg Idea" had some effect during 1916 was aviation. Here the military had much to gain from civilian initiative, for the government had done practically nothing to encourage flying prior to the First World War. Whatever advances had come were due to individual pioneers and branches of the Aero Club of America. The National Defense Act of June 1916 attempted to rectify the situation by making aviation a part of the army's Signal Corps, and subsequently Congress voted funds for twelve National Guard Aero Squadrons. The wheels of bureaucracy moved slowly, however; and it was necessary for interested civilians to devise a temporary expedient. General Wood proved cooperative, with the result

[124]William Greenough to Perry, June 8, 1920, ibid.; see also Perry, *Plattsburg Movement,* pp. 139-40.
[125]Clark to Perry, May 25, 1920, Perry MSS.

that by the second week in June 1916 a civilian flying school, or "Air Plattsburg," was being operated on the military reservation at Governor's Island.[126]

Raynal Bolling and Philip Carroll began the new experiment. Both were ardent Plattsburgers. Bolling had organized the Motor Machine Gun Troop at the 1915 camp, while Carroll, along with Clark and Ted Roosevelt, had first suggested the businessmen's camps. Bolling had participated in military aviation in the autumn of 1915 when, at the request of General John F. O'Ryan, he helped form the First Aero Squadron of the New York National Guard; and when the Guard was mobilized in June 1916 he spent the summer teaching volunteers to fly rickety biplanes at a field near Hempstead Plains, Long Island. The Governor's Island school did not have official status, though Wood was able to provide instructors. At the outset only seven men enrolled. Private funds purchased the two Curtiss J. N.-4 Tractors used in pilot training.[127] The program picked up as the summer wore on, and by mid-September over forty civilian pilots had received training — with only one minor accident in two thousand practice flights.[128] "Your work and the work of Philip Carroll," Wood told Bolling, "has been very valuable; in fact, it is about the only work in the air we have done which amounts to anything. . . . It is unfortunate aviation is attached to the Signal Corps. It must eventually be an independent corps."[129]

Wood expanded the Plattsburg training in other directions that summer. The first two weeks in September he arranged to offer a course in military medicine, open to any licensed doctor or third-year medical student for a fifteen dollar fee.[130] Even more interesting was the special instruction camp which he set up for the New York Police Department. Beginning on May 27, 1916, some 2,509 pa-

---

[126]Regulations for the Aviation Branch of the Plattsburg Camp of Instruction, Governor's Island, N.Y., June 8, 1916 (copy), Wood MSS.

[127]Carroll to General George A. Scriven, June 24, 1916 (copy), Wood MSS.

[128]Bolling to Henry A. Wise, September 14, 1916 (copy), ibid.; see also *New York Times,* September 9, 1916.

[129]Wood to Bolling, September 14, 1916, Wood MSS.

[130]*New York Times,* July 28, 1916.

trolmen underwent two weeks of intensive military drill under Regular Army officers at Fort Wadsworth on the eastern end of Staten Island. The city supplied food and uniforms; the army provided rifles and other equipment. The training camp lasted four months, with groups of approximately 350 policemen attending at one time, before a citywide transit strike in early September called everyone back to his beat. "It is a Plattsburg camp," the general explained to Police Commissioner Arthur Woods, the essential purpose being to "turn out a fairly efficient infantry soldier in a police uniform."[131] Overlooking the narrow entrance to Upper New York Bay, Fort Wadsworth was an ideal site to study problems of harbor defense.

Another army installation with even wider implications for the Plattsburg movement lay more than a hundred miles to the east—Fort Terry, on tiny Plum Island just off the northeastern tip of Long Island. There, under command of Colonel Andrew Hero, Jr., twelve hundred youths from 324 different secondary schools took five weeks military training, July 6 to August 10, 1916.[132] Fort Terry represented a departure for the training camp movement, extending Regular Army instruction for the first time to boys under eighteen. The success of this camp and others like it would further the cause of universal military training even more than Plattsburg. According to Wood, the camp on Plum Island was "the beginning of a series of camps which in the end will include each year hundreds of thousands of youths in all portions of the country."[133]

The man who first proposed a camp for boys was Samuel S. Drury, headmaster of St. Paul's School, Concord, New Hampshire. Like so many educators, Drury had been impressed by Plattsburg and the college camps and was

[131]Wood to Arthur Woods, May 5, 1916; see also Arthur Woods to Wood, May 3 and September 28, 1916, Wood MSS; and *New York Times*, April 26, 1916.

[132]See two pamphlets published by the MTCA: Archibald G. Thacher, *The Cadets at Plum Island* (New York, 1916); and Horace C. Stebbins, *Federal Training Camps for Boys: A Story of the Camp at Plum Island with an Outline of the Plans for Camps in 1917* (New York, 1916). A camp newspaper, *The Range Finder*, was published at Fort Terry; there are copies in the Clark MSS.

[133]Wood to Henry S. Hooker, August 28, 1916, Wood MSS.

eager to get General Wood's cooperation in holding a special course at St. Paul's during the summer of 1916.[134] Wood thought it a splendid idea and enlisted local MTCA leaders (among which were Horace C. Stebbins, James D. Williams, and Archibald G. Thacher).[135] Interest in the camp grew quickly, with two thirds of the preparatory and high schools in the New York area endorsing the idea, so that by the end of March 1916 Wood decided to hold the camp at Fort Terry.[136] The MTCA formed a Junior Division, set up recruiting offices at 475 Fifth Avenue, and urged that branches in other sections of the country do their part. The results were encouraging; boys from twenty-three states and Hawaii eventually paid their $50 training fees. Though a majority of the trainees came from Eastern private schools, there were enough boys from different backgrounds and locales to belie charges of aristocratic favoritism—a fact which camp publicists never neglected to point out.[137]

Wood and the MTCA gave extra attention to Fort Terry. One of Wood's aides, Captain Charles Kilbourne, was detailed to assist Colonel Hero, and each of the eight student companies into which the camp was divided was commanded by first lieutenants and captains of the Regular Army. West Point cadets, who gave up summer leave, served as seconds in command, with a select group of Plattsburg veterans as the other company officers.[138] A

[134]Drury to Wood, October 13, 22, November 15, 23, December 1, 1915, Wood MSS. See also Clark to Drury, January 12, 1916, Clark MSS. "A school camp should not be restricted to boarding school boys. It is absolutely essential to make the movement successful that it be made democratic and all vestiges of caste and exclusiveness be excluded."

[135]Comprising the Executive Committee of the Junior Division of the MTCA were Stebbins (chairman), Williams (secretary-treasurer), Thacher, Henry S. Hooker, W. DeLancey Kountze, John H. Prentice, T. Douglas Robinson, Fred N. Watriss, and George L. Wrenn.

[136]Wood Diary, March 27, 1916.

[137]See Perry, *Plattsburg Movement*, pp. 115–19; and Ernest H. Abbott, "The Boys at Fort Terry," *Outlook* (July 26, 1916): 951–54.

[138]"General Wood feels that it is a very necessary thing that there should be some influence over the boys besides that of the Regular Army." T. Douglas Robinson to Kenneth P. Budd, May 8, 1916, Clark MSS. Compare Archibald G. Thacher to Charles K. Cummings, May 12, 1916, ibid.

strict military regimen was followed, perhaps too strict in some instances.[139] Instruction was progressive, consisting of calisthenics, manual of arms, close and extended order drill, target practice, personal hygiene and camp sanitation, use of the shelter tent, and rudimentary tactics. As Colonel Hero put it, the purpose of the camp was "not only to give these cadets the necessary military training but also to quicken their interest in our country." The officers therefore put emphasis on smartness and military protocol, and the youngsters seemed to respond more favorably to discipline than did their elders.[140]

The trainees were teenagers, and the instruction had to take cognizance of this fact. There were rest periods after two hours of drill, as well as before and after meals; and, except when assigned to kitchen or guard duties, a cadet had three free hours every afternoon to participate in some form of supervised recreation. A large YMCA tent served as the camp's social center, providing concerts and movies, as well as ice cream sodas. On Sundays a special ferry brought parents and visitors from the mainland. Extra precautions were taken in regard to health; in fact, a second camp scheduled for Fort Terry during August had to be canceled because of a polio epidemic in the Eastern states. There was no polio at the July camp, however; the worst malady in the five weeks of training seems to have been a single case of tonsilitis.[141]

The Fort Terry camp attracted a few important visitors. An associate of Bishop Brent, the Reverend R. B. Ogilby of Bazenio in the Philippines, conducted Sunday services after the first week of training.[142] One of the editors of the *Outlook,* Ernest H. Abbott, came out for a few days to view

---

[139]E. H. Abbott's article in the *Outlook* described an occasion when some West Point cadets deliberately harassed boys on sentry duty, to see if they would hold their ground when approached without the proper password (pp. 252–53). Wood, when he read the article, quickly saw to it that the West Pointers were reprimanded. Wood to Abbott, July 24, 1916, Wood MSS.

[140]Andrew G. Hero, Jr., to Theodore Roosevelt, June 26, 1916, Roosevelt MSS.

[141]Perry, *Plattsburg Movement,* p. 117; *New York Times,* July 18, 1916.

[142]*New York Times,* July 18, 1916.

the proceedings, became a convert, and went back to New York to write a series of laudatory articles. Another *Outlook* editor visited Plum Island on July 25 — but to exhort, rather than to write. As the cadets lined up in review, Theodore Roosevelt told them the facts of military training. "The man who isn't fit to fight for his country isn't fit to vote," he proclaimed. The students now knew what military service entailed, what fine men their officers were, and how far-fetched the idea was of a million men springing to arms overnight. Roosevelt urged them to help counter the arguments of pacifists, those "nice old women of both sexes," who were like an old Belgian acquaintance of his, blind to any need for preparedness until it was too late. For Roosevelt, the only equitable solution was universal military training.[143]

Wood also spoke to the boys about universal military training. He came to Fort Terry for a surprise inspection just two days after Roosevelt. "Spent day until 2:20 watching work of boys," he wrote in his diary. "Review, etc. Are doing splendid work. Excellent camp. All going well."[144] The general's speech was short, with all the familiar arguments and allusions. Then he returned to Governor's Island and from there went up to Plattsburg.

That Wood spent far more time with the militia and at Plattsburg during 1916 did not diminish the importance of the Plum Island camp. The war in Europe and the crisis with Mexico made it imperative that emergency efforts be aimed at training men of military age. Nonetheless, the boys' camp had potential. "These officers are excellent," one Plattsburger remarked to Clark. "I believe this boy's movement promises big & they, as they grow older, will spread abroad our game with an enthusiasm lacking in an older man."[145] The MTCA planned further camps for boys in 1917, but the war intervened. When the training camps

---

[143]Ibid., July 29, 1916.

[144]Wood Diary, July 26–27, 1916.

[145]Horace C. Stebbins to Clark, July 23, 1916, Clark MSS; see also Henry S. Hooker to Woodrow Wilson, December 1, 1916, Wilson MSS.

resumed after the war, the so-called Citizens' Military Training Camps (CMTC) for young men aged seventeen to twenty-four were more along the lines of Plum Island than of Plattsburg.

SEVEN

Captain John R. Kelley wrote from Plattsburg that "the September camp—in my opinion—is far ahead of the prior ones this year. . . . [There] is no undercurrent of criticism. Dorey is the big chief and the camp is being run like those of last year. There is a big difference."[146] Mayor Mitchel was able only to acknowledge this news from his Plattsburg commander. He had done his soldiering that summer at the August camp and was embroiled at the time in a countywide strike of transit workers. He could not accept Kelley's invitation to come up for a weekend.

But General Wood was able to enjoy thoroughly this last camp of the season, from September 8 to October 5, 1916. Most of the difficulties in the National Guard mobilization were past, and for the moment Wood's political discontents were subdued by what seemed the imminent election of Charles Evans Hughes. The general found time to relax, to visit the Canadian officer training camp at Valcartier near the city of Quebec, and to see his younger son, Osborne, settled in Cambridge as a Harvard freshman. During the last week of September and the first week of October, he managed to unwind while following the Tenth Training Regiment on its hike through the countryside north and west of Plattsburg.[147]

As Captain Kelley stated, this autumn camp was different. With Dorey in command and fewer than a thousand trainees in attendance, the instruction succeeded in bringing out the same close-knit enthusiasm and *élan* that so characterized the 1915 Business Men's Camp. Cooler weather and an early harvest made it possible for the

[146]Kelley to Mitchel, October 1, 1916, Mitchel MSS.
[147]Wood Diary, September 7–27, 1916.

rookies to spend more time on maneuvers over terrain that closely resembled European battlefields. Eleven days— more than in any previous camp—were given over to war games; and, as always, the men thrived on such work. The volunteers were mostly 1916 vintage: clerks, salesmen, groups of sponsored employees, the unknown Browns, Kelleys, Olsons, and Smiths. These men were the first to have their expenses paid under the 1916 Army Appropriation bill. There were a few famous names on the roster, such as Jim Barnes, the African explorer and author, and Jacob Gould Schurman, Jr., son of the president of Cornell University. But all submerged their identities in military discipline. One of the September privates, Allen French, later published a novel, *At Plattsburg,* which described in eloquent detail this process by which individuals of all sorts acquired a common military bond.[148]

The autumn weeks seemed to affect Wood as never before. Perhaps it was the combination of beautiful weather and a long overdue holiday. Or maybe he had some premonition that war would come to America before another camp could be held at Plattsburg. Whatever the reason, the general's usually terse diary becomes almost lyrical in its lengthy description of frosty evenings by the campfire, horseback rides along trails blazing with autumn foliage, daily skirmishes between regular and civilian troops. As the hike swung back toward Plattsburg, the Training Regiment made camp on October 4 near Cadyville, a small town several miles to the west. Wood's diary describes the scene: "A clear splendid night. Made a talk to the men on universal service and went over generally the work of the camp. The men then got together brushwood and timber from all directions and built some large bonfires, around which they danced and sang until late in the night. A very pretty sight—hundreds of men dancing in circles about the great fires."[149]

The rookies paraded back into Plattsburg the next

[148]*At Plattsburg* (New York, 1917).
[149]Wood Diary, October 4, 1916.

morning, were reviewed and mustered out with certificates of training. Wood spent two days with Dorey and the regular troops straightening up the Plattsburg Barracks. Then, for one last excursion before returning to Governor's Island, the general and his daughter Luisita took an automobile trip north to Silver Lake. It was "as fine a day as I ever saw," the air "clear and cool," with "the entire mountains covered with wonderful colors." The experience inspired Wood to sum up the results of the summer's work. The training camps were going to be far-reaching, he told his diary, "as the men came from all over the union and are an able, efficient, progressive lot. Their teaching is bound to bear fruit and will probably be shown in the legislation looking to universal service." Wood concluded with a somber prediction: "These camps have laid the foundation for good material for training officers and men in case of war, which every day seems more and more inevitable."[150]

[150]Wood Diary, October 5–7, 1916.

VII.

The Plattsburg Philosophy &
Universal Military Training

In his *Annual Report* for 1916, published at the end of the year, General Scott reprinted his testimony before the House Military Affairs Committee the previous January wherein he had advocated compulsory military training for all able-bodied men between eighteen and twenty-one years of age. He went on to explain the necessity of such a policy: how the United States might be dragged into the European war and why it was impossible to recruit sufficient manpower through voluntary enlistment alone. Military service was an obligation of citizenship, Scott argued, an obligation which entailed training in time of peace. Without going into details, he pronounced "the volunteer spirit . . . moribund" and urged immediate passage of universal training legislation. To do otherwise and send untrained men into battle would constitute "criminal neglect."[1]

The words of the chief of staff were a trial balloon sent up by the Wilson administration at a time when the electorate was expressing a manifest desire to keep out of war.[2] A few weeks later, in February 1917, Secretary Baker forwarded a General Staff plan for universal military training to Congress, but without recommending its passage. At this time, too, the War Department drew up plans for wartime conscription, but it was not until after the declaration of war against Germany in April 1917 that the Wilson administration gave full backing to any program of military reorganization. As in the winter of 1915–1916, the presi-

dent emphasized peace and diplomacy before preparedness.

The issue of universal military training nonetheless received much discussion in the months prior to war. The
Senate Military Affairs Committee held hearings during
December 1916 and January 1917 on a bill written in part
by the Military Training Camps Association. The first number of *National Service,* a journal "Devoted to the Cause of
Universal Military Training," appeared in February 1917,
financed, edited, and published by the MTCA. Other patriotic societies, such as the Association for National Service,
the Universal Military Training League, and the National
Security League increased their activities; and, as war approached, public opinion seemed to swing in favor of some
plan for compulsory training.[3]

These months represented a kind of culmination for
the Plattsburg movement, a time when urgency and previous accomplishments offered hope that fundamental
changes might suddenly be made in America's military
system. The Governing Committee of the MTCA resolved
in November 1916 "that the object and policy of this Association is to bring about a system of universal obligatory
military training and equal service for the young men of
the United States under exclusive federal control, and that
this policy be publicly announced and followed as the policy of this organization."[4] Numbering nearly twenty thousand by this time, the Plattsburgers by virtue of their personal demonstration occupied a philosophical position
apart from other preparedness groups. Their purpose was
military reform, and yet at the same time they intended this
reform to have consequences for the whole of American
society.

As it turned out, only a part of what the MTCA wanted

[1]*War Department Annual Reports, 1916* (Washington, D.C., 1916), 1:160–63.

[2]Woodrow Wilson to Newton D. Baker, November 20, 1916, Baker MSS.

[3]Public opinion and universal military training are discussed in Chase C.
Mooney and Martha E. Layman, "Some Phases of the Compulsory Military Training Movement, 1914–1920," *Mississippi Valley Historical Review* 38 (March 1952):
640–47.

[4]Perry, *Plattsburg Movement*, p. 148.

was realized when the war came, namely, the Selective Service Act of May 1917. Nevertheless, the Plattsburg idea was a major factor in the passage and wartime success of the draft law. The Plattsburg movement stood for universal military obligation, and the United States accepted this principle in the spring of 1917.

ONE

In one of the best articles about Plattsburg in 1915, the *New Republic* wrote, "The associates of this camp do not propose to militarize the American nation. They seek rather to civilize the American military system. They do not propose to turn civilians into mere automatons. They seek rather to attach soldiering to citizenship; and they seek to do it in such a way as to make the soldier really a civilian." The article spoke of the "real danger of national disintegration," how democracy in America was identified too much "with having one's own way" and not enough with the responsibilities of citizenship. The ideal of "national service" put forth at Plattsburg might serve as a "social hygiene" if applied judiciously. Such service would not mean war necessarily, but might become, in William James's phrase, "the moral equivalent of war."[5]

That such a favorable editorial should appear in the leading progressive journal of the day, the journal of Herbert Croly, Walter Lippmann, and Walter Weyl, helps to place the Plattsburg movement properly in the reform tradition. The men who went to camp in 1915 and 1916 may have been wealthy and predominantly Republican, but many were part of what the historian William E. Leuchtenburg has identified as the imperialist side of the Progressive movement.[6] Many of these earnest young men had stood

[5]"The Plattsburg Idea," *New Republic* 4 (October 9, 1915): 247–49. Willard Straight was probably the author of this article.

[6]Leuchtenburg, "Progressivism and Imperialism: The Progressive Movement and American Foreign Policy, 1898–1916," *Mississippi Valley Historical Review* 39 (December 1952): 483–504. It should be noted that Leuchtenburg's thesis applies most accurately to Eastern Progressives, many of whom were graduates of Harvard and Yale; see also Charles Hirschfield, "Nationalist Progressivism and World

with Theodore Roosevelt at Armageddon in 1912, and they followed Leonard Wood three years later—and would support him for the presidency in 1920.[7]

There were other links to the Progressive tradition, besides devotion to the leader. The Plattsburgers believed that their cause was just, that if enough persons could be persuaded of the need for universal military training, then reform would come about through the democratic process. They had what Grenville Clark called a "naturally optimistic standpoint"—at least to the extent that they conceived of their program as a practical reform in an imperfect world.[8] This was why the camps emphasized propaganda so much, especially in 1916. Those who attended became converts and influenced others. "When a man is willing to make personal sacrifices," DeLancey Jay wrote, "he is not only himself ever afterwards a keen devotee of the cause for which he made the sacrifice, but his doing so has considerably more weight with the community . . . than the mere dissemination of literature and presentation of arguments."[9] Clark explained to one member of Congress that "we have proceeded on the theory that the only way to put into effect the only effective and democratic system, namely that of universal service, is through getting the young men of the country interested by actually going through the experience of military service themselves."[10]

Wood and other Plattsburg writers always pushed the idea that Americans were ignorant of things military, that the true facts of the nation's military past were obscured by

War I," *Mid-America* 45 (July 1963): 139–56; and Walter I. Trattner, "Progressivism and World War I: A Re-appraisal," *Mid-America* 44 (July 1962): 131–45.

[7]Grenville Clark and Willard Straight were perhaps the two most prominent Plattsburg leaders who were also Bull Moosers in 1912. In 1920 most of the Plattsburg leadership enlisted in General Wood's campaign for the Republican nomination. DeLancey Jay and William Cooper Procter were the most active volunteers.

[8]Harvard College, *Class of 1903, Twenty-fifth Anniversary Report* (Norwood, Mass., 1928), p. 185. For further discussion of the reformist implications of universal military training, see John P. Finnegan, "Specter of a Dragon: Military Preparedness in the Progressive Era, 1911–1917" (Ph.D. diss., University of Wisconsin, 1969), chapt. 7.

[9]Jay to Mrs. Whitelaw Reid, January 5, 1916, Clark MSS.

[10]Clark to Senator Frank B. Brandagee, May [?], 1916, Clark MSS.

false prophets (pacifists) and patriotic euphoria. "This country has never, single-handed, engaged in war with a first-class power prepared for war," the general would say.[11] Franklin D. Roosevelt, arguing in favor of the "Naval Plattsburg" cruises in 1916, put it this way: "Really, the fundamental trouble with those poor idiots who make harangues against the Navy and preparedness in general [is] that they simply lack education. If one could take them individually and show them the real facts with their own eyes they would stop handing out untruthful hot air." By dramatizing the truth through history, humor, and the Plattsburg example, the movement fully expected to win over public sentiment.[12]

A corollary to this Plattsburg belief in persuasion was the tendency to overestimate its effect. During the summer of 1916 several public opinion indicators, including a survey by the United States Chamber of Commerce, had shown a growing momentum in favor of compulsory military training.[13] The Plattsburgers, particularly General Wood, took this to mean that the country was willing to accept the principle of universal military obligation. "You saw the vote on the referendum sent out by the National Chamber of Congress," Wood exulted in August 1916. "Forty-three out of the forty-four states voting carried it, over thirty of them unanimously."[14] Later that autumn, notwithstanding President Wilson's reelection, the general took heart in that "despite the large foreign element in the

[11]Leonard Wood, *Universal Military Training* (New York, 1917), p. 24. "The country is thoroughly unready. The people are filled with ignorance and a cheap conceit as to their military ability, which has been catered to and built up by fakers of the Bryan type. . . . Their teachings are preparing us for a great disaster." Wood to Robert Bacon, June 28, 1915, Wood MSS.

[12]The Plattsburg literature is large, most of it propaganda of one sort or another. There are three fictional accounts by Plattsburg veterans: Arthur S. Pier, *The Plattsburgers* (Boston, 1917); Allen French, *At Plattsburg* (New York, 1917); and O.N.E. [John B. Barnes], *Letters of a Plattsburg Patriot* (Washington, D.C., 1917). The last is a humorous piece. See also Harold T. Pulsifer, "ABC of Soldiering," *Outlook* 113 (July 19, 1916): 651–53; Ralph Barton Perry, "Impressions of a Plattsburg Recruit," *New Republic* 4 (October 2, 1915): 229–31. Roosevelt to Eckford DeKay, May 24, 1916, RG 10, Box 16, Franklin D. Roosevelt MSS.

[13]*New York Times,* July 24, 1916.

[14]Wood to George Wharton Pepper, August 4, 1916, Wood MSS.

Eastern population and the fact that the East is the seat of the munitions industry, of high wages and everything which has come in the way of prosperity resulting from the war, all the area which has been thoroughly covered by the propaganda of universal service, the area . . . most thoroughly reached by the Training Camps Association, went Republican. The only state that did not is New Hampshire . . . [where] practically no work was done in the way of working up the training camps."[15] In Wood's eyes especially, compulsory training legislation should follow as a matter of course.

This reasoning was correct, in a sense, as the success of the draft in 1917–1918 subsequently attested. Even though wartime conscription was selective rather than universal, the country did accept the necessity of a compulsory military system during war. But so long as the United States remained at peace, the likelihood of Congress's reaching a favorable decision on universal training was extremely poor. Better than General Wood, the Military Training Camps Association understood this fact of political life and concentrated on building up the summer camps. Not until the autumn of 1916 did the MTCA formally endorse universal training and service, and even then Clark and other civilian leaders had doubts as to any immediate success.[16] Wood, however, was inclined to attribute sinister motives to those who seemed to thwart the public will. "If we can [only] induce a few gentlemen who have the courage of their convictions to tell the truth," he complained in December 1916, then "Universal Service" might be accomplished.[17] "We are now no better off than we were three years ago," the general grumbled on another occasion. "Academic pinheads . . . are still talking about experiments and declining to use the best Europe has produced in the struggle for life and death. Of course, in a democracy preparedness is a hard thing unless there is a real leader in

[15]Wood to Frederic R. Coudert, November 15, 1916, ibid.

[16]"It will be a long step forward if we can get the matter seriously discussed in Congress." Clark to John A. Farley, December 5, 1916, Clark MSS.

[17]Wood to General Clarence R. Edwards, December 20, 1916, Wood MSS.

a position of authority."[18] Convinced of his own righteousness and superior knowledge, Wood refused to debate with pacifists for fear of giving their "degenerate" argument "a dignity and standing [to] which it is not entitled."[19]

Nationalism was another tenet of the Plattsburg philosophy, and as such it fitted in better with the New Nationalism of Roosevelt and Croly than with the New Freedom of Wilson. Plattsburgers exalted the principle of federal control in military matters. MTCA members who belonged to the National Guard maintained that the latter organization should relinquish its connection with the various states of the Union and argued that a vast majority of Guardsmen favored such an arrangement.[20] When the National Guard Association continued in 1916–1917 to oppose military reorganization, Wood contended that "ninety percent of the Militia are now for universal training; perhaps ninety-five. . . . The five percent . . . represent the men who are financially or politically interested in the maintenance of the present condition of Militia organization. They are like the man in the crowd on whose toe you tread; you hear more from him than from the thousand others present."[21] The Plattsburgers had little fear of a centralized military establishment subverting individual liberties, because, they argued, with universal training the professional army would turn into a citizen army. Compulsion did not seem a basic question. Believers in manliness, patriotism, responsibility, duty, the Plattsburgers had an almost mystical attachment to national service. Their favorite metaphor was to describe military obligation as a tax, the logical corollary to manhood suffrage, and to say that the nation could no more meet its responsibilities through voluntary military training than it could through voluntary taxation.[22] Once adopted, compulsory training would justify itself. As one of the men drafting legislation

[18]Wood to Colonel Jennings C. Wise, November 16, 1916, ibid.

[19]Wood to Mrs. S. L. Cromwell, November 25, 1916, ibid.

[20]See Clark to Senator William E. Borah, December 5, 1916, Clark MSS.

[21]Wood to Basil Miles, January 23, 1917, Wood MSS.

[22]Leonard Wood, "Universal Military Training," *National Educational Association Proceedings, 1916* (New York, 1916): 161–62.

put it in early 1917: "If the camel, in the shape of any reasonable Bill for universal military training, gets its head under the tent, I do not fear for the camel."[23]

Universal training would help to unify a divided nation. "Heat up the Melting Pot," Wood liked to say.[24] "Yank the hyphen out of America," admonished Henry Breckinridge.[25] By putting the poor with the rich, the immigrant with the native born, and letting each rise according to merit, military training broke down artificial class barriers. The Plattsburg literature, particularly in 1916, was replete with stories of the Boston Brahmin who shared a tent with the butcher from Elmira, of the washerwoman's son who became chums with the Groton student.[26] No doubt, much of this was hot air, especially Theodore Roosevelt's oft-quoted remark about "the dog-tent" being a "cradle of democracy."[27] The army discouraged Negroes from attending camp prior to 1917.[28] Nor were the educational requirements at Plattsburg exactly geared to the more humble elements of society. Yet the Plattsburgers believed sincerely in the democratizing and Americanizing benefits of universal training. Their own experience among hand-picked officers and fellow enthusiasts left a feeling of brotherly exaltation which many could recall more than fifty years later.

Having been a doctor before joining the service, Wood had come to love the army and liked to tell of its human-

[23]Edward Harding to Wood, January 10, 1917, Wood MSS.

[24]Leonard Wood, "Heating Up the Melting Pot," *Independent* 87 (July 1917): 15.

[25]*New York Times,* May 19, 1916.

[26]See, especially, Archibald G. Thacher, *The Cadets at Plum Island* (New York, 1916).

[27]*New York Times,* October 13, 1915.

[28]See memorandum of August 15, 1916, RG 98, "Records of the Plattsburg Barracks, 1916." "In the United States Army, colored and white regiments are distinct and no colored men are enlisted in white regiments. It was supposed that the same principle would apply to training camps. . . . This question came up several times and it was intended to establish a camp for colored men in case a sufficient number enrolled and troops were available but neither condition was fulfilled." The memorandum is signed by Leonard Wood and Halstead Dorey. See also George Wharton Pepper to Halstead Dorey, March 10, 1916, and Dorey to Pepper, April 11, 1916, ibid.; and J. E. Springam to Wood, March 28, 1917, Wood MSS.

itarian work in Cuba and the Philippines.[29] Similarly he
would point out how military training promoted economic
efficiency, lowered the crime rate, and instilled democratic
spirit.[30] Opponents who saw a threat to civil liberties said
that "military training is animal training" and argued that
any decision in the matter should be based on military
necessity, not on any supposed benefits to the individual.[31]
Whether or not military training brought salutary results
was not the main issue, however. Convinced that compulsory training was a military necessity, Wood and the
Plattsburgers made the best possible case for it. They believed their own arguments, because at the Plattsburg level
their experiment seemed to have worked.[32]

The proverbial "blue nose" was another Progressive
trait shared by Plattsburgers. During the winter of 1916 a
radical student magazine at Columbia University ran a
story to the effect that Plattsburg was a haven of vice and
dissipation, complete with gin mills and prostitutes.[33] The
charge scandalized the Training Camps Association, and
pious denials were issued. President Drinker demanded an
investigation.[34] A realist, Wood at first tried to smooth the
matter over — "You might as well prevent men from coming
to Columbia because within a mile or two there are thousands of dissolute women, gamblers, etc." Besides, it was
only a question of one or two saloons, nothing illegal.[35] The
summer of 1916 with its large crowds and growing com-
mercialization changed Wood's mind. The next winter he
and the MTCA put pressure on the Plattsburg Chamber of
Commerce, and a bill was introduced in the New York state

[29]Leonard Wood, *The Military Obligation of Citizenship* (Princeton, N.J., 1915).

[30]See Wood to General S. B. M. Young, May 5, 1916; Wood to H. H. Gross,
June 20, 1916; Wood to editor of the *New York Times,* December 22, 1916, Wood
MSS.

[31]See statement of John Dewey, U.S., Congress, Senate, *Universal Military Training . . . Hearings on S 1695* (Washington, D.C., 1917), pp. 560–71.

[32]Senate Hearings, *Universal Training,* p. 142.

[33]See Silas Frank Seadler, "The Menace of Plattsburg," *Challenge* (March 1916).
There is a copy in "Records of the Plattsburg Barracks, 1916." See also *New York
Times,* February 22, 1916.

[34]Henry S. Drinker to Wood, May 29, 1916, Wood MSS.

[35]Wood to Drinker, May 31, 1916, ibid.

legislature prohibiting the sale of liquor within a quarter mile of the military reservation. "I wish the members of the state legislature," one of Wood's subordinates wrote, "could see this line of saloons, with their electric signs, their back rooms, and their music running full blast." It was a "vile" place to send the sons of American mothers.[36] The bill passed in April 1917.[37]

Probably the most legitimate Plattsburg claim to being "democratic" or "progressive" was their argument that universal training and service was the only fair policy. "There is an enthusiastic response by a certain proportion of the best elements in the early days of war," Wood wrote, "but this response cannot be counted upon to continue throughout a longer war involving severe strains upon the population, nor is it right or just to throw the burden of military service upon a portion of the population."[38] The volunteer spirit was fine, but as a system it was unfair. As Grenville Clark pointed out: "Jones will not do it while the man across the street is left to get ahead of him in business. Why should he? That is the fundamental trouble." [39]

There was a certain paradox in that the Plattsburg camps became a strictly voluntary means for advertising the principle of universal obligation. The Plattsburg method seemed different from the Plattsburg philosophy. That Wood and the MTCA should keep the camps voluntary was a matter of good sense and good politics. Prior to the 1916 Defense Act, the Plattsburgers had to pay lip service to voluntarism because the Congress had not authorized camps of instruction. Any premature endorsement of compulsory training would have killed the movement. "The system has got to be allowed to develop normally," Clark wrote, "and in accordance with civilian feeling, otherwise it will break down. If too much is asked to start with it will

[36]Captain J. A. Baer to Senator Wallace H. Pierce, March 1, 1917, ibid.; see also Wood to Pierce, March 3, 1917, ibid.; Clark to John Purroy Mitchel, March 7, 1917, Clark MSS; Wood to W. B. Jacques, March 12, 1917, and Jacques to Wood, April 14, 1917, Wood MSS.

[37]Jacques to Wood, April 14, 1917, ibid.

[38]Wood, *The Military Obligation of Citizenship* (Princeton, N.J., 1915), p. 10.

[39]Senate Hearings, *Universal Training*, p. 830.

prevent ultimate progress. The civilians have got to be educated up to it gradually."[40] The MTCA played down the issue of compulsory training until the autumn of 1916, by which time the movement had accumulated enough prestige to insure survival. When the Plattsburg Volunteer Force was being formed in the summer of 1916, nearly the entire MTCA leadership viewed it as little more than a paper organization—intended to forestall criticism from the National Guard, not to fight in Mexico.[41] The question came up again during the Army Appropriations Hearings at the end of the year when Congressman Julius Kahn urged the War Department to require future service of persons who volunteered for federal training camps.[42] The MTCA objected on the principle that all citizens were obligated to serve when called and that to single out Plattsburgers would be to perpetuate an iniquitous system. They would volunteer for camp, but were opposed to the volunteer system. At these same hearings even Secretary Baker admitted that 99 percent of the men who went to Plattsburg would enlist in time of national emergency; "they would beat the rest of us to it."[43] The intent of the Plattsburg movement was that the nation should not have to rely on the spirit of the 99 percent.

T W O

The universal training legislation which the Plattsburgers finally supported in 1916–1917 originated elsewhere. A military training bill had been introduced in the Senate in December 1915, sponsored by Senator George E. Chamberlain of Oregon. A short, stocky man with a reputation for candor, Chamberlain sometimes seemed like a Democratic version of Theodore Roosevelt with his pince-nez, white mustache, and passion for preparedness. The bill

[40]Clark to Moseley, June 10, 1916, Clark MSS.
[41]Clark to John R. Van Horne, July (?), 1916, Clark MSS.
[42]U.S., Congress, House, *Army Appropriations for 1918* (Washington, D.C., 1917), pp. 812–13.
[43]Ibid., p. 723.

had called for compulsory training of all able-bodied males, whether citizens or declarants, between the ages of twelve and twenty-four. The young men thus trained would form a Citizen Cadet Corps, Citizen Army, and Citizen Army Reserve, according to age.[44] The plan was too revolutionary. Congress saw the "ghost of militarism in anything that squints at universal military training," Chamberlain complained to Wood.[45] Nevertheless, the bill did provoke some discussion before it disappeared in the arguments over the National Guard and Continental Army; and with Chamberlain as chairman of the Military Affairs Committee, an amended bill could expect further hearings when the moment was more propitious.

To help draft an acceptable plan, Chamberlain obtained the services of Captain George Van Horne Moseley of the General Staff. A tall, severe-looking officer of Midwestern background, Moseley had been one of Wood's protégés, having first served on the General Staff in 1911 where he had assisted in writing the report on "The Organization of the Land Forces of the United States."[46] He was reassigned to the General Staff in the summer of 1915 at Wood's request.[47] Confined at first to routine duties at the War College Division, Moseley was detailed by General Scott in December 1915 as adviser to the Senate Military Affairs Committee. Moseley and Chamberlain hit it off immediately. Since officers at this time were still under President Wilson's edict not to speak publicly about preparedness, nor to talk with congressmen unless requested, the Senator told Moseley to read his mind and always assume that he, Chamberlain, wanted his advice. The result was an arrangement whereby Moseley became a kind of

[44]U.S., Congress, Senate, *Congressional Record,* 64th Cong., 1st sess., 1915, p. 223.

[45]Chamberlain to Wood, January 6, 1916, Wood MSS.

[46]See Moseley, "One Soldier's Journey," Moseley MSS.

[47]Wood used his influence to bring Moseley, John McAuley Palmer, Douglas MacArthur, and several other reform-minded officers to Washington in 1915 where they might have some say in forthcoming preparedness legislation. See Wood to James G. Harbord, April 23, 1915; Wood to Moseley, June 23, 1915, Wood MSS.

liaison between civilian preparedness groups and the Senate committee. Working quietly at his house, the young officer would receive visits from Clark, Drinker, and leaders of other civilian groups, tell them the latest congressional and War Department developments, and listen to their proposals.[48] In an informal way Moseley tried to arrive at a consensus.

As he worked on a new training bill in the spring of 1916, Moseley received special encouragement from two newly formed preparedness organizations. One group, located in Washington, was the Association for National Service, with Lieutenant General (retired) S. B. M. Young as president—the first defense organization to agitate exclusively for the principle of universal training. "It has been my experience," Young wrote, "that it takes about fifteen or twenty minutes to convince any thinking and reasonable man that Compulsory Military Training is the only safe and sane principle upon which to base a Military Policy. The trouble has been that our people have not been giving the matter more serious consideration."[49] Under the supervision of E. B. Johns (also editor of the *Army–Navy Journal*), the Association for National Service was planning a nationwide referendum of newspaper editors regarding universal service that summer and an even more extensive publicity campaign later in the year.[50] The problem was finding a specific plan on which Wood, Moseley, Chamberlain, and all the civilian groups could agree. The Universal Military Training League, under the leadership of John T. Pratt, provided the answer. A veteran of the 1915 Plattsburg camp and a good friend of Grenville Clark, Pratt had become interested in compulsory training when the MTCA leadership declined to endorse the principle early in 1916. Along with fellow Wall Street lawyer Edward Harding and

[48]Moseley, "One Soldier's Journey," 1:128–32.

[49]Young to John T. Pratt, April 12, 1916, Wood MSS. Other officers of the Association for National Service were H. H. Sheets, secretary-treasurer; Major Duncan C. Phillips, first vice president; Gutzon Borglum, second vice president; E. B. Johns, corresponding secretary; and Charles L. Frailey, legal counsel.

[50]Young to Wood, May 10, 1916, Wood MSS.

the Chicago Progressive Howard H. Gross, he decided to
form a separate organization which would draw up "a
definite plan of Compulsory Military Training" and "start a
campaign of education." They did not intend, he told
Wood, "to build up a large membership, but rather to work
through the present patriotic organizations as far as possible."[51] They would also undertake to raise large sums of
money. Wood put Pratt and his friends in touch with
Young's group and with Moseley.[52] Progress was swift. By
the end of June when Moseley accepted a commission in
the Pennsylvania National Guard and left for the border he
had completely rewritten the Chamberlain bill.[53]

The new draft, as Moseley later described it, was "simply this: Train all able-bodied young men in the calendar
year they become eighteen (or nineteen) years of age. After
this training they are permitted to go free, except in the
event of an emergency or war they would be called to the
colors *for service* by yearly *classes*, the youngest first."[54] Because of the National Guard mobilization and the presidential campaign, however, it was difficult to make much headway during the summer of 1916. Still very cautious, Clark
and the MTCA decided not to participate in the publicity
effort planned by the Association for National Service.[55]
Clark did not want to commit the Plattsburg movement to
universal training until after the summer season, but did

[51]Pratt to Wood, May 4, 1916, ibid.

[52]See Wood to E. B. Johns, April 17, 1916; Wood to Young, April 4, May 5,
1916; Wood to Pratt, April 18, 1916; Pratt to Wood, June 26, 1916, ibid.

[53]Moseley, "One Soldier's Journey," 1:130–32; Moseley to H. H. Gross, June 6,
1916, Moseley MSS. For Wood's comments on the Moseley bill, see Wood to
Howard H. Gross, June 20, 1916: "The training proposed . . . is in accordance
with the best thought of the day on the subject and will, so far as the individual is
concerned, turn out a better man physically, intellectually and morally; it will make
him a better man from the economic standpoint because of the habits of promptness, thoroughness and exactness. He will be a better all around citizen. It will give
him that self control, respect for the flag, for the authorities and for the rights of
others which are so much needed. It will serve to impress upon him a sense of his
responsibility towards the nation and teach him to think in terms of the nation
rather than in terms of the individual or locality. It will tend to national solidarity.
It will make America what she must be, a real melting pot, fusing the various
unassimilated elements into one mass of real Americans." Wood MSS.

[54]Moseley to Henry L. Stimson, December 1, 1916, Moseley MSS.

[55]Clark to S. B. M. Young, July 18, 1916, Clark MSS.

admit the importance "for the different people who are working in this direction to keep in close touch with each other and work in harmony."[56] The task of Pratt and his associates was to circulate copies of Moseley's draft bill among interested individuals in the hope of getting unified support in the autumn.[57]

The prospects for universal training increased markedly at the end of the summer. Not only were the polls conducted by the United States Chamber of Commerce and the Association for National Service favorable, but reports began to filter in from Texas of disenchantment among the rank and file of the National Guard and a growing sentiment in favor of universal training and service.[58] Encouraging also was the campaign by Robert Bacon for the Republican nomination for the Senate in New York. President of the National Security League and a prominent Plattsburger, Bacon ran on a strong preparedness platform which included universal military training. Although he lost the primary election in September (partly due to the eleventh-hour nature of his candidacy), his favorable showing convinced many advocates of preparedness that the time for caution was past.[59] Then, too, there was the success at Plattsburg. The ten thousand young men who took the training and demonstrated their willingness to serve made their impression on Wood. "These men are going to put the universal training proposition over," he boasted.[60]

Backed by the "unanimous" campfire pledges for universal training, Grenville Clark was ready by mid-August 1916 to have the Military Training Camps Association com-

[56]Clark to Moseley, June 10, 1916, ibid. Clark cooperated with the Association for National Service by allowing Young to circularize the members of the First Training Regiment (the 1915 Plattsburgers).

[57]See Pratt to Wood, November 14, 1916, Wood MSS.

[58]See John R. Van Horne to DeLancey Jay, September 9, 1916; Julius Kahn to Clark, December 1, 1916, Clark MSS; Major George T. Langhorne to Wood, August 3, 1916, Wood MSS. See also Report of the Executive Committee of the Mayor's Committee on National Defense, *The Mobilization of the National Guard 1916: Its Economic and Military Aspects* (New York, 1917).

[59]See Scott, *Robert Bacon*, pp. 256-72; H. H. Sheets to Clark, September 28, 1916, Clark MSS.

[60]Wood to James G. Harbord, July 18, 1916, Harbord MSS.

mit itself.[61] His approach was, first, to get a favorable resolution from the MTCA Governing Committee at its biannual meeting in November and then publicize the Plattsburg position by publishing its own magazine. Unlike the *Bulletin of the First Training Regiment,* this would be a journal of professional quality and national circulation. Already Clark had interested Captain John McAuley Palmer, a close friend of Moseley and a prominent army intellectual, in becoming the magazine's editor.[62] General Wood also promised his support.[63] Preparations went ahead during the next few months — both on the magazine and on the November meeting of the MTCA Governing Committee.

While the Plattsburgers made plans, the Association for National Service and the Universal Military Training League continued their efforts at coordination.[64] By the end of September 1916, Pratt's organization had gathered enough expert opinion to make the Moseley bill more "simple and definite."[65] Their revised draft, approved by Wood, called for "universal military service for all who are physically and mentally fit for the irreducible minimum of six months."[66] When Pratt showed the bill to Clark in mid-November, the latter replied: "You are very much to be congratulated. . . . What would you think of our publishing the bill in the first or second number of the magazine? . . . We shall want to throw the influence of all the [MTCA] membership behind it when the bill is introduced."[67]

The MTCA meeting in New York on November 24,

[61]See Clark to Theodore Roosevelt, Jr., August 21, 1916, Clark MSS.

[62]Palmer to Clark, August 25, 1916, ibid.; see also Clark to Professor Theodore Lyman, June 12, 1916; and Clark to DeLancey Jay, September 9, 1916, ibid.

[63]Wood thought the magazine "a splendid idea. If there is anything I can do to help it I shall be glad to do it." Wood to DeLancey Jay, August 27, 1916, Wood MSS.

[64]See H. Sheets to Clark, September 28, 1916; and Clark to Sheets, October 10, 1916, Clark MSS; John T. Pratt to Moseley, November 27, 1916, Moseley MSS.

[65]H. H. Gross to Wood, September 28, 1916, Wood MSS.

[66]Wood to Gross, October 2, 1916, ibid.

[67]Clark to Pratt, November 15, 1916, Clark MSS.

1916, promised to be a unique gathering.[68] Because of the proposed endorsement of universal training, Clark wanted as many MTCA representatives as possible to attend. He therefore scheduled the meeting for the weekend of the Harvard-Yale football game. Plattsburgers would conduct their business on Friday afternoon and then take the train on Saturday morning to New Haven where the MTCA had reserved a block of tickets on the fifty-yard line. (Or, alternatively, one could go with General Wood and his entourage up to West Point for the Army-Navy game.)[69] It all went as Clark had planned — "a great success."[70] More than a hundred Plattsburgers attended from some twenty-five states, with representatives from Fort Oglethorpe, Fort Douglas, Monterey, and all the 1916 camps. The universal training resolution, proposed by William Marshall Bullitt of Louisville and seconded by Mayor Mitchel, passed unanimously.[71] On Sunday afternoon some of the Plattsburgers and their wives were treated to a cruise around the Battery in one of Mayor Mitchel's police boats, after which there was a reception at Governor's Island where "Phil Carroll gave a first-rate flying exhibition."[72] Clark wrote, "I believe that . . . [the weekend] will have important results that do not show on the surface in the way of making everyone pull together and stimulating interest."[73]

THREE

Chamberlain's subcommittee planned to open hearings on universal military training on December 16, 1916. Although Clark saw little hope of positive legislation in the

[68]Clark to Drinker, October 3, 1916, ibid.
[69]See Clark to Members of Committees, October 10, 1916, ibid. Anyone who lived more than 500 miles from New York City would be the guest of the MTCA Executive Committee.
[70]Clark to Mitchel, November 28, 1916, ibid.
[71]Clark to Drinker, November 27, 1916, ibid.
[72]Clark to Mitchel, November 28, 1916, ibid.
[73]Clark to Drinker, November 27, 1916, ibid; see also "Minutes of the Meeting of the Governing Committee of the Military Training Camps Association . . . , November 24, 1916," ibid.

current session of Congress, he did think it would be a long step forward if they could get the matter seriously discussed.[74] Accordingly, he helped organize a dinner at the University Club in New York on December 14, where representatives of the MTCA, National Security League, Association for National Service, Universal Military Training League, and Maryland League for National Defense could confer on strategy. There were still differences of opinion over the right kind of bill, he told Henry L. Stimson, and he believed that a meeting might produce a "consensus as to the best form."[75] A controversial point which the various representatives threshed out was the length of time a citizen should be obligated to train under a universal system. Clark thought that six months was the maximum that would be seriously considered and possibly accepted, and the other preparedness leaders concurred.[76] Despite this agreement, there was still confusion when the Senate committee began hearings—confusion resulting from the several versions of the original Chamberlain bill and the fact that the General Staff was drawing up its own program based on a training period of twelve months.[77]

Hearings lasted for six weeks, until February 1, 1917. More than a hundred witnesses testified, including army officers, doctors, pacifists, college students, diplomats, and advocates of preparedness. Though both sides of the question were debated, a majority of speakers favored some form of universal military training. The Plattsburg position was well represented.

Wood was one of the first to appear, on December 18. He gave his usual candid testimony, a catalog of past and present mistakes, a stern sermon about where America's military responsibilities lay. He used Plattsburg to drama-

[74]Clark to J. A. Farley, December 5, 1916, ibid.
[75]Clark to Stimson, December 5, 1916, Stimson MSS.
[76]Clark to John McAuley Palmer, December 16, 1916, Clark MSS.
[77]See the drafts of the various bills being considered: Senate Hearings, *Universal Military Training*, pp. 4–65. See also "Memorandum on Moseley Bill, as Modified by John T. Pratt and Edward F. Harding, November 4, 1916," Mitchel MSS. There are several of these drafts in the Mitchel MSS.

tize universal training, calling it "a voice to a slumbering people" and "the most hopeful thing I have seen." Citing the approval of prominent university presidents as well as the fifty-odd clergymen at Plattsburg in 1916, Wood took pains to emphasize "the pure democracy of that association." Plattsburg showed that intelligent men could be made into soldiers in less than six months by using intensive and progressive methods — "there is no comparison between this kind of training and that followed . . . at most of our scattered garrisons."[78] Wood demonstrated through statistics how much less per man a system of universal training and citizen reserves cost in comparison to the existing Regular Army and National Guard. He recommended that the latter organization be relegated to its previous status of state militia and replaced by Federal Reserve regiments organized territorially. These reserve units would be comprised of young men who had completed six months of intensive training at age eighteen or nineteen and would undergo short periods of refresher training and summer maneuvers until age twenty-nine, after which they would pass into an inactive reserve.[79] The general did not press hard on specifics which "should be left to Regulations . . . promulgated . . . by the Secretary of War as the interests of the situation develop." He sought rather to impress upon the senators that military training was a necessary proposition, not something to be feared. The times required courage.

"Went to Congress and had a full hearing on Universal Service," Wood wrote in his diary. "Much interest. I made a very frank statement. . . . Many press men. Keen interest."[80] The general was heartened enough by the re-

---

[78]Senate Hearings, *Universal Military Training*, pp. 130–32, 142.
[79]Ibid., p. 145.
[80]Wood Diary, December 18, 1916. To John T. Pratt, Wood wrote: "I have advocated substantially the provisions of the . . . Moseley Bill with some of your proposed suggestions and have urged in the meantime that steps be taken looking toward the physical training of youth under the general provisions of the Australian system so we may be able to eventually evolve a well rounded system which will cover the preparatory stage as well as the stage of specialized military training." December 19, 1916, Wood MSS.

sponse to inform Theodore Roosevelt that "we could put it over even in this Congress if the President would come out and endorse it."[81]

The MTCA was not scheduled to testify until mid-January, and Clark wanted its position to coincide with Wood's. "I think we ought to advocate something like the Moseley Bill," he told Mayor Mitchel, "that is, a single period of intensive training at 18 or 19. I believe this is the only project that would work. The period should not exceed six months. General Wood considers that sufficient."[82] In this same vein, Clark tried to persuade Captain Palmer to have the training period in the General Staff plan lowered from twelve months to six. The General Staff scheme might be militarily feasible, but it was politically impossible — "it is like saying that a lawyer should take no account of a practical business situation when he gives advice, but restricts himself purely to the rules of law."[83] Even more important were Clark's efforts in coordinating MTCA testimony with that of the other preparedness groups. Conferring with Edward Harding and General Wood on Governor's Island in early January, he and Archibald Thacher arranged a slate of witnesses and subjects to be covered by the MTCA and National Security League. These two organizations would speak the loudest.[84]

A parade of witnesses using the Plattsburg example to justify universal training appeared during the first weeks of January 1917. George S. Hornblower, one of the organizers of the first Business Men's Camp, testified for the National Security League and compared the Plattsburg spirit and training to that of the National Guard, in which he had served on the Texas border in 1916. "I knew the

[81]Wood to Roosevelt, January 5, 1917, ibid.

[82]Clark to Mitchel, January 3, 1916 [1917], Mitchel MSS.

[83]Clark to John McAuley Palmer, December 27, 1916, Clark MSS. "This whole question cannot be treated entirely as a military question. It is partly military and partly political — I mean by 'political' what the public will stand for." Clark to Palmer, December 16, 1916, ibid.

[84]See Clark to Harding, January 5, 1917; Harding to Clark, January 4, 1917; Thacher to Clark, January 3, 4, 1917, ibid. Thacher's law partner, Herbert Barry, was in charge of the National Security League's presentation to Congress.

solemnity of 'colors' at evening in the Plattsburg camp," he recalled,

> when 1200 red-blooded Americans stood rigid in the ranks, with eyes to the front, gazing into the ominous future that the morning news of the *Arabic* sinking had made so plain to men who could think and look ahead. At Van Cortlandt Park [where the New York Guard regiments had mobilized in 1916] it was different. It was not as if the flag were calling us to our country's need. It was rather as if the country crawled behind and pushed us forward, saying "Here, you go ahead and do the dirty work; we are going about our business, making money or taking our summer vacations." . . . It was like saying to us, "You were patriotic; now take your punishment."[85]

Allen T. Klots, another Plattsburger who had joined the Guard, testified in a similar manner.[86] Other training camp witnesses included two Harvard students and a five-man delegation from Lehigh, all of whom repudiated charges made by an earlier group of students that Plattsburg training hardened rookies and made them militarists.[87]

The results of the testimony seemed favorable. General Scott reiterated his endorsement of universal military training before the senators and requested the War College Division of the General Staff to prepare its own elaborate plan, the plan which Secretary Baker forwarded to Congress in February 1917 and which subsequently became the basis for the wartime Selective Service Act. During the Senate hearings, also, the National Security League conducted a poll of newspaper editors and mayors scattered throughout the country and found a majority in favor of compulsory training.[88] Even Secretary Baker spoke tentatively of how "the obligation to defend one's country is universal."[89]

[85]Senate Hearings, *Universal Military Training*, p. 399.
[86]Ibid., pp. 403–10. Klots later became an assistant secretary of state in the Hoover administration.
[87]Ibid., pp. 917–30.
[88]Perry, *Plattsburg Movement*, pp. 160–61.
[89]House Hearings, *Army Appropriations for 1918*, p. 717.

And yet, in spite of what seemed possible on the surface, there was virtually no chance that either the administration or Congress would accept new defense legislation. Germany had not yet resumed unrestricted submarine warfare, and the crisis with Mexico had eased to the point where the preparedness rationale — for defensive purposes only — seemed to have little relevance. When a delegation from the Maryland League for National Defense (some of them Plattsburgers) carried a petition to the White House condemning the Defense Act of 1916, President Wilson rebuked them for using unrestrained language and *ex cathedra* arguments.[90] The president was then in the last stages of his diplomacy to keep America out of the European war by mediating that conflict. Rightly or wrongly, he believed that additional efforts at preparedness would serve mainly to stir up interventionist opinion, thereby antagonizing Germany and making war more likely. Neither Wilson nor Baker could accept compulsory military training as other than a last resort.[91] Even if the administration had pushed more vigorously, antipreparedness minorities in Congress possessed enough strength to block major legislation. When the Senate Military Affairs Committee reported out the Moseley bill favorably in early February, there was no discussion of it on the floor.[92]

The facts of the situation became painfully clear to the Military Training Camps Association when the official delegation appeared before committee on January 22, 1917. The Plattsburgers had prepared carefully for their hearing, with Mayor Mitchel giving a detailed statement on the failures of the National Guard mobilization, and Grenville Clark a shorter statement on how universal training worked and how much it cost. "We take it for granted that Congress is going to adopt some radical change of policy," Clark declared confidently, going on to describe Plattsburg as "a crusade for universal training and . . . an example

[90]*New York Times,* January 25, 1917.
[91]See the excellent discussion in Daniel R. Beaver, *Newton D. Baker and the American War Effort, 1917–1919* (Lincoln, Nebr., 1966), pp. 25–30.
[92]See Clark to Drinker, March 2, 1917, Clark MSS.

that something must be done."[93] Henry S. Drinker, Alfred Roelker, and G. Edward Buxton also spoke.

That same morning the Plattsburgers had visited the secretary of war "with the object of urging him to get behind compulsory training legislation; or at least to push the Plattsburg camp idea as against . . . the National Guard." Baker was noncommittal and took the position that, inasmuch as the Defense Act had passed Congress after full debate in June 1916, he had no choice but to administer the system as it was. He would not initiate new legislation. Mitchel, whose placid exterior covered up an Irish temper, proceeded to give Baker "a very still talk, in the course of which he said that rather than be Secretary of War and compelled to operate under a weak system, he should resign as Garrison did." Baker did not reply.

Later in the afternoon the MTCA representative sat in the Senate gallery listening to an address by President Wilson. It was one of Wilson's great state papers, his famous "peace without victory" speech, in which he set out the terms of a viable European settlement and described how the United States would help to guarantee such a peace by participating in a League of Nations. The subtleties of the speech were lost on the Plattsburgers, who saw only that Wilson was going to do nothing in the way of preparedness. By now Mitchel "had become very much disgusted." As Clark remembered it, the mayor "kept making audible remarks" and "when the 'peace without victory' phrase came out, he said that it was an insult to the country" and that the entire speech "would precipitate war."[94] The mayor walked out of the building in a huff.

FOUR

The war which Mitchel predicted was closer than he or Wilson suspected; the Imperial Government in Berlin announced a week later, on January 31, 1917, that it was

[93]Senate Hearings, *Universal Military Training*, pp. 817–22.
[94]Clark to Ralph Barton Perry, April 29, 1920, Perry MSS; see also Clark to Henry Breckinridge, January 29, 1917, Clark MSS.

resuming unrestricted submarine warfare in the Atlantic and Mediterranean war zones. What ensued is a familiar story: how Wilson, despite the German declaration, continued his efforts to avoid war, how he hoped against hope that German U-boats would refrain from overt acts, how his attempts at even moderate defensive measures, such as the arming of merchant vessels, were thwarted by "willful" minorities in Congress. The picture is of a reluctant and humane president, agonizingly aware of the horrors of war, trying desperately to avoid the decision he finally reached on April 2, 1917.

If less sensitive to war's horrors than was Wilson, the Plattsburgers were much more aware of what was required to wage war. Their attitude was in sharp contrast to administration activity in the weeks prior to war, and the continued Plattsburg insistence on compulsory training helped to facilitate Wilson's military policy when he finally decided to move.

General Wood had just testified a second time before the Senate subcommittee when he heard the news. "The German note . . . came out this P.M.," he wrote in his diary on January 31, "and will cause even a W[ilson] to act. General indignation, and are now to receive the coward's reward: ducking." Three days later he noted: "Relations broken off with Germany. General feeling of satisfaction that after years of international cowardice we have had the decency to resent this last and most insulting note."[95] Wood's satisfaction was short-lived, and within a few days he became disgusted at Wilson's unwillingness to ask for an immediate declaration of war. He sneered at continued opposition to preparedness:

> Think of poor, foolish Henry Ford opposing preparedness but stating if war comes he will give his shops and factories. It is a good deal like a ship owner who refuses to spend money for life boats but when the storm is on and the ship is going down offers the ship's carpenter his entire fortune for

[95]Wood Diary, January 31, February 3, 1917.

a boat. These people are really the most dangerous type. They appeal to the cheap emotionalism of the people when an emergency is upon us but contribute assiduously to bringing it about by their failure to help and back up the common sense policy of preparedness which would render a situation of this sort impossible.[96]

He deplored the lack of defenses: "They have started to dismount the 6″ guns at West Point and rush them to Rockaway. These guns there are about as good as a pea shooter in a bull fight. We are now absolutely dependent . . . upon the forbearance of our enemies and the active support of our well armed but not over enthusiastic friends. It looks as though we should surely drift into war unless we have been kicked into such a state of callousness that future thumps will not be painful."[97] Wood was determined to speak out. "To tell the truth," he wrote to a friend, "is not to give away secrets because every foreign country knows exactly what our condition of preparedness is. The only people who do not know are our own people and until they know they will not be active in providing defense."[98]

And so the general continued to talk. What he said was no more provocative, no more insubordinate than what he had said previously. Certainly he said nothing to match his statement of the previous year—"Gentlemen, we have no leadership in Washington."[99] Condemning pacifists, pointing out the lack of men and material, contending for universal military training, Wood was the same outspoken officer he had been since 1914. He was not unaware of what might happen. "As a soldier," he said, "I am supposed to risk my life in the service of my country. Should I not be willing to risk my commission?"[100] He knew that his activities violated the spirit, if not the letter, of an officer's

[96]Wood to John H. Iselin, February 16, 1917, Wood MSS.
[97]Wood to Frank R. McCoy, February 17, 1917, ibid.
[98]Wood to Iselin, March 15, 1917, ibid.
[99]Hagedorn, *Leonard Wood*, 2:200.
[100]Ibid., p. 199.

loyalty to his commander-in-chief.[101] But he was able to convince himself that loyalty to the army and the country as a whole compelled him to speak out. Besides, Wilson had not seen fit to challenge him — except through an occasional rebuke from the secretary of war.[102]

It was in such a context that the events of March 24–25 took place. Wilson had decided on war by this time and was writing his message to Congress, making last-minute preparations.[103] On the evening of March 24 an order, signed by the adjutant general, arrived at Governor's Island removing Wood from command of the Eastern Department. The department was being broken up into three separate commands, the order stated, and Wood had the choice of taking command of either the new Southeastern Department with headquarters at Charleston, South Carolina, "or the more important one at Manila or Hawaii."[104] Not wanting to leave the country, Wood telegraphed the next morning: "I prefer Charleston."[105] The general made no public response to this sudden change of events, accepting his orders like a soldier. Inwardly he seethed. "This division of command means an enormous amount of work," he confided to a friend. "It takes me absolutely out of Plattsburg, divides the Atlantic Coast into three independent commands, means a division of all our records. . . . How much easier it would have been to send me to Chile to look into the nitrate situation, to have made a personal investigation of the Cuban elections or to have gone to Alaska to see about the railroad and how much less dangerous to the military organization of our defenses."[106]

Wilson's reasons for removing Wood are not entirely

[101]See Wood Diary, January 3, 1917; and Wood to Theodore Roosevelt, January 5, 1917, Wood MSS.

[102]See Hagedorn, *Leonard Wood,* 2:196–210.

[103]On March 24 Wilson ordered the withdrawal of all American officials from Belgium and authorized the Navy Department to begin conversations with the British Admiralty. And on March 25 and 26 he called most of the National Guard into federal service; see Link, *Woodrow Wilson and the Progressive Era,* pp. 276–77.

[104]Adjutant General to Wood (telegram), March 24, 1917, as quoted in Hagedorn, *Leonard Wood,* 2:206.

[105]As quoted in ibid., p. 207.

[106]Wood to Frederic R. Coudert, March 1917, Wood MSS.

clear, for the president maintained a dignified silence.[107] Whatever military explanation the administration might make, however, it seems likely that political considerations weighed heavily on Wilson's decision. "First Blood for Politics," ran the headlines.[108] In some ways the situation was similar to President Harry S. Truman's firing of General Douglas MacArthur nearly forty years later: like Truman, Wilson was dealing with a general who would not follow the policy he had set forth; the principle of civilian control of the military required some action. But the irony in Wood's case was that the president chose to punish him at the very time when the administration was adopting Wood's position. About to ask the country to go to war and to accept military conscription, Wilson might well have won Wood over with a conciliatory approach. Instead, he relegated the troublesome general to a secondary role for the duration of the war, and Wood's bitterness and hostility increased accordingly.

The historian is tempted to speculate on what might have happened if Wilson had acted more like Abraham Lincoln and had made greater efforts to understand his military commanders. In view of the opposition the president was to arouse in 1919 and 1920, it was a real tragedy that Wilson could not make use of Wood's talents. If they could have seen the strength of the other's point of view (and the weaknesses of their own), there might have been some fruitful compromise: Wilson might have pursued his diplomacy during the neutrality years from a basis of strength and have deterred Germany from renewing U-boat warfare in 1917; and Wood might have campaigned

[107]None of the major studies of Wilson and his administration, with the exception of Hagedorn's biography of Wood, go into any detail on Wood's removal. When they deal with the problem of Wood, they do so in connection with Wood's separation from his division in 1918 and the refusal to let him go to Europe. The earlier (and perhaps more important) episode of March 1917 is left relatively unmentioned; see Link, *Wilson*, 5:408–11; Ray Stannard Baker, *Woodrow Wilson: Life and Letters*, 8 vols. (New York, 1927–1939), 7:69–71; Arthur Walworth, *Woodrow Wilson*, 2 vols. (New York, 1958), 2:103. For the official (and unconvincing) War Department explanation of Wood's transfer, see Frederick Palmer, *Newton D. Baker and America at War*, 2 vols. (New York, 1931), pp. 163–65.

[108]Hagedorn, *Leonard Wood*, 2:210.

for preparedness with more of a realization that military requirements had to be balanced with diplomatic and political needs. But there was no compromise. Both men failed. The United States did go to war in 1917, and the country was unprepared militarily. Perhaps Wood's failure was more tragic because, unlike Wilson, he had no opportunity to rectify his mistakes.

Although Wood suffered personally in the spring of 1917, he could take pride in the success of the MTCA. Always more cautious than the general, the Plattsburgers steered clear of controversy. "Derby hears from Palmer by telephone," Clark wrote on February 6, "that the G[eneral] S[taff] is doing what they can" to push for some form of compulsory training. Clark thought it would be best for the MTCA not to agitate, but to continue recruiting trainees for the 1917 camps. Plattsburgers who were eager for action could take examinations for the Officers' Reserve Corps.[109] "It is hard to tell how the German situation will affect the camps," he wrote a week later. "I am inclined to think . . . that they will be held in the present form if there is not war, and as officers' training camps if there is war and a large land force is needed."[110] As far as Clark was concerned, the Plattsburg movement would continue step by step.[111]

Part of this "business as usual" policy included the new MTCA magazine, *National Service.* The first issue came out in early February and was an impressive beginning: articles by Charles W. Eliot, General Wood, Newton D. Baker, Sidney Brooks, John McAuley Palmer, Hermann Hagedorn, and Louis L. Babcock.[112] The initial editorial pledged

[109]Clark to Anson Conger Goodyear, February 6, 1917, Clark MSS.

[110]Clark to Drinker, February 13, 1917, ibid.

[111]Clark to Edward A. Sumner, February 6, 1917, ibid.

[112]To publish *National Service,* the MTCA leaders formed the Military Training Publishing Corporation, with $50,000 authorized in shares of $5 each. The Editorial and Managing Board consisted of Grenville Clark, J. Lloyd Derby, Nelson Doubleday, Anson Conger Goodyear, DeLancey K. Jay, Theodore Roosevelt, Jr., Willard Straight, and E. Frank Strother. As Clark put it, "the magazine is not underwritten by any group but depends for its success on the support of a large body of stockholders. The corporation will be managed by a board of directors representing various parts of the country and including a number of those

that the magazine's "hopes and aims are bound up with the cause of equal obligation for the defense of the country, equal service in performing that duty, and universal training to fulfill it."[113] Far from being a shrill propaganda organ, *National Service* exemplified Clark's reasoned and moderate approach. "I think it has a place in educating our crowd of people and promulgating authentic information and statements of policy," he told Drinker. "We have only 2,000 subscribers now, but they are beginning to increase and I think we can work it up to 7,000 or 8,000 within a few months. After that figure it ought to be nearly self-supporting."[114] The idea was to put across the Plattsburg philosophy in the best possible manner. It did not matter if *National Service* had a small circulation; what mattered was that the right people read it. Congressman Richard Olney II of Massachusetts was so taken with the article "Muddling Through" (concerning England's conversion from volunteers to conscription in 1916) that he read it into the *Congressional Record* and had 40,000 copies printed, franked, and mailed out to his constituents.[115]

The MTCA also continued recruiting for the summer camps "just as if conditions were normal."[116] This was the most important work the Plattsburgers could do, even though the 1917 camps were never actually held. Recruitment kept the MTCA organization intact, added new names to the Plattsburg roster, and helped maintain a cordial working relationship with the War Department.[117] Building on their experience of the previous year, the

---

prominently identified with the Federal Training Camps. . . . The magazine is not planned as a commercial venture. It will doubtless be run at a loss for the first year and even if it is successful financially later, it will be the policy of the magazine corporation to pay only a moderate return on this stock and devote any surplus to advancing the cause of universal training and service. Subscriptions are asked only on this basis and with this understanding." Clark to Archibald G. Thacher, December 23, 1916, Clark MSS.

[113]"National Service," *National Service* 1 (February 1917): 2.

[114]Clark to Drinker, February 23, 1917, Clark MSS.

[115]Olney to Wood, March 20, 1917, Wood MSS.

[116]Arthur F. Cosby, "Bulletin #11," March 26, 1917, Clark MSS.

[117]See DeLancey Jay to Adjutant General, December 20, 1916; and Jay to Newton D. Baker, January 10, February 27, 1917; RG 94, AG2486469.

MTCA planned speaking campaigns, national advertisements, selective mailing lists, moving pictures, employer
pledges, and "endless chain" recruiting—wherein Plattsburgers promised to enlist personally at least two new trainees.[118] The army cooperated by setting aside some
$100,000 of the 1917 training camps appropriation for
recruiting purposes; this enabled the government to print
all enrollment blanks and circulars and to employ a force of
clerks and stenographers at Governor's Island (something
which the MTCA paid for in 1916). "The army people are
acting in their usual inefficient way about spending this
money," Clark informed Drinker, "but it will be a material
help."[119] Recruiting went particularly well for the nine junior camps authorized for 1917: by the end of March more
than 70,000 applications had arrived at Junior Division
Headquarters in New York.[120] Before the declaration of
war changed everything, the MTCA was even planning to
hold a segregated training camp for Negroes during the
summer, as well as a special camp in October for major
league baseball players.[121]

In addition to recruitment, the Plattsburgers kept up
their winter training and correspondence courses. While
the War Department assumed direction of the correspondence program, winter drill remained pretty much a local
affair, as in 1916, with Plattsburg groups getting together
evenings and weekends at a nearby armory, or wherever
they could find facilities and supervised instruction.[122] The

[118]The MTCA published a roster of all the men who had attended the federal
training camps, 1913–1916. This was done at private expense. The roster was a
valuable assistance in locating officer candidates in April-May 1917, since it was the
only complete record of camp attendance.

[119]Clark to Drinker, February 23, 1917, Clark MSS.

[120]Perry, *Plattsburg Movement*, pp. 132–33. See also John Nobel to Archibald
Thacher, January 3, March 5, 1917, Clark MSS; James D. Williams to Halstead
Dorey, March 15, 1917, RG 98, "Records of the Plattsburg Barracks, 1916,"
National Archives.

[121]On the Negro camp, see J. E. Springam to Wood, March 28, 1917, Wood
MSS. For the baseball camp, see T. L. Huston to Wood, February 12, 1917; and
Wood to Huston, February 13, 1917, RG 98, "Records of the Plattsburg Barracks,
1916." Huston was co-owner of the New York Yankees.

[122]"Memorandum for the Chief of Staff," December 26, 1916, RG 94,
AG2450169.

best known were the drills conducted on Governor's Island by Wood's staff and MTCA organizer A. L. "Tiger" Boyce. Nicknamed "Boyce's Broomstick Brigade" because of the shortage of army rifles, the training became so popular that by mid-March some 2,000 civilians were marching in formation every afternoon between four and six o'clock. Not only did these drills provide experience for officer candidates in handling men, but they continued to publicize the need for trained men. Home Defense Leagues and training corps in various businesses in the New York area sprang up in imitation.[123] The program was so successful and the enthusiasm so keen that Clark had to caution against forgetting the Plattsburg commitment to universal training — as opposed to training simply for the purpose of becoming reserve officers.[124]

The Plattsburgers refrained from any direct pressure on Washington until it became clear what Wilson was going to do. On March 25, the day after Wood's transfer order from the Eastern Department, Clark heard from friends in the War Department that the president would ask Congress for 500,000 volunteers and reject universal service.[125] The MTCA immediately moved into action. A telegram went to the White House the next day urging the adoption of the Chamberlain Universal Service bill "or its equivalent."[126] The Executive Committee alerted MTCA branches throughout the country, recommending that wires, resolutions, and letters in favor of universal service be sent to Washington before April 2.[127] Special emphasis was put on getting pressure from areas other than the East, where preparedness opinion was only too well known to the Wilson administration. The response was swift. The Illinois

[123]See Wood Diary, February 17, 1917; and Arthur F. Cosby, "Bulletin #11," March 26, 1917, Clark MSS.

[124]See Clark to Drinker, February 23, 1917; Clark to Benjamin H. Dibblee, March 14, 1917, ibid.

[125]Clark to Pierce Anderson, March 25, 1917; to Anson Conger Goodyear, March 26, 1917; to Benjamin H. Dibblee, March 26, 1917, ibid.

[126]Perry, *Plattsburg Movement*, pp. 165–66.

[127]See Langdon P. Marvin to members of the Harvard Club, March 27, 1917, Clark MSS.

State Senate and the City Council of Chicago passed resolutions favoring conscription, as did a meeting of 10,000 persons in Salt Lake City. Telegrams and letters poured into Washington from San Francisco and other Western cities, and the Chicago branch of the MTCA persuaded a dozen prominent Democrats to write directly to the president.[128] At General Wood's suggestion, President Emeritus Eliot of Harvard also wrote directly to Wilson.[129]

Perhaps Wilson was persuaded, for in his message to Congress on April 2 he recommended "the immediate addition to the armed forces of the United States . . . at least five hundred thousand men, who should, in my opinion, be chosen upon *the principle of universal liability of service.*"[130] This was the principle which the Plattsburg movement had stood for, and which presently became law in the Selective Service Act of May 18, 1917. Sponsored by Senator Chamberlain and Congressman Julius Kahn, the legislation authorized the president to recruit the Regular Army and National Guard to full war strength, permitting him to raise 500,000 men immediately through the draft and another 500,000 when he deemed appropriate. Further wartime legislation granted authority for still additional levies. The law stipulated that the Regular Army and National Guard be recruited by voluntary enlistment, but that the draft should be used to raise a National Army.[131] To the disappointment of Plattsburgers who wanted a permanent system of universal training and service, the formal title of the draft law was "An Act to Authorize the President to Increase Temporarily the Military Establishment of the United States." One of its provisions stated specifically that compulsory service would remain only for "the period of the existing emergency."[132]

[128]Perry, *Plattsburg Movement*, pp. 166–67; Anderson to Clark, March 27, 28, 31, 1917, Clark MSS.

[129]Charles W. Eliot to Wilson, April 3, 8, 1917, Wilson MSS.

[130]Albert Shaw, ed., *The Messages and Papers of Woodrow Wilson*, 2 vols. (New York, 1924), 1:376. Italics added.

[131]U.S., *Statutes at Large*, vol. 40, pp. 76–83.

[132]See Clark to Benjamin H. Dibblee, April 4, 1917, Clark MSS; and Wood Diary, April 5, 1917.

FIVE

How much did the Plattsburg movement have to do with the passage of selective service in 1917? Why did President Wilson finally accept conscription as his military policy? The actual bill was drafted at the president's request in early February 1917 by the judge advocate general Enoch H. Crowder and two of his assistants. The universal training plan proposed by the War College Division of the General Staff—not the Chamberlain-Moseley-Harding bill sponsored by the MTCA—served as a convenient basis.[133] But there is some question as to whether Wilson considered Crowder's bill as anything more than standby legislation, in case the volunteer system failed to provide sufficient manpower. More than likely, the final decision came in March. By then General Scott had converted Secretary Baker to the logic of universal liability to service, and it is probable that their combined influence, plus the last-minute campaign by the MTCA, helped make up Wilson's mind in the critical days prior to April 2. As Clark put it, "it would be going a little far to say that the training campers' activities had much to do with the President's recommendation for universal service . . . but one can never tell. The agitation certainly did no harm and may have done considerable good."[134] Even after the decision was made, the administration still did not accept all the Plattsburg program, since selective service was to be only for the duration of the war, not a permanent military system.[135]

[133]David A. Lockmiller, *Enoch H. Crowder: Soldier, Lawyer, and Statesman* (Columbia, Mo., 1955), pp. 152–54.

[134]Hugh L. Scott, *Some Memories of a Soldier* (New York, 1928), pp. 557–59. Clark to Pierce Anderson, April 3, 1917, Clark MSS.

[135]The difference between the Plattsburgers and the Wilson administration is seen most clearly in a letter Secretary Baker wrote in response to criticism of the MTCA's advocacy of universal military training. Baker wrote this letter on April 3, 1917, the day after Wilson's war message. "The Military Training Camps Association, from whose literature you quote, . . . is a private association, made up of enthusiastic young men who are, as they say, devoted to the idea of universal obligatory military training and service. The Plattsburg camp and the other camps maintained by the Government are not, at least expressly, maintained upon any such theory, but rather for the purpose of training men as possible officer material in the event of great emergencies. I hardly know how to answer your question, therefore, as to whether the object stated in this literature is the real object. It is

Recent scholarship has indicated another, ironic reason for Wilson's conversion to conscription. As soon as the United States severed diplomatic relations with Germany in early February 1917, Theodore Roosevelt had begun to clamor for permission to lead a volunteer division in France. Romantic that he was, Roosevelt wanted to repeat the glory of 1898, and if the president adopted the volunteer principle there would have been no stopping the Rough Rider. After a close study of War Department records and relevant personal papers, the historian Daniel R. Beaver has concluded that Wilson and Baker supported selective service as much for political as for military reasons—because Roosevelt could not raise a volunteer division under such a system.[136] The fact that Wood was removed from Governor's Island at the same time lends credence to Beaver's political interpretation. Nor was the administration alone in considering politics. During the subsequent debates in Congress over selective service, it was Roosevelt's Republican friends (even more than antipreparedness progressives) who delayed the passage of the law by insisting on some kind of volunteer provision under which Roosevelt could qualify.[137]

Once war was declared and the compulsory principle decided upon, the Plattsburgers gave only secondary attention to the arguments on Capitol Hill. Within days of Wilson's war message, the MTCA was busy launching the next

---

undoubtedly the object of the Training Camps Association; it is undoubtedly the object . . . of interest in the camps of many of the Regular Army officers and prominent civilians who have patronized the movement. And yet, neither the President nor I, as the official head of the War Department, have [*sic*] ever taken an affirmative ground on this subject, believing that the present was not a time to form a permanent military policy for the nation, but that we ought rather to meet the existing emergency; and when the world war is over and the conditions of national life are normal, we would have a less distorted view of both our place in the world and our task, and then could more calmly address ourselves to such a question. I can see no reason why you should not go to Plattsburg on your own theory and take advantage of the training which the Government thinks it valuable to give at such camps." Newton D. Baker to J. G. de Roulhac Hamilton, April 3, 1917, RG 94, AG2566254.

[136]Beaver, *Newton D. Baker*, pp. 28–30.

[137]Seward W. Livermore, *Politics Is Adjourned* (Middletown, Conn., 1966), pp. 15–31.

stage of the Plattsburg movement, that of training officers for the great mass of conscripts soon to be selected. However much they may have sympathized with Roosevelt's desire to command a division, the Plattsburg philosophy that officer candidates must demonstrate their capacity to lead through intensive training ran counter to Roosevelt's romanticism.[138]

Logically, the Plattsburg belief in universal military obligation was in accord with the Selective Service Act. Selective service was not universal service, but it did operate on the assumption that every male citizen of military age, even if he was not selected, had a military obligation. Plattsburgers regretted only that the principle was not made permanent policy. MTCA spokesmen later claimed that the wartime success of selective service, due in part to its system of local administration, was also the consequence of their own repeated demonstrations for universal training. They had educated the people for national service, and thus there were no draft riots as in the Civil War.[139] No one can judge accurately how important the training camp propaganda was in this respect. Certainly the men who went to camp in 1915–1916 believed in its philosophy; an estimated 90 percent saw military service during World War I, most of them as line officers.[140] If universal military training and service was the philosophy of the Plattsburg movement, the willingness to serve personally was its central tenet.

[138]Theodore Roosevelt, Jr., resigned from the MTCA Executive Committee in March so as to be able to devote more time to his father's military schemes. Clark encouraged his resignation. See Clark to Drinker, March 19, 1917, Clark MSS. Wood, too, was privately critical of the former president's plans; see Wood Diary, March 4, 1917, Wood MSS. The Chicago branch of the MTCA resolutely opposed the TR Division; see Pierce Anderson to Clark, May 15, 1917, Clark MSS.

[139]Perry, *Plattsburg Movement*, pp. 171–72.

[140]Arthur F. Cosby to Perry, March 27, 1920, Perry MSS.

VIII.

The MTCA & the War

Shortly after the Armistice in 1918, two officers, French and American, were reminiscing about the battles and sacrifices which had culminated in victory. "I know you recruited over 3,000,000 men in 19 months," the Frenchman commented. "That is very good but not so difficult. But I am told also that, although you had no officers' reserve to start with, you somehow found 200,000 new officers, most of them competent. That is what is astonishing and what was impossible. Tell me how that was done."[1]

The American was able to describe how it was done because he himself had earned his commission at one of the famous "ninety-day" Officer Training Camps in 1917. These officer camps, a logical outgrowth of the prewar training camps, became the basic contribution of the Plattsburg movement to the American war effort. Not only did the Military Training Camps Association first suggest the idea of officer camps to the War Department in April 1917, but a majority of the prewar Plattsburgers also won commissions at these camps and eventually led troops on the Western Front. Moreover, despite the loss of so many men to active service, the MTCA maintained its organization at home for the duration of the war, helping the army recruit for the officer corps and the technical services, providing card files and clerical assistance, and generally acting as "a liaison between the War Department on the one hand and the civilian population on the other."[2] Having talked and demonstrated for military preparedness before 1917, the Plattsburgers showed that they were ready when war came.

O N E

Wilson's war message on April 2, 1917, galvanized the Plattsburgers into action. For the previous two months MTCA leaders had been recruiting candidates for the summer camps on the assumption that they would be held as planned, or, if war intervened, they could be converted into officer camps. One Plattsburger had visited the War Department just prior to Wilson's speech and found the army sympathetic but without any definite plan for training officers.[3] Thus, when they learned of the president's decision for war, the MTCA Executive Committee called an emergency meeting and on April 5 sent the following telegram to Secretary Baker:

> Recognizing the importance of securing officers for increased Army in large numbers as soon as possible, we respectively suggest that the citizens' military training camps be turned into officers' training schools. They could not only supply material for officers' reserve corps, but could act as professional training ground for men now commissioned or recommended for commissions [in] officers' reserve corps. Suggest all applicants attending such camps be obligated to accept commissions . . . if found qualified and to whatever grade recommended. Suggest all camps be opened May first for two or three months of instruction . . . to be continued in relays thereby securing officers while raising of new armies is progressing. This plan can be executed under law already invested in you subject only to your changing regulations under authority you now have under section fifty-four national defense act.[4]

The secretary of war replied favorably, and a Plattsburg delegation was soon en route to Washington to assist in working out details.[5]

[1][Grenville Clark], "The Emergency Officer," *National Service* 5 (April 1919): 198.
[2]Arthur Cosby to Ralph Barton Perry, June 17, 1920, Perry MSS.
[3]Clark to Pierce Anderson, April 4, 1917, Clark MSS.
[4]MTCA Executive Committee to Newton D. Baker, April 5, 1917, RG 94, AG2567076.
[5]Baker to MTCA Executive Committee, April 6, 1917, ibid.

The next ten days were hectic. Unprepared for the demands of war, the army seemed confused. What little planning there had been on officer training was done by two officers in the Adjutant General's Office, not by the General Staff.[6] No one was certain yet how Congress would react to Wilson's request for selective service, or how officer training could be coordinated with a draft. The Plattsburgers and Major Dorey (sent by General Wood to represent his views) urged that officer camps be opened on May 1 and that recruiting begin as early as possible, but the army seemed overwhelmed by the magnitude of the project.[7] Grenville Clark, who took part in these preliminary discussions, noted that "everyone has his own idea and no one really knows because they can't tell what Congress will do. Things are very much confused in Washington and the organization of military forces looks like it would go very slowly. . . . [The] red tape and inertia are disheartening."[8] After conferring with the department commanders, the army finally announced its plans on April 17: there would be sixteen officer camps, lasting three months, to be held in various geographical areas and attended by 2,500 men each. The camps were to begin on May 8.

It was significant that this officer program could come into existence more than a month before the passage of the Selective Service Act on May 18. The Officer Training Camps of 1917, as the Plattsburgers suggested, were legally the citizens' training camps authorized by Section 54 of the National Defense Act and already provided for in the War Department Appropriation bill for 1917. The MTCA's legislative effort in 1916, as well as the initiative in April, thus made it possible for the War Department to act so decisively. As one Plattsburger put it: "The public will never know but . . . thanks to section 54 so valiantly fought for by [this] band of hopefuls the Army . . . has gotten the jump on Congress."[9]

[6]Perry, *Plattsburg Movement,* pp. 179–81. Captain A. W. Bjornstadt and Captain Robert O. Van Horn were the two officers.

[7]Halstead Dorey to Ralph Barton Perry, June 9, 1920, Perry MSS.

[8]Clark to G. Edward Buxton, April 16, 1917, Clark MSS.

The MTCA's initiative was also crucial in the interval between the announcement and opening of the camps. The task of recruiting 40,000 officer candidates within three weeks was so staggering that the army could not do it alone. There was the sheer physical job of drafting and printing application blanks, bulletins of information, medical certificates, and forms for examination reports. Somehow recruiters had to arrange medical examinations for all applicants, make certain that the best 2,500 men were chosen for each camp, get notices prepared and sent to all successful candidates, send all relevant information to the camp commanders, and see to it that all 40,000 candidates reached camp on schedule. The army had neither the money, the manpower, nor the organization to do all these things; the MTCA did.

As soon as the general orders authorizing the camps arrived at Governor's Island on April 17, the MTCA Executive Committee moved into action. Consulting with the new department commander, General J. Franklin Bell, the Plattsburgers quickly drew up the necessary application forms and bulletins, which they rushed to printers in New York City. By the evening of April 19, 40,000 circular letters and application forms were in the mail to MTCA branches from Maine to Alabama. Regional MTCA headquarters in Chicago and San Francisco, having been alerted previously by the New Yorkers, carried out similar duties. By cooperating with local army recruiters (some of the larger states had only two or three) and army medical officers, the MTCA was able to begin recruitment throughout the country on Monday, April 23. Even with the quick start, the obstacles were such that the opening of the camps had to be pushed back a week to May 15.[10]

Recruitment caused "many heart burnings," as one officer phrased it, because "everything has been put off until the 11th hour and some things . . . are going to be put off until the 13th hour."[11] Although army recruiters, in

---

[9]Pierce Anderson to DeLancey Jay, May 15, 1917, Clark MSS.

[10]Arthur Cosby, report to MTCA Executive Committee, May 14, 1917, ibid.

[11]A. W. Bjornstadt to Clark, April 30, 1917, ibid.

some cases, regarded cooperation with the Plattsburgers as "a sort of necessary nuisance," the alliance quickly proved indispensable.[12] That the army had too few officers to process 40,000 applicants was obvious at the outset, so emergency recruiters were commissioned and sent into the field. Unfortunately, the army's instructions to these new officers did not always coincide with the bulletins of information circulated by the MTCA, and several days were wasted because of the mix-up.[13] Because the War Department had limited funds, the MTCA hired clerical assistance, provided office space, and drummed up numerous volunteers. The mailing lists which the MTCA had circularized for the 1916 camps were used again, as was the MTCA roster of more than twenty thousand persons who had attended federal training camps. The Plattsburgers were particularly helpful in getting local doctors to volunteer as medical examiners. In the Midwest, approximately forty-five doctors took a special two-day crash course in army procedures in Chicago and then went back to their respective locales to conduct preliminary examinations.[14] Notwithstanding the fact that the government frank was supposed to cover all official correspondence, it became necessary to use MTCA funds for bulk mail, telephones, and telegraph. In Chicago, for example, the MTCA phone bill amounted to $300, while other expenses totaled $35,000.[15] The estimate for the entire country was $350,000, none of which was repaid.[16]

The MTCA's role was most prominent in New York and Chicago. More than 9,000 applications were received at MTCA headquarters at 19 West 44th Street, where army examiners were given separate offices. The New Yorkers obtained some forty volunteer physicians, who examined applicants in groups of five in three-hour shifts from 8 A.M. to 12 midnight, including Sundays. During the last week of recruiting the crowds became so large that police reserves

[12]Pierce Anderson to Clark, May 15, 1917, ibid.
[13]Arthur Cosby, report to MTCA Executive Committee, May 17, 1917, ibid.
[14]Anderson to Clark, May 15, 1917, ibid.
[15]Wharton Clay to Clark, May 10, 1917, ibid.
[16]Cosby, report to MTCA Executive Committee, May 17, 1917, ibid.

had to be called out to keep order.[17] In Chicago the army became even more dependent on the Association, as the department commander, General Thomas H. Barry, found himself swamped with more than 75,000 applications in eighteen days. The Chicago branch of the MTCA, headed by Wharton Clay and Pierce Anderson, solicited offices and stenographical help from downtown businesses, and within a few days some seventy typewriters were in operation. General Barry later paid tribute to the civilian effort:

> To meet the necessity approximately one thousand Branch Chairmen of the Association voluntarily converted their offices and their homes into auxiliary recruiting stations and points of distribution for the literature furnished them; physicians associated with the organization gratuitously examined local candidates to insure physical fitness and thus avoid costly journeys for disqualified men to and from the location of Examining Boards; widespread publicity to all matters which might help the public understand and to act quickly was accomplished through the press; the members of the Association at Department headquarters were tireless in their labors; while business houses, civic organizations and municipal officers freely helped by furnishing clerical assistance to handle the work.[18]

So effective was the MTCA recruiting in the Midwest that, as Pierce Anderson reported, "the military authorities out here are strongly in favor of holding the thing together and developing it."[19]

An important factor in this early success was the presence in Washington of Grenville Clark. Leaving Arthur Cosby and Langdon Marvin to run things in New York, Clark took a suite at the New Willard Hotel. Beginning on April 12 Clark worked closely with officers in the Adjutant General's Office in drawing up the general orders which

[17]Ibid.; Perry, *Plattsburg Movement*, pp. 184–85.
[18]Barry to Executive Committee and Branch Chairmen of the MTCA, June 6, 1917, in *War Record of the Military Training Camps Association of the United States* (Central, Western, and Southern departments), pamphlet in Clark MSS and in John J. Pershing MSS, Library of Congress.
[19]Anderson to Clark, May 15, 1917, Clark MSS.

authorized the camps. It soon became apparent that the War Department might offer commissions to a limited number of civilians to help with the organization of new forces. Pressed by his friends, Clark reluctantly applied, took the necessary examination ("my showing was not brilliant"), and was eventually commissioned as a major in the Adjutant General's Office in mid-May.[20] At first he thought that other training camp leaders such as Wharton Clay and Benjamin Dibblee could obtain similar commissions, but, as he told Pierce Anderson, "I have run up against a situation . . . and I find that Army etiquette, red tape, etc., make it necessary to use a great deal of tact and go slow."[21] So Clark acted as a liaison between the army and the MTCA, listening to complaints from local branches and making tactful suggestions in Washington. Near the end of the recruiting period Clark submitted a long memorandum to Secretary Baker which summed up the experience of these first weeks and recommended changes for subsequent officer camps.[22] This memorandum served as the basis for the second series of camps which began in September.

TWO

"Like old times," one officer candidate wrote from Plattsburg. "Everybody was jolly . . . a very earnest crowd of men, and the only real handicap will be one of time. . . . There are so many Roosevelts that you can't turn around without stumbling over one."[23] This particular candidate, a veteran of the Plattsburg camps of 1915 and 1916, was typical of the 43,000 men, ages twenty-one to forty-five, who attended the first camps on May 15. As DeLancey Jay reported from Plattsburg, the quality was "about

---

[20]Clark to John M. Palmer, April 15, 1917, ibid.; see also Elihu Root to Henry P. McCain, April 12, 1917; and Henry S. Drinker to Newton D. Baker, April 10, 1917, ibid.

[21]Clark to Anderson, April 25, 1917, ibid.

[22]Clark to Baker, memorandum, May 14, 1917, ibid.

[23]Quincy S. Mills to Mrs. Mills, May 11, 13, 1917, Mills MSS.

between the 1915 and 1916 camp," the same core of patriotic elites who had organized the Business Men's Camp,
plus an additional influx of equally enthusiastic rookies of
humbler background.[24] The press called these trainees
the "First Ten Thousand," although 27,341 of them eventually earned commissions. Because they gave up their civilian positions and volunteered immediately, because they
were recruited largely from MTCA lists and did not wait
for the draft, and because they competed for commissions
without regard for favoritism or political wire-pulling,
these first officer candidates represented something special.[25] Practically the entire MTCA leadership from New
York attended the May camps at Plattsburg: DeLancey Jay,
Archibald Thacher, Kenneth Budd, Philip Carroll, Ted
Roosevelt, Horace Stebbins, James D. Williams. No one,
exulted a successful graduate of the Presidio camp in San
Francisco, showed "a finer spirit than those who had practically thrown their business affairs to the winds . . . with no
thought of anything than having a part in the greatest
game provided for men since history has been written."[26]

The sixteen camps, numbering approximately 2,500
candidates in each, were held at the following sites: two
camps each at Plattsburg; Fort Benjamin Harrison, Indiana; and Fort Sheridan, Illinois; one at Fort Niagara,
New York; Madison Barracks, New York; Fort Myer, Virginia; Fort McPherson, Georgia; Fort Oglethorpe, Georgia;
Fort Logan H. Roots, Arkansas; Fort Riley, Kansas; Fort
Snelling, Minnesota; Leon Springs, Texas; and the Presidio
of San Francisco. Each camp had fourteen regular companies (nine infantry; three artillery; one cavalry; and one
engineering company) to provide instruction, with at least
one regular officer who had experience at the earlier civilian camps. When the three-month course ended on August
15, the successful graduates were commissioned: 18,929 as

[24]Jay to Clark, May 16, 1917, Clark MSS.
[25]James G. Steese, "Procurement of Commissioned Personnel in War," *National Service* 5 (May 1919): 263–75.
[26]Silsby M. Spaulding to Benjamin H. Dibblee (copy), June 1, 1920, Perry MSS.

second lieutenants, 4,452 as first lieutenants, 3,722 as captains, 235 as majors, one as a lieutenant colonel, and two as colonels. Some graduates went into the Regular Army, some into the National Guard, and some were retained as instructors for the second series of officer camps in September. Most of the new officers, however, were ordered to the new cantonments being built to train the first group of draftees beginning in September. They became, in effect, the officers and instructors of the new National Army.[27]

The course of instruction in the 1917 camps, while extended to three months and continually modified in light of overseas experience, was essentially the same kind of intensive and progressive training begun by General Wood in 1913 and perfected in subsequent summers.[28] Nevertheless, because of the greater urgency in 1917 and the difficulty of coordinating officer training with the larger task · of creating a National Army, unforeseen obstacles inevitably arose. The haste with which the army assembled the camps caused problems, especially with regard to equipment shortages and inadequate housing.[29] Nor were there enough officers experienced in dealing with civilians, and the result in some instances was that officer training too closely resembled recruit training, without sufficient scope for developing leadership qualities. Another complaint was aroused when the War Department announced early in the training course that only 671 men from each camp would receive commissions, a number sufficient to officer only a single division and an additional cavalry regiment. The army's expanding manpower demands eventually reversed this policy, but not before causing damage

[27]Steese, "Procurement of Officers," pp. 268–69; Perry, *Plattsburg Movement,* pp. 189–90.

[28]There are numerous articles about the officers' camps in *National Service* in 1917. A convenient firsthand account by a perceptive rookie can be found in Quincy S. Mills's letters to his mother in the Mills MSS at the University of North Carolina. See also Edward M. Coffman, *The War to End All Wars* (New York, 1969), pp. 54–58; H. Reed, "The First Ten Thousand," *Independent* 40 (June 9, 1917): 465–66; W. Menkel, "Making Officers for Our New Army," *Review of Reviews* 56 (July 1917): 58–62.

[29]See John Purroy Mitchel to William B. Meloney, June 1, 1917, Mitchel MSS; Mills to mother, May 20, 1917, Mills MSS.

to trainee morale.[30] Delays in congressional appropriations also created confusion about the pay and status of reserve officers, and these problems were not settled until after the beginning of the camps.[31]

Ironically, one of the bitterest critics was none other than General Wood. Transferred from Governor's Island to Charleston at the beginning of the war, Wood felt a sense of loss at not being at Plattsburg, and he took out his resentment by criticizing nearly everything the War Department did. His own work in recruiting for Fort Oglethorpe and other camps in the South could not overcome his anger at being unable to initiate policy. He was annoyed when Halstead Dorey and Gordon Johnston were not selected to command any of the camps; and when he received mildly critical letters from other officers and men who had been at Plattsburg, he grew even more resentful.[32] (One ex-Plattsburger wrote of the "keen disappointment the old Plattsburg men felt at the lack of your presence this year. . . . I am not criticizing the camp—but the old men knew the difference.")[33] As a result, Wood vented his frustration in long letters to Clark and other MTCA leaders, always emphasizing that the "powers that be" could do more if they only had enough imagination. The training was "not satisfactory," he wrote. "It savors too strongly of the theoretical rather than the practical. . . . I am sorry to note a tendency to exclude all men who have had any Plattsburg training or experience." In Wood's mind, there was "a startling failure to visualize the magnitude of the war. They go at it as though it were an Indian campaign or another Spanish-American proposition, and they do not realize that this first draft is only the beginning of a very big job."[34] Such criticisms, while they stemmed in part from

[30]Of course, the belief that only a small percentage of the trainees would receive commissions also helped to increase incentive to work hard.

[31]Perry, *Plattsburg Movement*, pp. 188–89.

[32]For example, J. M. Chapple to Wood, June 25, 1917; Dorey to Wood, September 5, 28, 1917; W. B. Jacques to Wood, August 10, 1917; H. J. Slocum to Wood, May 29, 1917; Ralph M. Parker to Wood, May 17, 1917, Wood MSS.

[33]Julian A. Ripley to Wood, December 11, 1917, ibid.

[34]Wood to Clark, July 23, 1917, Clark MSS.

Wood's own personal circumstances, served as a goad for MTCA policy throughout the war.

Given the general state of unpreparedness in April 1917, one must conclude, however, that the snarls and confusion of the first camps were unavoidable. Red tape, shortages, complaints, sudden changes in policy—all were the inevitable result of having to improvise. Despite the criticism of General Wood, the camps did produce some 27,000 officers who later proved their mettle in battle. If some in the army were slow and unimaginative, there always seemed to be officers ready to take the necessary initiative—men like Captain George C. Marshall, aide to General Bell, who in May 1917 disregarded all normal procedures by purchasing "blankets, mattresses, and things of that sort," and shipping them express to Plattsburg without informing the quartermaster.[35] Far outweighing the drawbacks to the program was the very fact that it existed. "No single thing is more fraught with the possibilities of disaster," the editors of *National Service* observed, "than the volunteer untrained officer. . . . To send untrained troops into the field is manslaughter, but to despatch troops with untrained leaders is murder in the first degree."[36] The first 180,000 draftees who arrived at the cantonments in September 1917 would have had no leaders at all if it had not been for the officer camps. The War Department's official history of the personnel system in World War I admitted that "in many ways, the Army [in 1917] faced a more difficult problem in securing officers than in securing men."[37] Without the officer camps the army could not have begun to solve either problem.

THREE

Once the camps were launched, the task of the Plattsburg movement shifted to that of improving the program as

---

[35]Pogue, *Marshall: Education of a General,* pp. 140–42.

[36] "The President's Policy and What It Means," *National Service* 1 (May 1917): 203.

[37]Committee on Classification of Personnel in the Army, *History of the Personnel System* (Washington, D.C., 1919), p. 34.

much and as quickly as possible. The MTCA had four central premises: that commissions should come only after a prescribed training course and observation by professional officers; that officer candidates should be recruited from civilian life as well as from the ranks; that training should occur in advance of the mobilization of draftees; and that planning should be sufficient to provide for a maximum force. The Plattsburgers continued to cooperate with the army on officer matters throughout the war, although at times they tended to be critical and impatient. As evidenced by *National Service* editorials which constantly urged the "need for greater efforts," the Plattsburgers were the "hawks" of their day, desirous of winning the war quickly and willing to subordinate all other considerations.[38] While the War Department did not accept all of their advice, it did accept a good deal.

Grenville Clark's activities in Washington were largely responsible for the MTCA's influence. Because the Plattsburg leader had the knack of locating and using power amidst all the army red tape, his commission in the Adjutant General's Office was a godsend. "Everything is so *slow*. They take *too long* to get around to things," he complained at first, but before long he was telling his wife that "I have not been at my desk all day but around the building trying to figure out a method of keeping records."[39] Arriving early at his desk in the old War, State, and Navy Building and staying late, Clark was able to learn which officers had initiative and which did not. He struck up friendships with Ralph Hayes, private secretary to Newton D. Baker, and Frederick B. Keppel, the former Columbia dean who became Baker's assistant in charge of personnel.[40] He also kept up a steady correspondence with Wood and MTCA leaders. Clark's relationship with Keppel proved useful in

[38]"Need for More Strenuous Effort," *National Service* 2 (November 1917): 237–38. Nearly every article and editorial in *National Service* during the war stressed the necessity of greater efforts, particularly in the area of making larger numbers liable for military service.

[39]Clark to Mrs. Clark, n.d. [June 1917], Clark MSS.

[40]Clark also renewed old friendships with Felix Frankfurter and Walter Lippmann, both of whom worked for the War Department in 1917.

June 1917 when the MTCA, following Clark's advice, went directly to the secretary of war with the suggestion that the Plattsburgers conduct their own inspection of the various officer camps. Keppel handled the matter personally, thus bypassing Clark's prickly superior in the Adjutant General's Office, Colonel A. W. Bjornstadt, who was "as meek as a lamb."[41] Keppel told Clark that he "hoped I wouldn't be too sensitive about doing things direct [because] the situation was too big to consider the feelings of [individual] people."[42] This willingness to do things direct enabled Clark to assume more and more responsibility. When general orders for the second series of officer camps were issued on June 4, 1917, the Plattsburg imprint was obvious. "Don't congratulate me," Bjornstadt muttered to a General Staff officer. "Congratulate Clark; he did the real work."[43]

As Clark emphasized to General Wood, the essence of the MTCA's policy was embodied in the first section of the War Department's orders, which Clark wrote himself: "To provide officers for the drafted forces of the National Army, the War Department has adopted the policy of commissioning *all new officers of the line* (Infantry, Cavalry, Field and Coast Artillery) purely *on* the *basis* of demonstrated ability after three months' observation and training in the Officers' Training Camps. Thus, the appointment of the new armies will be made entirely on merit and free from all personal or other influences."[44]

The Plattsburgers regarded as sacred this principle of not commissioning officers without prior training. Clark noted: "Some of the political outfit are getting on to the fact that there is no way *at all* to get a commission except by going to camp and working for it."[45] So strongly did Clark believe in this axiom that when a plan surfaced in mid-July to commission a limited number of civilians as lieutenant colonels, he did all he could to kill it. He went to the

[41]Clark to Mrs. Clark, June 21, 1917, Clark MSS.
[42]Clark to Mrs. Clark, n.d. [June 1917], ibid.
[43]Ibid.
[44]Memorandum of information," June 4, 1917, enclosed in Clark to Wood, July 16, 1917, Wood MSS.
[45]Clark to Mrs. Clark, June 25, 1917, Clark MSS.

adjutant general, Henry P. McCain, "worked myself up to a white heat & gave him some straight talk, breach of faith, loss of lives, [which would work to the] everlasting discredit of the War Department."[46] If the plan were not revoked, the MTCA would send a delegation to protest in Washington, "and failing satisfaction do so publicly."[47] Properly chagrined, McCain promised to talk to Secretary Baker. As a result, no civilians were ever commissioned directly as line officers.[48]

While successful in holding the line against direct commissions, Clark was disappointed that the second series of camps envisaged only 16,000 officers. "I don't see how we could go wrong in training more officers," he complained.[49] As Clark saw it, the army would be better off having more officers than it needed, rather than face a crisis where more officers were needed than available. General Wood agreed. "Many thousands of officers will be needed in addition to those the Department is now talking of," he wrote to Clark. Wood wanted greater numbers and was particularly concerned that the army seemed to be neglecting ROTC units at various colleges, where he regarded much of the training as superior to the officer camps. "There is no reason why this should not be done," he growled, "and every reason why it should, and it can be done."[50] Clark assured the general that he would do everything possible for college training, but army priorities and the fact that the draft applied only to twenty-one-year-olds and older made it difficult to place much emphasis on the colleges at present.[51] As it turned out, pressure from the MTCA helped persuade the army that the number commissioned

[46]Clark to Mrs. Clark, n.d. [July 1917], ibid.

[47]Clark to Wood, July 16, 1917, Wood MSS.

[48]Clark was pleased at McCain's response, observing: "I don't think Mc[Cain] ever means badly; only not quite big enough & needs a rod stuck up his --- to stiffen him occasionally." Clark to Mrs. Clark, n.d. [July 1917], Clark MSS. Officers were commissioned without prior training in the various staff corps and special services. Clark himself was a case in point. Gradually, however, the principle of prior training was adopted throughout the army. Steese, "Procurement of Commissioned Personnel," p. 271.

[49]Clark to Wood, July 9, 1917, Wood MSS.

[50]Wood to Clark, July 21, 1917, ibid.

[51]Clark to Wood, July 9, 22, 1917, ibid.

from the second camps should be increased from 16,000 to 22,000. The extra 6,000 were of immediate use.[52]

Looking beyond the second series of camps, Clark submitted in August 1917 a "Plan for Maintaining a Continuous Supply of Officers."[53] The goal was to provide 160,000 commissioned officers a year in consecutive three-month camps (40,000 in each series). Once the draft was underway, Clark envisioned two basic sources of officer material—men from the ranks, and men from civilian life. He thought that half the officer candidates should come from the ranks. The rest could be obtained from outside the service, especially from the 150,000 potential officers still in college and ineligible for the draft. ROTC units, which had been discontinued that spring when all regular instructors were called to active duty, could be revived by assigning reserve officers as instructors. As Clark put it, the colleges constituted a "unique . . . advantage if we employ it."[54] The colleges could supply two-fifths from civilian life, with older men accounting for the rest. Moreover, as a reaction to criticism against the aristocratic bias of the Officer Training Camps, Clark recommended that the American Federation of Labor act in conjunction with the MTCA in recruiting civilian candidates. Educational qualifications should be deemphasized in favor of leadership ability, and the best of all classes should have ample opportunity to win commissions.[55]

Clark's plan was powerful enough to win the tentative approval of General Bliss, the acting chief of staff.[56] He submitted further memoranda and was seconded by General Wood and the MTCA.[57] The War College supported a

---

[52]Perry, *Plattsburg Movement,* p. 201.

[53]"Plan for Maintaining a Continuous Supply of Officers," August 14, 1917, Clark MSS.

[54]Ibid.

[55]For criticism of the camps, see Beaver, *Newton D. Baker,* p. 38 n.; "I had a long jaw with a Labor Union guy sent by Lippmann complaining that no laboring men were getting into the Officers' Camps." Clark to Mrs. Clark, August 8, 1917, Clark MSS.

[56]Bliss memo, attached to Clark's "Plan for Maintaining a Continuous Supply of Officers," August 14, 1917, Clark MSS.

[57]Clark memo for Chief of Staff, August 31, 1917, ibid.; Langdon Marvin to

similar plan. The opinion prevailed in the Adjutant General's Office, however, that future camps should be limited to men in the ranks and that commissions should be restricted to the number of vacancies available.[58] Clark argued in vain that "too many officers would [not] be trained, because I think that it is likely that during the next year we are going to have a very large army, since it is becoming more apparent every day the war cannot be ended unless the U.S. goes at it on a very large scale."[59] Wood, of course, was disgusted at the army's unwillingness to act boldly. "The situation," he observed to Theodore Roosevelt, "reminds one of a green man in an automobile, with one foot on the clutch and the other on the accelerator. The engine is whirling around and a tremendous noise is being made, but there is no appreciation of power and so it goes."[60]

When the War Department announced officially in September 1917 that the third series of officer camps would recruit exclusively from men already in the service, the MTCA Executive Committee, at the urging of Clark and Wood, made a strong effort to block the change. In a long memorandum to Secretary Baker on October 25, Langdon Marvin, Clark's successor as executive secretary of the MTCA, reiterated earlier arguments and added some new ones. He characterized the Plattsburg position as "unselfish . . . simply what is best for the Army and the Country." The MTCA believed that

> no consideration, no questions of justice or injustice to one group of men or another, [should] have any basis for consideration. The college graduate has no better right to be an officer than the laboring man, unless his training and character better fit him for the position; and the laboring man of higher efficiency than the college graduate or business man should, of course, be given prior consideration. But education, business experience and leadership in civilian life must

Clark, August 24, 1917, ibid.; Wood to Adjutant General, October 22, 1917, Wood MSS.

[58]Perry, *Plattsburg Movement,* pp. 204–5.

[59]Clark memo for Colonel Johnston, September 7, 1917, Clark MSS.

[60]Wood to Roosevelt, September 10, 1917, Wood MSS.

not be overlooked. We believe that all questions of class should be eliminated and that the only question is one of efficiency. We must have plenty of officers of the best possible qualifications, and where they come from, so long as we have the best, is immaterial.

Marvin did not object to promotion from the ranks, only "the exclusion of civilian volunteers and the abandonment of the plan now in operation." He thought that the War Department, by estimating officer needs conservatively, was losing sight of the fact that England had lost some 52,000 officers in battle during the past year. And "if this country is to fulfill its mission of bringing the War to a successful and prompt conclusion, it should pour into Europe an army fully as great as the British Army, and fully as well officered." Marvin did not think that restricting officer procurement to the ranks was the correct method. It excluded men between thirty-one and forty-five who might make excellent officers but preferred not to enlist as privates. Marvin and the MTCA had lists of hundreds of such men, and "they should not be permitted to waste their abilities." In sum, the MTCA recommended that officer camps be continued under the same procedure as the first two series.[61]

Vocal arguments were added to the written word, as a delegation of Plattsburgers tried to convince Secretary Baker in person on November 14. The meeting was congenial, wide-ranging, and unproductive. Baker informed the MTCA that the third series of camps would be restricted to men from the ranks, although "if not enough available material should be developed in this way he might open the camps to some civilians." This was not necessarily a permanent policy. The secretary of war said that "it was his full expectation to have a fourth and probably a further series . . . on the same basis as the first and second camps." For the present, however, the new policy was set. "I suppose," Marvin complained, "that we must abide by the

[61]Marvin memorandum for Secretary Baker, October 25, 1917, Clark MSS.

result."[62] Arthur Cosby, who thought that the army would be forced to recruit civilians when manpower needs became more pressing, told Wood that in a few months "I am in hopes there will be a reconsideration."[63] The reconsideration did not occur until the summer of 1918, when losses on the Western Front led the War Department again to adopt Plattsburg methods.

Despite General Wood's comment that "the whole thing represents a failure to visualize what is needed in training an army," the army's opposition did not stem solely from bureaucratic obscurantism.[64] Complaints about aristocratic bias in the first two series made the War Department understandably receptive to more egalitarian methods of officer procurement, and selecting candidates from the ranks seemed to provide a solution. The army also thought it necessary to coordinate officer training more closely with the training of the new National Army divisions. By training officers alongside draftees at the twenty-odd divisional cantonments, there would be no dilution of Regular Army discipline, and Regular officers attached to the divisions could be used more effectively as instructors. Such procedures gave the army greater control than before. As it turned out, the third series of Officers' Training Camps (or "schools," as they were then called), held at the divisional cantonments from January 5 to April 19, 1918, produced only 11,657 officers, all of them commissioned as second lieutenants.[65] Although the need for greater numbers forced a return to civilian recruitment and Plattsburg methods, the War Department preferred its own policy. And when the army began its preparations for World War II some twenty years later, officer procurement was based not on the Plattsburg idea, but on the experience of

[62]Marvin to Wood, November 17, 1917, Wood MSS.

[63]Cosby to Wood, November 16, 1917, ibid.; see also Henry S. Drinker to members of the MTCA, November 22, 1917, ibid.

[64]"You must remember in dealing with the Army that it is still a bureaucratic establishment. The fighting line is only an incident. The Bureau's first thought is itself." Wood to Cosby, November 19, 1917, Wood MSS.

[65]A Plattsburg Graduate, "The Reason for the Divisional Training Camp," *National Service* 4 (September 1918): 102–6; Perry, *Plattsburg Movement*, pp. 206–7.

January-April 1918. Instituted in the spring of 1941 and requiring all candidates to have undergone five months of basic training, the Officer Candidate Schools (OCS) became a permanent and popular fixture of American military policy.[66]

FOUR

The army's decision to exclude civilians from officer candidacy brought up the question of whether or not the MTCA ought to continue its activities. The primary object of the association—universal military training—had been held in abeyance since Congress passed the Selective Service Act in May 1917. Most prewar Plattsburgers of military age had long since gone into the service, and President Drinker talked of dissolving the MTCA "for the duration," had it not been so important to recruit for the officer camps.[67] The army's decision seemed to imply that the MTCA's recruiting role would cease. Langdon Marvin told General Wood that he was "very much discouraged" and thinking of joining a Red Cross mission in Italy.[68]

The MTCA Executive Committee met in Washington on November 21, and the decision was unanimous to keep the organization intact. Efforts would continue with respect to persuading the army about officer procurement, although in the meantime the MTCA would concentrate on other matters.[69] Given their general willingness to serve, the Plattsburgers' determination to carry on rather than sulk was understandable. Much remained to be done. Since June 1917, for example, a MTCA delegation headed by Arthur Cosby and C. Willing Hare had been inspecting

[66]Robert R. Palmer, Bell I. Wiley, and William R. Keast, *The Army Ground Forces: The Procurement and Training of Ground Combat Troops* (Washington, D.C., 1948), p. 95.

[67]Drinker to Wood, August 10, 1917, Wood MSS; MTCA Bulletin #31, July 30, 1917, Clark MSS.

[68]Marvin to Wood, November 23, 1917, Wood MSS.

[69]Henry S. Drinker to members of the MTCA, November 22, 1917, copy in Wood MSS. Attending the executive committee meeting were Drinker, Clark, Cosby, Marvin, Pierce Anderson, Willing Hare, and Tompkins McIlvaine.

officer camps and divisional cantonments, reporting directly to the secretary of war. Notwithstanding the larger differences over officer training, "the particular value of these inspection reports," in Cosby's words, "has been in our obtaining the ear of the Secretary and has enabled us to make one or two recommendations of rather·large importance."[70] Furthermore, as long as Grenville Clark occupied an important position in Washington, it was foolish for the MTCA to disband. *National Service* was another reason for continuing. Although the entire editorial board had gone off to war that spring, the MTCA magazine had "drifted honorably but gently."[71] The opportunity still existed to publicize the Plattsburg viewpoint on officer matters and universal military training, and in early 1918 a new editorial staff, vigorously led by Tompkins McIlvaine, took up the challenge.[72]

Perhaps the major reason the MTCA continued in existence was the recent expansion of the organization at local levels, particularly in the Midwest. The urgent demands of the officer camps had resulted in the establishment of MTCA branches where none had existed before. By the end of 1917 committees had sprung up in some 1,300 towns and cities, all under the jurisdiction of the Chicago branch of the MTCA. Many committees had only nominal connections with the prewar training camps, perhaps one or two members who had attended a camp in 1916. So many temporary members were added that by March 1918 the MTCA decided to establish associate memberships. (A typical example was the MTCA branch at Fond du Lac, Wisconsin, formed on April 17, 1917, when the commanding general at Fort Sheridan telegraphed local business leaders. Before long there existed a Committee of 16 which

[70]Cosby to Wood, November 16, 1917, Wood MSS.

[71]Marvin to Wood, April 11, 1918, ibid.

[72]Throughout 1918 the tone and content of *National Service* became increasingly more sensational. War news predominated. At times, editorials verged on endorsing superpatriotic, "kill-the-Hun" attitudes. There remained, however, many restrained and informative discussions. For an example of wartime excess, see George F. Arps, "Atavistic Character of the Behavior of U-Boat Crews," *National Service* 2 (November 1917): 256–62.

raised $2,800 and recruited forty-three candidates for the first two camps at Fort Sheridan.)[73] These committees helped sponsor Liberty Loan Drives, provided preliminary military instruction for drafted men, organized home defense battalions, and acted as general bureaus of information.[74] In Chicago, MTCA leaders even commissioned the Zenith Motion Picture Company to produce a documentary film of the first officers' camps, entitled "Who Leads the National Army?" Approved by the Creel Committee on Public Information, the movie received nationwide distribution and became an integral part of the War Department's public relations effort in 1918.[75] Even without recruiting for the officer camps, the Plattsburgers had much to keep themselves busy.

An area in which the MTCA proved especially useful was in helping the army obtain specialists for the staff corps and technical services. It became apparent in November 1917 that the draft had failed to provide a sufficient number of technicians for the American Ordnance Base Depot in France. Following the pattern established with the officer camps, the army sent its recruiters to work with local committees in several cities. Within three weeks some 7,000 skilled mechanics had enlisted. Methods in Chicago were so refined that army recruiters obtained thirty motorcycle riders and seventy-five electricians (all that was desired) in one day.[76] In a letter to Wharton Clay of the Chicago Branch, the Ordnance Department hailed "the splendid response made by you and other patriotic men . . . to meet the immediate emergency requirements."[77]

[73]Military Training Camps Association, Fond du Lac branch, *Report of Activities* (Fond du Lac, 1919), pp. 10 – 12.

[74]MTCA, *War Record; The Fort Sheridan Association: Its History and Achievements* (Chicago, 1920), pp. 20–23; S. C. Roettinger to Wood, August 4, 1917; and Claude L. Matthews to Wood, May 1, 1918, Wood MSS.

[75]Wharton Clay, "Who Leads the National Army?" *National Service* 2 (November 1917): 240–41.

[76]"The Conventions of the Military Training Camps Association of the United States," *National Service* 2 (April 1918): 126; Clay, "A Record of National Service," *National Service* 2 (April 1918): 129–30.

[77]D. M. King and A. W. Maish to Clay, December 18, 1917, in MTCA, *War Record.*

The Ordnance accomplishment led to similar efforts. During the winter of 1917-1918 the army asked the MTCA to provide, if possible, hundreds of "expert instructors" who were to help streamline production and prevent sabotage in munitions plants. The Chicago branch managed to obtain 1,095 candidates in twenty-one days.[78] Through MTCA auspices in 1918 thousands of officer candidates and technicians for the Engineer Corps, Quartermaster Corps, Chemical Warfare Service, and Air Service were also recruited. When the army decided to organize a Tank Corps in March 1918, the MTCA supplied more than 3,000 applicants. "I came into Chicago with nothing but orders to recruit a certain number of skilled specialists," one officer marveled, "and your Association furnished me with publicity and office help, which enabled me to get these men in record time, and at no expense."[79] During this period the Central Department of the MTCA also cooperated with a British-Canadian recruiting mission, the Field Ambulance Service, the Public Service Reserve, and the War Service Exchange of the Adjutant General's Office. In each instance, the Plattsburgers responded to direct appeals; they neither received nor expected pay for their efforts.[80]

This "splendid achievement" inevitably resulted in a closer official relationship between the MTCA and the War Department.[81] There had been a movement afoot during February 1918 to get more Plattsburg leaders appointed to staff positions and even to have Grenville Clark made a special assistant to Secretary Baker, but the effort failed.[82] Recruitment provided another opportunity. As the need for specialists and technicians increased, personnel responsibilities had gravitated within the War Department to the

[78]*War Record.*

[79]W. H. Allen to Clay, March 15, 1918, *War Record.*

[80]Perry, *Plattsburg Movement,* pp. 222-23.

[81]C. G. Garland to Clay, June 3, 1918, in *War Record.*

[82]Clark memo, February 4, 1918; Marvin to Baker, February 5, 1918; Pierce Anderson to Baker, February 6, 1918; Henry S. Drinker to Baker, February 6, 1918; Franklin D. Roosevelt to Marvin, February 8, 1918, Clark MSS.

War Service Exchange, which in turn had come to depend on the MTCA for recruiting help. In a gradual way, the MTCA, with its network of local committees throughout the country, thus became unofficial representatives of the Washington bureaucracy. So logical was this arrangement that in May 1918 the secretary of war granted permission to the adjutant general to issue Civilian Aide Certificates to recruiting representatives of the War Service Exchange. Such certificates authorized the use of franking privileges and enabled the MTCA and the army to deal with one another through regular channels.[83] In June 1918, moreover, C. Willing Hare, head of the MTCA inspection committee, was attached to the office of Assistant Secretary of War Benedict Crowell, thereby bringing the MTCA's views on training camp procedures more sharply into focus.[84] These accretions of power did not endear the MTCA to all members of the military establishment, and one old colonel on the General Staff called the Plattsburgers "grafters and politicians." An angry Langdon Marvin protested that there was never an organization "more free of politics [or] any thought of personal gain," to which Assistant Secretary Keppel soothingly replied: "you need not worry about our appreciation of the unselfish and invaluable service which the Training Camps Association is performing."[85] The MTCA, it seemed, was making itself indispensable.

FIVE

This resurgence of strength prompted the MTCA to make another effort for officer training. In a memorandum to Secretary Baker, dated March 12, 1918, Marvin reiterated arguments used the previous autumn for continuous officer camps, open to civilians as well as to men from the ranks. He tried to counter the notion that the army had a surplus

[83]*History of the Personnel System*, pp. 498-99; MTCA Executive Committee minutes, May 1, 1918, Clark MSS.

[84]Hare to Ralph Barton Perry, June 17, 1920, Perry MSS.

[85]Marvin to Clark, June 3, 1918; Marvin to Keppel, May 28, 1918, and Keppel to Marvin, May 31, 1918, Clark MSS.

of officers by pointing out that "with Russia removed from the war, it is obvious that the responsibility of this country will become greater and greater. . . . Officers would have to be trained before additional forces are raised, and the longer they can be trained, the better they should be."[86] Marvin also stressed the possibility of commissioning older men (ages thirty-one to forty-five) in grades above that of second lieutenant.[87] Despite supporting letters from Clark and General Wood, the army decided to continue the Officers' Training Schools on the same basis as before.[88] These schools, Marvin was told, "are furnishing sufficient basic officer material for present needs. . . . The necessity for resorting to civil life for candidates for commissions does not appear at the present time."[89]

The Plattsburgers' disappointment did not last long, because the German offensive on the Western Front soon forced the War Department to revise nearly all its plans. The original estimate to place an army of thirty divisions in France by early 1919 mushroomed to the point that by June 1918 General Pershing was asking for one hundred divisions at the earliest possible date.[90] A new and more vigorous chief of staff, General Peyton C. March, assumed command in Washington that spring and did much to energize the army's sluggish bureaucracy. Clark, who had been working on personnel and ROTC questions since the previous autumn, immediately noticed the difference. "I am doing what I can to hurry up the mobilization," he wrote to Wood in mid-May, "and it seems to me there is a distinct waking up among the staff people in the direction of raising a bigger Army."[91]

[86]Marvin, "Memorandum for War Department in regard to Officers' Training Schools or Camps," March 12, 1918, Clark MSS. See also Marvin to Baker, April 4, 1918, Wood MSS.

[87]Ibid.

[88]Clark memorandum for General McCain, March 4, 1918, Clark MSS; Wood to McCain, April 3, 1918; and Wood to General Peyton C. March, April 3, 1918, Wood MSS.

[89]Benedict Crowell to Marvin, April 8, 1918; and General William S. Graves to Marvin, April 6, 1918, Clark MSS.

[90]Quoted in Coffman, *The War to End All Wars*, p. 177.

[91]Clark to Wood, May 15, 1918, Wood MSS.

The urgent pressure for more divisions caused complications in the fourth series of officer schools, which began on May 15 and had 13,114 candidates enrolled in twenty-four divisional cantonments. It was obviously difficult to obtain uniform standards with so many schools, and, even worse, officer training was often subordinated to the more immediate task of training and organizing the divisions. Morale and efficiency suffered accordingly. When the new divisions went overseas ahead of schedule, the majority of candidates stayed behind and finished their training course in the new "Central Officers' Training Schools."[92] Another serious obstacle was the decline in quality of officer candidates. Just as the MTCA had argued, the number of men in the ranks with sufficient education and leadership capacities proved to be limited. The auxiliary services were draining off many of the best candidates, while the Field and Coast Artillery Corps, which required a basic knowledge of physics and mathematics of all officers, found the existing procurement system particularly unsuitable. If the army was to provide qualified officers for its new forces, some changes would have to be made.[93]

The Military Training Camps Association continued to press for a larger officer program and the admission of civilians to candidacy. More memoranda went forth, and in mid-May another delegation visited Secretary Baker. The Philadelphia branch of the MTCA circulated a petition signed by men between the ages thirty-one and forty-five, urging the army to institute special officer courses (open to civilians) for the infantry, artillery, engineers, and cavalry.[94] This pressure, combined with Pershing's increased demands, led to permanent abandonment of the divisional schools in early June, to be replaced by Central Officers' Training Schools. Essentially what the MTCA had advo-

[92]Some 2,418 candidates from the fourth series finished their courses in France and received their commissions there.

[93]Perry, *Plattsburg Movement*, p. 208.

[94]Arthur Cosby, *Military Training Camps Association, Annual Report for 1918*, pamphlet in Clark MSS.

cated since August 1917, five infantry schools were begun at Camp Pike, Arkansas; Camp Grant, Illinois; Camp MacArthur, Texas; Camp Lee, Virginia; and Camp Gordon, Georgia. The army also set up a school for machine gunners at Camp Hancock, Georgia; a cavalry school at Leon Springs, Texas; and a school for field artillery at Camp Zachary Taylor, Kentucky. The numbers ranged from 1,000 candidates at Leon Springs to 6,000 at Camp Taylor. The instruction was to be continuous, with classes graduating and new classes being added at monthly intervals. At the outset the new schools were not open to civilians, but this policy soon changed.[95]

Because of the dearth of qualified candidates, the field artillery school at Camp Taylor was the first to admit applicants from civilian life. Following the practice of the technical services, the chief of field artillery appealed for MTCA assistance in recruiting and instructed all recruiting officers to place themselves under the guidance of local Plattsburg committees.[96] By a fortunate coincidence, the assistant adjutant at Camp Taylor happened to be Lieutenant Colonel Benjamin H. Dibblee, formerly head of the San Francisco branch of the MTCA. Dibblee was personally acquainted with many MTCA committeemen, and his presence helped to establish an excellent recruiting service based in approximately 120 cities. The capacity at Camp Taylor gradually increased over the summer to 14,000, of which some 5,000 candidates were provided through MTCA auspices. According to Dibblee, this working relationship between the MTCA and field artillery proved so effective that the other branches of the service, "purely as a matter of self-protection," were forced to recruit civilians and ask for MTCA cooperation.[97]

When the infantry officers' schools were opened to civilians in July, the army at first attempted to make professors of military sciences and tactics at selected colleges respon-

[95]Perry, *Plattsburg Movement*, pp. 109–10.
[96]General William J. Snow to MTCA, July 16, 1918, *War Record*.
[97]Dibblee to Ralph Barton Perry, June 2, 1920, Perry MSS.

sible for recruiting. This method failed. The professors had other duties to perform, were not geographically distributed, and lacked any working organization. Even with five infantry schools the military professors managed to provide only one-fourth as many candidates as the Plattsburgers recruited for Camp Taylor, notwithstanding the fact that educational requirements were stiffer for the field artillery. Finally, to eliminate confusion, the War Department instructed all military professors to make use of MTCA machinery and personnel in every phase of recruiting.[98]

New problems arose when Congress, on August 8, 1918, amended the Selective Service Act to extend the age range from eighteen to forty-five years. Recruitment of civilian officer candidates ceased for more than a month, so as not to take key men from defense industries until the new registration could be completed. During this period the MTCA continued to process applications and give provisional examinations, and when the army revoked the ban on civilian enlistment in mid-September, the Association had in readiness a long list of candidates who were immediately admitted.[99] A week later, September 20, the Coast Artillery requested MTCA help in enlisting older men for its new central officer school at Fort Monroe, Virginia. Success was similar to that obtained at Camp Taylor, and recruitment continued at a quickened pace until the end of the war in November.[100] The Armistice also cut short an even more ambitious project: the army announced in late October that a new infantry school would be set up at Camp Fremont, California, open to civilian candidates, with a capacity of 20,000 trainees, and the course of instruction reduced to two months. Although the camp was never begun, it represented the most extensive application of what the MTCA had been preaching since the spring of 1917.[101]

[98]Ibid.; Perry, *Plattsburg Movement*, pp. 224-25.
[99]C. W. Jones to Wharton Clay, August 14, 1918, *War Record*.
[100]Perry, *Plattsburg Movement*, p. 225.
[101]Ibid., p. 210.

The Plattsburgers watched these late developments with a certain amount of self-satisfaction. General Wood, then training the Tenth Division at Camp Funston, Kansas, informed Clark how pleased he was that the army had readmitted civilians, particularly older men, to officer camps. "If this had been done from the start there would be no officer problem." Wood went on to pay tribute to Clark's influence: "I know that your attitude has been for thorough training. I know what a struggle you have had to get anything done. . . . I think we are all to be congratulated that you have remained in the Department. . . . Your views have been sound throughout."[102] Obviously touched by the general's remarks, Clark later replied: "It is extraordinary (though always obvious to me) how the course of events in the last six months of the war entirely vindicated the position you took in this matter all through."[103] Even if the MTCA's criticism of the War Department was sometimes too harsh, their view that the war would require men and officers in ever-increasing numbers had proved correct.

SIX

Another wartime measure which attracted the close attention of MTCA leaders was the Students' Army Training Corps (SATC). Described by Clark as "mostly my scheme in its origins," the SATC was established on August 24, 1918, as an attempt to mobilize the nation's colleges.[104] Because of their Ivy League backgrounds and because of their interest in the prewar ROTC, it was inevitable that the Plattsburgers should become involved.

The MTCA had been pressing the War Department to make greater use of the colleges since the summer of 1917.

[102]Wood to Clark, October 14, 1918, Wood MSS; Clark had written Wood earlier: "C. Willing Hare . . . got hold of your letter to the Adjutant General on this subject [more officers] and put it before Mr. Crowell, and I think it was the determining factor in getting things opened up on a permanent basis." Clark to Wood, September 20, 1918, ibid.
[103]Clark to Wood, April 23, 1919, Clark MSS.
[104]Clark to Wood, August 5, 1918, Wood MSS.

According to the National Defense Act of 1916, however, only Regular Army officers with five years' experience commanding troops could be placed in charge of ROTC units, and the army had reassigned all such officers to active duty at the outbreak of war. The MTCA talked of substituting retired officers or civilian instructors, but without success. Beginning in November 1917, the Association's Advisory Board of University Presidents negotiated with Secretary Baker about amending the law. The result was a Joint Resolution of Congress on April 20, 1918, which made 1,000 temporary officers eligible for ROTC detail.[105] Simultaneous to these developments, the General Staff established in February a Committee on Education and Special Training, which also concerned itself with obtaining officers from the universities. Representing the Adjutant General's Office and serving as the committee's secretary and chief executive officer was Grenville Clark. Major Ralph Barton Perry, Harvard professor and former Plattsburger, also sat on the committee.[106] Following the committee's recommendations, Secretary Baker announced on May 8 that military training would resume during the academic year 1918–1919 at all colleges attended by one hundred or more able-bodied male students. The purpose was twofold: "to develop as a great military asset the large body of young men in the colleges; and . . . to prevent unnecessary and wasteful depletion of the colleges through indiscriminate volunteering."[107] "I got up this plan and wrote the announcement," Clark confided to Wood, "and I am now working on the detailed plan which I believe will go through."[108]

Plans matured during the spring, and on June 29 the adjutant general issued a circular which officially replaced

---

[105]Perry, *Plattsburg Movement,* p. 231.

[106]Lieutenant Colonel D. I. Rees was chairman of the Committee and C. R. Mann of MIT was chairman of a Civilian Advisory Board. See Mann to Clark, December 19, 1918, enclosing "Reminiscences of the Educational Work of the Committee on Education and Special Training," Clark MSS; Ralph Barton Perry, "The Students' Army Training Corps," *National Service* 6 (August 1919): 77–84.

[107]Baker to College Presidents, May 8, 1918, circular letter in Wood MSS.

[108]Clark to Wood, May 15, 1918, ibid.

ROTC with the Students' Army Training Corps. Under the new system, the army was authorized to enlist 150,000 young men of college age and to place them in SATC units on furlough status without pay. When the trainee turned twenty-one, he would register with his local Selective Service board and become subject to the draft. Ten hours each week would be devoted to military training, with the rest of the curriculum taken up with regular academic pursuits. To provide the necessary instructors, it was decided to hold special camps at Plattsburg, Fort Sheridan, and the Presidio of San Francisco, open to selected students, faculty, and civilian volunteers. These camps, numbering 8,000 trainees, began on July 18 and were to run for two months.[109]

Then came the announcement in early August that the draft age would be lowered to eighteen. The original plan for the SATC was now obsolete. For more than a week the Committee on Education and Special Training debated whether or not to jettison the idea. It was Clark's emphasis on officer shortages which finally determined the committee to convert the SATC into "one large reservoir . . . from which candidates for officers' training camps might be supplied in numbers sufficient to meet the very large demands."[110] The committee resumed work and on August 20 submitted a revised plan to the chief of staff which was approved and became part of the Manpower bill passed by Congress nine days later. The plan envisaged fundamental educational changes. In essence, colleges were to become army posts. All able-bodied students over eighteen would be placed on active duty, with housing, uniforms, pay, and subsistence provided by the government. Students would remain in school, follow a course of instruction organized to provide officer candidates according to the needs of the various services and then be subject to transfer whenever and wherever the army needed them. Twenty percent of all future officer candidates would come out of the SATC. When the units were activated on Octo-

[109]*History of the Personnel System,* p. 536.
[110]C. R. Mann, "Reminiscences," Clark MSS.

ber 1, 1918, some 518 colleges became part of the system, involving more than 135,000 students.[111]

The SATC never had much chance to develop, since the Armistice put an end to the program some seven weeks after it had begun. Even in this short period, participants had to endure equipment shortages, the inevitable conflict between civilian and military philosophies, and an influenza epidemic which halted training for three weeks at most institutions.[112] These drawbacks notwithstanding, the experiment seemed to provide some interesting possibilities. Admission to the SATC, for example, remained the responsibility of the various colleges until October 1, after which time the Committee on Education and Special Training undertook to select replacements from young men already in National Army training centers. Such a policy would not only maintain a constant supply of officer candidates, but it would also, in Clark's words, "remove any criticism as to lack of democracy, and the exceptional boy, physically or personally, who happens to lack the technical standard of education, will not be excluded."[113] As C. R. Mann put it, the SATC became "a genuine national university—the University of Uncle Sam, in which every boy had an opportunity with every other boy to render his utmost service to the nation."[114] While such claims may have been exaggerated, the war did not last long enough to determine that.

From the military standpoint, moreover, the SATC epitomized the kind of comprehensive measure for recruit-

[111]Perry, *Plattsburg Movement*, pp. 212–13.

[112]One young professor at Hamline University in Minnesota later remembered: "The program was of course unworkable: there is good authority for the dictum that no man can serve two masters. What can a distracted teacher do when an army sergeant appears at his classroom door, interrupts the proceedings with a loud command for Private So-and-so to report to such-and-such place p.d.q., then departs noisily, followed by the uneasy victim. . . . We all tried hard to make the proper adjustments, the President, the faculty, the students, and the somewhat unlettered military commandant, but it just couldn't be done. The college authorities knew nothing about how to run an army post, the army knew nothing about how to run a college." John D. Hicks, *My Life with History* (Lincoln, Nebr., 1968), p. 106.

[113]Clark to Wood, September 20, 1918, Wood MSS.

[114]Mann, "Reminiscences," Clark MSS.

ing civilian officer candidates which the Plattsburgers had always urged. With the Committee on Education and Special Training serving as coordinator, the SATC provided a means for allocating civilians with special skills according to the overall needs of the military and naval services. It removed the necessity for haphazard recruiting campaigns and brought a vital segment of the civilian population — the universities — into a close working relationship with the War Department. As Ralph Barton Perry later wrote, the SATC "was based on a quantitatively adequate estimate of future needs. It sought to draw into the service, and to use in accordance with their individual fitness, those civilians who were best qualified for leadership by education, inheritance and experience. Finally it proposed that all candidates for commissions should be assembled, trained, and judged by direct observation."[115] This was what the MTCA had stood for all during the war.

Perhaps the most important consequence of the SATC from the Plattsburg point of view was that it led to an expanded ROTC in the nation's colleges after the war. Clark had predicted to Wood in August 1918 that the SATC would be "a long step towards a permanent military training policy because I don't believe that most of the colleges will ever give it up."[116] He was right. When the war ended and SATC lapsed, the War Department during the winter of 1918 – 1919 reconstituted the ROTC system begun in 1916. Whereas there had been only 115 ROTC units in April 1917, by 1920–1921 some 334 units were in existence at 244 universities, colleges, and secondary schools, involving approximately 100,000 students. A subject of some controversy during the interwar years, ROTC nevertheless provided the army with a reserve of officers sufficiently numerous and capable to avoid a repetition of the worst mistakes of 1917.[117] The MTCA's Advisory

[115]Perry, *Plattsburg Movement*, p. 214.
[116]Clark to Wood, August 5, 1918, Wood MSS.
[117]Ralph Barton Perry to Wood, January 22, 1919, ibid.; Gene M. Lyons and John W. Masland, *Education and Military Leadership: A Study of the ROTC* (Princeton, N. J., 1959), chapt. 2.

Board of University Presidents worked closely with the War Department in reorganizing ROTC, and after one of the meetings in 1919 President John Grier Hibben of Princeton reported to Wood: "I took occasion to state that in my opinion we would either be fighting Germany at this time or overcome by its brutal tyranny had it not been for your foresight in establishing summer camps beginning in 1913. It was not only that these camps furnished a nucleus of young officers for our army, but it started a propaganda which convinced the sober minded and thoughtful people of the United States that we must enter the war and begin our preparation for it."[118]

SEVEN

And so the war ended for the Plattsburgers. They had performed well. In his *Annual Report* for 1918, written shortly after the Armistice, Secretary Baker expressed his "deep satisfaction" at the success of the army's officer program. "Thousands of our young men," he wrote, "left positions of responsibility and profit, dropped their personal affairs and devoted themselves wholeheartedly to the new business of war. . . . the results have exceeded our warmest hopes."[119] Baker did not mention the Military Training Camps Association by name, but his appreciation of the Plattsburg achievement was obvious.

The fact that so many Plattsburgers served in France magnified what was accomplished at home. (Some prewar leaders like Willard Straight, John Purroy Mitchel, Raynal Bolling, and Robert Bacon lost their lives.) By keeping an organization intact, continuing to publish *National Service,* and performing so capably as recruiters, the MTCA contributed as much to the war effort as any civilian organization. The army paid the Plattsburgers a supreme compliment by adopting, however reluctantly, the policy of

[118]Hibben to Wood, January 3, 1919, Wood MSS.
[119]*War Department Annual Reports, 1918* (Washington, D.C., 1918), 1:19.

training an ever-increasing supply of civilian officers. This alone was a considerable accomplishment.

And yet, notwithstanding the efforts of Clark in Washington, the growing relationship with the War Department, and the MTCA's expansion at local levels, there was a vague feeling that the war had diverted the Plattsburg movement from its principal object: universal military training. Langdon Marvin described some of this feeling in a letter to General Wood in December 1918. He had resigned from the MTCA that summer, he told the general, and had gone to England on a Red Cross mission. While in London, he had received a telegram from the Adjutant General's Office offering him a commission (and the opportunity to "work with Grenny Clark"), but before he could get back to the United States, the Armistice intervened. Marvin felt frustrated. Kenneth Budd and DeLancey Jay, both wounded in the war, had also returned to New York. Other Plattsburgers would be coming back shortly. Marvin told Wood that they would all have to begin working again. While everything was "pretty quiet at present," he promised that the MTCA will do "what it can to try to bring about universal training and service."[120]

[120]Marvin to Wood, December 19, 1918, Wood MSS.

IX.

Postwar Policy & the National Defense Act of 1920

"Let us begin the struggle for universal training," General Wood wrote to Theodore Roosevelt shortly after the Armistice. "We have these great cantonments and we must not let things slump. . . . You saw the other day the mob bearing the red flag coming into New York from the East Side. You see the same crowd in Germany today. The world is a bit upside down, and we want to begin to talk organization and preparation as we never talked before."[1] The prospect of fighting for universal military training would have pleased Roosevelt, but seven weeks later, January 6, 1919, the old Rough Rider was dead.

The death of Roosevelt brought intense grief to his followers. "Something went out of my life that has never been replaced," Harold Ickes wrote a quarter-century later.[2] "Sad, sad business, all of it," Wood wrote in his diary.[3] It was a prelude to the disappointment and disillusionment that pervaded practically all of America in the years immediately following the World War: an embittered Woodrow Wilson, broken, ill, unable to gain Senate endorsement of the League of Nations; Leonard Wood, frustrated again as the Republican professionals selected Warren G. Harding as their standard bearer at Chicago in 1920; a scandal in the 1919 World Series; strikes; depression; the Great Red Scare. Perhaps such confusion and disenchantment followed inevitably from the regimentation and moral exaltation of war.

A major casualty of the postwar reaction was the military program which Wood and the Plattsburgers had been advocating since 1915. All that had happened in the past two years—the raising and training of a National Army, industrial mobilization, the problems of transportation and supply, the experience of combat—made it imperative for Congress to pass legislation that went beyond the National Defense Act of 1916. Here, it seemed, was an opportunity for the Military Training Camps Association to realize its goal of a citizen army based on universal military training. But army reorganization became caught up in the whirlpool of confusion and prejudice that seemed to characterize all public questions in 1919 and 1920. Antagonism from the National Guard, differences within the Regular Army, mistaken ideas about militarism, economic concerns, politics—all worked against the desired solution. Universal military training, the heart of the Plattsburg program, was to be left out of the National Defense Act of 1920.

ONE

When the war ended on November 11, 1918, the duties of the Military Training Camps Association in connection with recruiting and examining officer candidates stopped. Grenville Clark resigned his commission in the Adjutant General's Office and went off to New England for an extended vacation (vowing to "retire or take a back seat in the agitating business").[4] In France, where a majority of the prewar Plattsburgers were still serving, Colonel Theodore Roosevelt, Jr., began to sound out fellow AEF (Allied Expeditionary Force) officers on the idea of forming a new organization of veterans, the American Legion.[5] Only the small group in charge of editing *National Service* kept up

[1]Wood to Roosevelt, November 15, 1918, Roosevelt MSS.
[2]Harold L. Ickes, *Autobiography of a Curmudgeon* (New York, 1943), p. 217.
[3]Wood Diary, January 6, 1919.
[4]Clark to Ralph Barton Perry, February 20, 1919, Perry MSS.
[5]Marquis James, *A History of the American Legion* (New York, 1923), pp. 15-19; Raymond Moley, Jr., *The American Legion Story* (New York, 1966), pp. 43-49.

any official MTCA function in the weeks immediately following the Armistice.[6] And with the motto — "Devoted to the Cause of Universal Military Training" — emblazoned on the journal's masthead, it was natural that these men should turn their thoughts in such a direction.

The *National Service* group had been thinking about postwar legislation, but their ideas were still tentative. Shortly after the Armistice Arthur Cosby sent a long letter to Camp Funston outlining their plans and asking advice.[7] "You speak of a nine months course," Wood replied. "This is too long. . . . These new National Army Divisions, after five months of training, are more efficient fighting machines than was our old army." He liked Cosby's suggestion about including vocational training along with military training, but was afraid that nine months would prove politically impossible. "The main thing now," warned Wood, "is to establish it."[8] Encouraged, the MTCA set up a Committee on Universal Military Training, with Tompkins McIlvaine as chairman.[9]

The man chosen to supervise the MTCA's legislative program in many ways exemplified the Plattsburg tradition. Tall, lean, and somewhat older than his colleagues at forty-nine, McIlvaine had been a National Guard officer in 1898, attended the first Business Men's Camp in 1915, and served as a major during the World War. Like many Plattsburgers, he was a lawyer and a Republican. A direct descendant of Daniel Tompkins, the sixth vice president of the United States, McIlvaine sometimes manifested aristocratic tendencies, and no one ever accused him of being shy or

[6]The editorial board in January 1919 consisted of Henry S. Drinker, Arthur S. Cosby, Donald R. Cotton, C. Willing Hare, Tompkins McIlvaine, Langdon P. Marvin, George Wharton Pepper, Charles B. Pike, Robert H. Perdue, Dean Sage, C. S. Walker, and Frederick N. Watriss.

[7]Cosby to Wood, November 15, 1918, Wood MSS; Cosby also sent a memorandum of their ideas to Grenville Clark, who submitted it to Frederick Keppel, the assistant secretary of war. See "Memorandum for the Third Assistant Secretary of War," December 5, 1918, Clark MSS.

[8]Wood to Cosby, November 18, 1918, Wood MSS.

[9]The committee members were McIlvaine, Arthur F. Cosby, Benjamin F. Dibblee, John C. Greenway, Landon Thomas, Langdon P. Marvin, George V. L. Meyer, Charles B. Pike, and C. S. Walker.

self-effacing. His editorial style and public manner were forceful, almost arrogant. Nonetheless, McIlvaine did have a broad knowledge of military affairs and a knack for writing well. Even better, he and his committee were able to formulate a program quickly.[10]

The first public statement of MTCA policy appeared as a memorandum (under McIlvaine's name) in the January 1919 issue of *National Service*. It was primarily an argument for "a short period of intensive training of all young men actually or potentially capable of receiving training and who are not the sole support of dependents." Six months at age eighteen or nineteen would enable them to "defend their country when necessary, and . . . Americanize them and . . . teach them habits of social discipline and respect for law and order, and incidentally . . . give them suitable training to fit them for industrial life." Moreover, the McIlvaine memorandum linked training to the larger questions of military reorganization, because without so doing it "would simply result in giving a certain amount of individual training to our young men, but would by no means relieve us of the necessity of maintaining a real military force sufficient to garrison the United States and its territorial possessions, and on any sudden outbreak of war, to provide the first line of defense until the nation would be mobilized."

Specifically, the memorandum proposed to substitute a Swiss-type citizen soldiery for the existing Regular Army, National Guard, and National Army. The plan would take a certain number each year from the class of young men undergoing six months' training. This number would be one-third of the strength considered essential for a first line of defense, and those recruited were to serve for two years. The percentage of trainees entering this first line would not be large, and the intention was to encourage voluntary recruitment through higher pay and industrial training. If

[10]For McIlvaine's somewhat inflated estimate of himself, see "Memo as to the Experience of Tompkins McIlvaine Regarding Military Matters," July 8, 1940, Record Group 46, Box 117, National Archives.

volunteers did not come forth in sufficient numbers, the memorandum recommended some form of selective draft. When a man had completed his two-year stint, he would pass automatically into a second line reserve where he would serve until age thirty. The second line, like the first line, was to be organized territorially with the reservists called out each summer for periodic maneuvers. Envisioned also was a third line of reserve, comprised of men who had passed through the first and second lines and of those younger trainees who did not opt for further service. Except in times of emergency, actual military duty with the third line was to be minimal.

To officer the new formations, the MTCA plan would employ future graduates of West Point, men qualified from the ranks, professionals transferred from existing forces, and ROTC graduates of approved colleges. Once the citizen armies had become a going concern, officer selection would be highly competitive with compulsory retirement for anyone who did not measure up. Such weeding out would be determined by a special Board of Officers "acting on all information, including officers' records of service, qualification cards," and the like. This whole proposal reflected the Plattsburg concern that officers of a citizen army be sympathetic to civilian needs and not form a separate caste. It also reflected the resentment which many returning veterans harbored against the pettifogging, bureaucratic type of Regular officer.[11]

The McIlvaine memorandum did not cause much immediate stir. The War Department had its own, quite different, ideas about military reorganization, and public opinion in general was not about to be shaken from its post-Armistice euphoria by a magazine article with such limited circulation as *National Service*. What McIlvaine wrote was still imprecise. The emphasis on "Americanization" and "law and order" seemed clearer than the military features, which lacked detail. Nor did it appear politic to advocate

[11]Tompkins McIlvaine, "Universal Training and Army Reorganization," *National Service* 5 (January 1919): 23–25.

such a drastic replacement of the Regular Army and National Guard.[12]

More work was needed. "Get in touch with those who have heretofore been interested in the plan," one Plattsburger wrote from France, "and arrange for a systematic support of the plan, which would not perhaps be under full way until . . . autumn when the forces now on this side return to the States."[13] Some of these persons already had arrived in New York: Kenneth Budd, DeLancey Jay, Archibald Thacher, Philip Carroll, John Farley, Robert Homans. By mid-February Langdon Marvin was reporting "weekly luncheons lately of many of these men to talk over questions of Universal Service."[14] Although the MTCA Executive Committee approved the McIlvaine program in substance at this time, the obstacles which loomed ahead were obvious.[15] As Grenville Clark observed: "the whole preparedness propaganda must be done all over again, large sums of money must be put up, many enthusiasts must give up their business and go to it. . . . Whether it will be done or not I don't know."[16]

While the Plattsburgers continued to work on legislation during the winter and spring months, it became clear that public sentiment was not altogether favorable. A few important voices did speak out in favor of universal training, such as President Emeritus Charles W. Eliot of Harvard and Assistant Secretary of the Navy Franklin D. Roosevelt. The National Security League, Army League,

[12]General Wood was critical of McIlvaine's anti-Regular bias. "McIlvaine's plan has many good points, and certain ones I think will have to be modified. The Regular Army, which is to do the police work of the country, all over the world, will have to be filled by voluntary enlistments as . . . at present. This will be the national training cadre also." Wood to Langdon Marvin, February 6, 1919, Wood MSS. "The main thing to bear in mind, as I see it, is that the permanent force must be Regular, ready for duty anywhere in the world, as at present. When we have the increments of the first five years trained and organized and ready, we can, of course, cut the permanent forces down at home to the minimum." Wood to McIlvaine, February 17, 1919, ibid.

[13]Anson Conger Goodyear to Wood, January 27, 1919, Wood MSS.

[14]Marvin to Wood, February 21, 1919, ibid.

[15]Tompkins McIlvaine, "A People's Army – Plan of the MTCA in Congress," *National Service* 6 (September 1919): 150.

[16]Clark to Ralph Barton Perry, February 20, 1919, Perry MSS.

and National Association for Universal Military Training were also active.[17] But opinion seemed to be swinging in the opposite direction. As the number of anti-preparedness magazine articles rose sharply from what had been the case during wartime, the National Security League's publicity director in the spring of 1919 bewailed the fact that opponents of universal military training were winning high school debates at a rate of two to one.[18] According to the *Nation,* troops were returning from Europe "with a stomach full of soldiering . . . with the greatest eagerness to get out of uniform, and with the minds of many men open to new ideas."[19]

This disposition on the part of veterans was particularly annoying to the Plattsburgers. From the beginning the MTCA leaders had high hopes for the new American Legion. They saw the Legion as a possible successor organization, an instrument "specifically to work for an adequate military policy based on universal obligation for service." Clark told Ted Roosevelt that "at the proper time the two organizations could be merged, and they should meanwhile be controlled by the same people; also the machinery of the MTCA could be used . . . to start the new association."[20] Despite these hopes and close planning between the two groups, the first caucus of the American Legion, held in St. Louis, May 8 – 10, 1919, made no mention of universal training and army reorganization.[21] McIlvaine and DeLancey Jay were present but remained in the background. "It was a disappointment to me," McIlvaine wrote, "that no

[17]*New York Times,* January 5, March 9, 1919.

[18]Chase C. Mooney and Martha E. Layman, "Some Phases of the Compulsory Military Training Movement, 1914–1920," *Mississippi Valley Historical Review* 38 (March 1952): 649.

[19]*Nation* 108 (June 21, 1919): 973.

[20]Clark to Roosevelt, February 11, 1919, Clark MSS. There was also a move afoot to make Ralph Barton Perry the permanent secretary-treasurer of the Legion. Perry was interested, even to the point of resigning his Harvard professorship, but Eric Fisher Wood took the position. Perry, at Clark's urging, then undertook to write a history of the Plattsburg movement. The details of these developments can be found in the Clark-Perry correspondence in either the Clark or Perry MSS. See also Clark to Ted Roosevelt, April 15, 1919, Clark MSS.

[21]McIlvaine, "The American Legion," *National Service* 5 (June 1919): 348–49.

action was taken about universal training. . . . It is the only thing that will make us a country."[22] To Wood McIlvaine lamented: "The chief reliance for effective . . . propaganda and active work in Congress must still be the Training Camps Association. The Association is out of funds, indeed in debt. We need at least $50,000 — if possible, more — to carry on the program we have outlined in the coming six or eight months."[23] Wood, who was stationed at Fort Sheridan and just beginning his campaign for the presidency, said he would "take up the question and see what we can do."[24]

The fact that public attention focused on the Paris Peace Conference was another reason the Plattsburg effort bogged down at the outset. While hopes remained high for the kind of peace envisioned in President Wilson's Fourteen Points, it was difficult to generate much enthusiasm for military matters. Secretary Baker discovered this when his request for funds to maintain a reduced army of 500,000 men for another year encountered a chilly reception from Congress during January and February 1919.[25] Once the participants in Paris began to haggle over colonies, boundaries, and reparations, however, the essentially nationalistic attitude of the Plattsburgers was bound to gain in popularity.

The MTCA position on international affairs was clear — whatever the "outcome of the Peace Conference . . . whether or not a League of Nations be formed, the United States will be required to maintain a considerable military force."[26] As expressed in *National Service* editorials, there was a continuing suspicion of Wilsonian foreign policy, a belief that the United States should safeguard such diplomatic traditions as the Monroe Doctrine and "no entangling alliances," that the collective se-

[22]McIlvaine to Ted Roosevelt, May 15, 1919, Theodore Roosevelt, Jr., MSS, Library of Congress.

[23]McIlvaine to Wood, May 15, 1919, Wood MSS.

[24]Wood to McIlvaine, May 17, 1919, ibid.

[25]John Dickinson, *The Building of an Army*, pp. 333–37.

[26]MTCA, *Reports of the Executive Secretary and Treasurer for 1918* (New York, 1919), p. 10. The reports were dated January 31, 1919.

curity provisions of the League Covenant might be unconstitutional, and that the whole trend of an internationalist
peace might be to embroil the United States in disputes
that had no bearing on the national interest. "We are feeling our oats just now," the editors put it, "but let us remember the warning of Gilbert and Sullivan and beware the lot
of the world policeman."[27] While in favor of a World Court
and avowedly neutral during Wilson's fight with the Senate
that summer, the Plattsburg position did not differ much
from that of Henry Cabot Lodge, Elihu Root, Henry L.
Stimson, and other Eastern Republicans.[28] The MTCA
hoped that the old slogan, "a wise man in time of peace
prepares for war," would attract additional support in Congress.[29]

TWO

Before they obtained sponsors for their universal training
program in Congress, the Plattsburgers thought it prudent
to learn the attitude of the War Department. There were
indications that Secretary Baker opposed compulsory training, having been converted to the idea of a large standing
army by the General Staff.[30] Because of his familiarity with
the inner workings of the Department, Grenville Clark
visited Washington early in April ostensibly to discuss an
article on ROTC being written for *National Service*. Unable
to see the secretary of war, he talked with Assistant Secretary Keppel, who assured him that "Baker's mind was entirely open on universal training but he could not commit
himself until the peace treaty situation has cleared up."[31]
Clark remained suspicious. Fearful that Keppel's state-

[27]"The Policeman's Lot," *National Service* 5 (May 1919): 262; e.g., "Punishment
or Restitution," 5 (January 1919): 35; "A League of Nations," 5 (February 1919):
89–90; "Peace and the League," 5 (May 1919): 262; "Long Distance Plotting," 6
(July 1919): 6; "Needed—Common Sense," 6 (August 1919): 69–70.

[28]Grenville Clark was a strong supporter of the League and eventually voted
for James Cox in 1920 on this particular issue. He was, however, a rarity among
the Plattsburgers.

[29]"A League of Nations," *National Service* 5 (February 1919): 89–90.

[30]Beaver, *Newton D. Baker,* pp. 241–43.

[31]Clark to John McAuley Palmer, April 16, 1919, Clark MSS.

ments were "camouflage to bolster up a permanent volunteer army policy," he had "no faith at all in the present war administration advocating what we want. . . . big results are to be achieved only by outside and probably political action."[32]

Clark's suspicions were confirmed when he renewed an old acquaintanceship with Lieutenant Colonel John McAuley Palmer. Recently transferred to the General Staff from the AEF where he commanded a corps for General Pershing, Palmer had known Clark in 1916–1917 when he had written articles for *National Service* and kept the MTCA informed about General Staff policies. The slight, professorial-looking colonel had acquired the reputation within the army of being one of the two or three foremost service intellectuals. His imaginative book, *An Army of the People*, published early in 1916, had placed him foursquare with Wood and the Plattsburgers in favoring a citizen reserve army over the Uptonian professional model.[33] Even better, he lacked Wood's ability to alienate, and while in France he was able to win over that supreme professional, General Pershing, who sent him to Washington after the Armistice to represent the AEF's views on postwar reorganization.[34]

But, as Palmer told Clark, since returning to Washington he had run into a stone wall in the person of General Peyton C. March, the chief of staff. A ramrod administrator whose abrupt manner did not encourage advice from subordinates, March had practically dictated the War Department bill sent to Congress in January 1919. It was the old

[32]Ibid. Clark added that they ought, however, to keep on good terms with the War Department, "instead of giving them up as absolutely hopeless enemies, according to the General Wood policy."

[33]Palmer had served under Wood during the latter's tenure as chief of staff and had been the principal author of "The Organization of the Land Forces of the United States." Palmer's book, *An Army of the People*, written in the Philippines during 1915, was published primarily through the efforts of Anson Conger Goodyear, the MTCA leader from Buffalo, who read the book in manuscript and persuaded a reluctant War Department to permit its publication. (Palmer dedicated the book to Goodyear.) And through Goodyear, Palmer came to know Clark and the other Plattsburgers. There is a convenient summary of their long relationship as "co-conspirators" in Palmer to Clark, November 28, 1947, Clark MSS.

[34]For a good discussion of Palmer's ideas, see Weigley, *Towards an American Army*, chapt. 13.

Uptonian idea of an expansible standing army: 509,909 men in peacetime, to be increased to 1,250,000 during an emergency.[35] March later added a provision for three months' universal training at age nineteen, but made no effort to connect this training to a system of citizen reserves.[36] Palmer was certain that Congress would reject the large regular establishment, and he did what he could from his position on the War Plans Division to urge alternatives. The chief of staff simply ignored his memoranda. "Your suspicions are completely justified," he informed Clark, "that the policy here is predicated not only on the idea that we are not to have universal military training, but that it is definitely aimed at killing the idea if practicable . . . I agree with you that the fight must be from the outside and I cannot help feeling that if I am to help I must get at it very soon."[37]

Palmer found himself in a delicate position. Convinced that the War Department plan for a large standing army was wrong, he could not speak out publicly without seeming disloyal to General March. He talked with Clark about resigning from the army. Perhaps the Plattsburgers could obtain a professorship at Harvard for him, or possibly he could get a salaried position with *National Service* or the American Legion. The difference between regular and retirement pay would be $250 a month, and Palmer did not feel he could make the financial sacrifice without some alternative commitment. Above all, he wanted to publicize universal military training. "I can present it," he told Clark, "so that all conflicting interests, National Guard, National

[35]For an excellent analysis of the General Staff bill, see Edward M. Coffman, *The Hilt of the Sword: The Career of Peyton C. March* (Madison, Wis., 1966), pp. 175–77. Wood's comment, when he first learned of the March plan, is interesting. "We have a lot of doddards toddling into the military situation now. The General Staff which is such only in name is quoted in last night's paper as being opposed to universal service and training and recommending a standing army of 500,000 men. These are on a par with the group of microcephaloids, who twice sent me when I was Chief of Staff, a unanimous recommendation from the War College in favor of a bounty system as against universal service." Wood to Theodore Roosevelt, December 12, 1918, Wood MSS.

[36]Under the March bill trainees would have no further peacetime obligation after three months, other than to file an annual written report for two years.

[37]Palmer to Clark, April 17, 1919, Clark MSS.

Army, regular army, all who are interested in preparedness will get onto the bandwagon."[38] Clark was sympathetic, and throughout the spring and summer he kept in close touch with Palmer.[39] Although the MTCA was short on funds for the moment and could make no final commitment, a tentative understanding was reached that whenever Palmer resigned the Plattsburgers would provide adequate remuneration.[40] In the meantime, Palmer continued to give Clark and McIlvaine advice about drafting legislation.

With the Sixty-sixth Congress beginning its first session in May 1919, the Plattsburgers kept busy revising and polishing their draft bill. McIlvaine was in "daily consultation with men of all sorts on the subject."[41] By early June, after much discussion, the legislation was ready.[42] Finding sponsors did not prove difficult, and the MTCA selected Julius Kahn (R.-California) in the House and George E. Chamberlain (D.-Oregon) in the Senate. Kahn, the amiable former actor who had sponsored the Selective Service Act in 1917, was particularly receptive. Now chairman of the House Military Affairs Committee, Kahn had gone to Europe during March and April to visit American troops and to observe firsthand the Swiss and Italian military systems. He had seen something of the bickering in Paris and was convinced more than ever that the United States needed a sound defense policy, which did not necessarily include a large standing army. He told a reporter in Coblenz that he would introduce legislation for universal military training on his return to the States.[43] Kahn accepted the MTCA bill eagerly, as did Chamberlain, who had sponsored similar training bills in 1916 and 1917.[44]

[38]Palmer to Clark, June 7, 1919, ibid.
[39]Clark to Palmer, April 10, 16, 18, 19, June 12, 1919; Palmer to Clark, April 18, June 7, 1919, ibid.
[40]Clark to Palmer, June 12, 1919; see also Clark to McIlvaine, April 10, MTCA Executive Committee minutes, March 10, 1920, ibid.
[41]McIlvaine to Charles B. Pike, May 1, 1919, MTCA records (Chicago).
[42]McIlvaine to Landon Thomas, June 6, 1919, Wood MSS; see also Wood to McIlvaine, April 29, 1919, Wood MSS; Clark to McIlvaine, April 12, May 7 (2 letters), May 20, 1919, Clark MSS.
[43]*New York Times*, April 6, 16, May 17, 1919.
[44]See Clark to George E. Chamberlain, April 4, 1919, Clark MSS.

Before having the bill formally submitted, the Plattsburgers made one last attempt to obtain War Department
backing. McIlvaine wrote to Secretary Baker, suggesting
that the General Staff, the Senate and House Military committees, representatives of the National Guard, MTCA,
American Legion, and other patriotic societies avoid
conflict by getting together and agreeing on one
all-inclusive plan for military reorganization. Baker expressed interest, but said that matters were unsettled at the
moment with President Wilson still in Europe. The Plattsburgers waited for the president's return, but no further
word came.[45] Thereupon Kahn and Chamberlain introduced HR–8068 and S–2961 on July 31, 1919.[46]

"The National Service Act," as the two bills were titled,
did not differ in essentials from the original McIlvaine
memorandum. Six months of training at age eighteen or
nineteen (preceded by a special three-month course for
aliens and illiterates) remained, as did the principle of a
citizen reserve organized and trained territorially according
to residence. The vocational training features were also
present. Where the proposed legislation did depart from
the earlier outline was in regard to existing organizations.
The MTCA bill would now maintain the Regular Army as a
small standing force sufficient to garrison outlying possessions, to provide for coastal defense and other emergencies, and to serve as a training cadre for the citizen
reserves. The National Guard would preserve its separate
identity, but would revert to its earlier status as strictly a
state militia. The new bill also envisaged local civilian
boards, similar to those set up under the Selective Service
Act, to administer the training system. The actual details of
the citizen reserve, aside from the stipulation that all trainees would have a ten-year reserve obligation, were not
spelled out as precisely as in the McIlvaine memorandum.
The words "under regulations to be prescribed" appeared

[45]See McIlvaine's testimony, U.S., Congress, Senate Hearings, *Reorganization of the Army*, 66th Cong., 1st sess. (Washington, D.C., 1919), p. 834.

[46]U.S., Congress, *Congressional Record*, 66th Cong., 1st sess., pp. 3390, 3462.

often, implying that the bill would receive careful scrutiny at the House and Senate hearings due to begin shortly.[47]

The evening after the Kahn-Chamberlain bill was introduced in Congress, the MTCA gave a dinner at the New Willard Hotel in Washington. Henry S. Drinker, chairman of the MTCA Governing Committee, presided, and more than a hundred notables attended. At the dinner, McIlvaine gave a general explanation of the proposed legislation. Kahn and Chamberlain made speeches in support, and were seconded by Howard H. Gross, chairman of the Universal Military Training League, and Henry L. West, representing the National Security League.

The principal speaker of the evening was Republican Senator James W. Wadsworth, Jr., of New York, chairman of the Senate Military Affairs Committee. Wadsworth, a balding, forty-two-year-old former National Guard officer and advocate of universal military training, talked about the work that lay ahead for the seven senators who would conduct military hearings. "No subcommittee has ever been confronted with a more difficult and more important task," he said. "Permanent reorganization of the military forces involves a tremendous revision of the entire system." Wadsworth cited the problem of the air service, what to do with the National Guard, how to strengthen the General Staff. He spoke of the psychology of the American army and the psychology of the American people, urging that they somehow be brought into harmony. "And we want you to help us," he told his listeners.

> We have an infinite amount of information to collect. We have got to listen to conflicting ideas and conflicting proposals of all kinds and descriptions. It must be all thrashed out in the most open public way, so that we may all be educated, and the public educated to the true situation, and when you help us, — and when I say *you* I mean officers of the regular service and officers of other services, the educators and the representatives of these civilian organizations — the people of

[47]The bill is printed in full in *National Service* 6 (September 1919): 161-65.

the United States will cheerfully respond and support intelligent and wise legislation.[48]

Colonel Palmer was one of several officers at the dinner. He was struck by Wadsworth's appeal for candor. If called to testify before Wadworth's committee, Palmer decided he would speak his mind.[49] "I am going to kick over the traces," he told a friend.[50]

THREE

Senate hearings began on August 7, 1919, House hearings on September 3. Hundreds of witnesses testified: Regular officers, pacifists, National Guardsmen, Plattsburgers, college presidents, practically everyone with a conceivable interest in military policy. The hearings continued well into the autumn, and, while they were sometimes overshadowed by the Senate debates on the Versailles Treaty, all shades of military opinion received full expression.

The first to represent the Plattsburg position was General Wood who appeared before the senators on September 10. He spoke out emphatically in favor of the MTCA bill. "It is essentially the old bill," he told Chamberlain, "which you took up and prepared in part when I was Chief of Staff and in part later. . . . It gives essentially the same amount of training." Wood contrasted it with the General Staff measure:

> I see no reason whatever for this large Army. I think it far wiser to limit our military forces not to exceed 200,000 to 250,000 men and to take up promptly whatever system of general training for national service that may be adopted. Our trained men should be put into reserve organizations, fully officered, and adequate supplies, arms and equipment of all kinds ready for them. Once this general system is in force, our Regular Army can be still further reduced. Any

[48]"Universal Military Training," *National Service* 6 (September 1919): 153–61. The article is a transcript of the speeches given at the New Willard Hotel.
[49]John McAuley Palmer, *America in Arms* (New Haven, Conn., 1941), p. 167.
[50]As quoted in Coffman, *The Hilt of the Sword,* p. 199.

Regular Army we may decide upon will be only a small fraction of what will be needed in case of a great war. The demands of a great war must be met by a National Army just as they were in this war.[51]

The Regular Army, in Wood's opinion, should constitute the nucleus of the training force, but between 80 and 90 percent of the officers should come from the reserves. It was important that reserves should have the dominant role; otherwise if "all the training is to be done by the Regular Army, you will have a system which will not meet with public approval; one which will be largely impracticable, and which is unnecessarily expensive."[52] Later in his testimony, the general vigorously endorsed the extramilitary benefits of universal training: "better coordinated mind and muscle . . . habits of promptness, personal neatness, respect for authority, respect for the law, respect for the rights of other people," a general education in citizenship.[53] He also praised the idea of vocational training.[54] Wood was saying nothing he had not said for years, but he said it well and the senators seemed impressed.[55]

Tompkins McIlvaine testified a week later, September 19. The MTCA spokesman was even more critical than Wood of the War Department bill, and he punctuated this criticism by reading into the record a recent letter to Secretary Baker. According to the McIlvaine letter, what Baker and the General Staff proposed was "thoroughly unsound and would perpetuate our worst mistakes," leaving the country "just where we were in 1917." He deplored the large standing army, saying it was "not only the most expensive system, but it is uneconomic, undemocratic, and un-American. It is opposed to the idea of a reduction in armaments and so is the antithesis of any League of Nations. And, finally, it is impracticable because of the impossibility of obtaining recruits in sufficient numbers." The

---

[51]Senate Hearings, *Army Reorganization*, p. 622.
[52]Ibid., p. 623.
[53]Ibid., pp. 634–35.
[54]Ibid., pp. 635–37.
[55]"Apparently made a good impression." Wood Diary, September 10, 1919.

universal training features of the Baker-March bill were also deemed valueless, because three months would not produce much benefit in terms of Americanization and economic efficiency, nor would it suffice from a purely military standpoint. Such a short period of instruction would result in a multitude of half-trained young men, who would not be organized into any territorial reserve, would have no opportunity to qualify as officers, and could not be called to the colors or organized into units until after a declaration of war. "As a whole," McIlvaine summed up, "the bill is really as bad as can be. It seems like patch-work — not the logical development of any practicable system."

McIlvaine then extolled the virtues of the MTCA's "National Service Act." He emphasized the democratic features of a citizen army, its principle of "equality of obligation and opportunity," the fact that Australia and Switzerland were successful models, and that officers would be promoted from the ranks. He described further the kind of reserve system that was envisaged: how each citizen would spend the first five years subsequent to training in an organized reserve with two or three weeks set aside every autumn for maneuvers, and how during the second five years each young man would pass into an unorganized reserve and be "subject to no further active service in time of peace but . . . required to make a periodical report and submit to medical inspection." And not only would such a system be more American and more democratic, McIlvaine argued, "but the cost will be less by hundreds of millions of dollars." This premise McIlvaine buttressed by noting the exorbitant cost of maintaining a professional soldier (food, clothing, pay) for one year, and comparing it to the much smaller amount needed to support a reservist during his two or three weeks of yearly maneuvers. (In subsequent testimony, McIlvaine estimated that a citizen army would require about $550,000,000 annually; a large standing army, $900,000,000.)[56] The letter concluded by urging abandon-

[56]Senate Hearings, *Army Reorganization*, pp. 843–44.

ment of the General Staff plan and assuring Baker of the continued cooperation of the MTCA.[57]

The "question-and-answer" portion of McIlvaine's hearing was mostly an elaboration of his letter, particularly in regard to expenses and the need for organized reserves. When asked about the National Guard, the Plattsburg spokesman responded with the old argument that it was unconstitutional to require federal service from the militia during peacetime and that training and reserves, therefore, should be part of a separate federal system. The militia should be retained as a state force.[58] McIlvaine also reiterated the nonmilitary benefits of universal training, estimating that 640,000 young men would undergo training each year, and of this total some 10 to 20 percent would be illiterate or "non-English-speaking" and thus eligible for special three-month introductory camps.[59] The rest of his testimony touched on such subjects as officer promotion, ordnance, what to do with the air service; at one point McIlvaine even advocated "having only one Cabinet officer for National Defense, to be called, let us say, the Secretary of National Defense, and . . . having the Secretary of War and the Secretary of any other department concerned with national defense as under secretaries."[60] In conclusion, McIlvaine repeated to the senators the same suggestion he had made to Baker, namely, that "the way to get a good bill is for all interested to unite in a little working committee, which will draft something to meet the general principles that you gentlemen of Congress should lay down as basically sound."[61]

The War Department plan, as Senator Wadsworth later put it, was taking "some pretty hard knocks."[62] Chamberlain, Wadsworth, and other members of the Senate com-

---

[57]Ibid., pp. 831–34; see also U.S., Congress, House Hearings, *Army Reorganization*, 66th Cong., 1st sess. (Washington, D.C., 1919), pp. 1389–92.

[58]Senate Hearings, *Army Reorganization*, pp. 834–37.

[59]Ibid., p. 841.

[60]Ibid., p. 857.

[61]Ibid., p. 856.

[62]James W. Wadsworth, Jr., "Introduction," in John McAuley Palmer, *Statesmanship or War* (Garden City, N.Y., 1927), p. xiv.

mittee were opposed to a large standing army, and they began to echo the testimony of Wood, McIlvaine, and General John F. O'Ryan of New York (who advocated a citizen army similar to that of the MTCA, except that it federalized the National Guard and made it an integral part of the training system).[63] Still, there was a feeling of confusion. General March and Secretary Baker had appeared and defended their handiwork. Other officers testified similarly. Some witnesses seemed unwilling to speak openly. Then, according to Wadsworth, just as the Senate committee despaired of ever obtaining a bill that both Congress and the army would accept, Colonel Palmer's name was mentioned by some of the younger staff officers who frequented the committee rooms. They spoke of Palmer's wide knowledge, his AEF background, and Pershing's confidence in him. Although he did not know Palmer personally, Wadsworth decided to call him before the committee.[64]

The frail-looking colonel appeared on the afternoon of October 9, carrying "a stack of papers a foot high." The senators groaned, shuffled their chairs, and prepared to go to sleep. But within minutes everyone was alert. "In half an hour he had us fascinated," Wadsworth remembered. "In an hour he had torn Peyton C. March's bill into scraps—figuratively speaking—and thrown it in the waste basket."[65] It was Palmer's assertion that the War Department plan was "not in harmony with the genius of American institutions" which startled the Senators.[66] Asked to elaborate, Palmer spent nearly two days detailing his objections to a large standing army and offering his alternatives. "He was not domineering," Wadsworth recalled, "he wasn't offensive but he was philosophical. He had studied 'way, 'way back and brought his thoughts up to date."[67] "I think I have never seen a witness create as deep an impression."[68]

---

[63]Senate Hearings, *Army Reorganization,* pp. 511–41.
[64]Wadsworth, "Introduction," p. xiii.
[65]James W. Wadsworth, "Memoir" (Columbia Oral History Project), pp. 307–8.
[66]Palmer, *America in Arms,* p. 168.
[67]Wadsworth, "Memoir," pp. 308–9.

As soon as his testimony ended on the second day, the committee met in executive session and voted unanimously to request the secretary of war to assign Palmer as their military adviser. Baker, after some hesitation, acceded.[69]

What Palmer said in his testimony was in direct support of the Plattsburg position. "I feel quite satisfied," he stated at one point, "that if a citizen army could be formed under the general provisions of the Kahn-Chamberlain bill, with a provision added giving it sufficient regular personnel to tide over the emergency, that we could work out under it a military policy of probably the maximum efficiency and economy."[70] Palmer agreed with the proposed six months of training and the ten-year reserve obligation. He went even further in emphasizing the territorial organization of any reserve—what he called "corps areas." There would be, ideally, sixteen such corps areas, or training centers, each maintaining a permanent staff and generating trained personnel that would comprise two or three divisions in time of war. At such a time, in Palmer's words,

> each corps area will be able to mobilize a complete army corps at full strength and to fill its replacement depots with trained replacements, and will have sufficient surplus strength in trained officers and men to form such new and unforeseen organizations as any particular military situation may require after necessary exemptions for war industries have been determined. The corps area with its territorial units and its training center thus becomes a continuously functioning machine through which, if necessary, the entire manpower of the nation can be mobilized promptly, effectively, and economically.[71]

There was some deviation from the MTCA plan with respect to the militia, since Palmer wanted to make the National Guard a straight federal force, in effect, "charter

---

[68]Wadsworth, "Introduction," p. xv.
[69]Baker did not want to embarrass General March. Wadsworth, "Memoir," pp. 309–10.
[70]Senate Hearings, *Army Reorganization*, pp. 1197–98.
[71]Ibid., p. 1192.

members" of the citizen army.[72] But this was a minor point; the upshot of Palmer's testimony was clearly favorable.

The cause of a citizen army received a final boost three weeks later when General Pershing made known his position. The AEF commander had returned to the United States in mid-September and had spent nearly six weeks resting up and learning all he could about army reorganization. His aide-de-camp, Major George C. Marshall, saw that Pershing read the galleys of Palmer's hearing; and when the General of the Armies came to Washington prior to his own testimony, he had formal conferences with twenty key officers, including the chief of staff.[73] Pershing also talked with Tompkins McIlvaine. The next day, October 31, standing before a joint House-Senate committee in the caucus room of the House Office Building, Pershing stated at the outset that "our traditions are opposed to the maintenance of a large standing army. Our wars have practically all been fought with citizen soldiery."[74] Although confusing and contradictory in places, the testimony that followed indicated approval of a 300,000-man standing army, a federalized National Guard, and a six-month universal training program with the trainees subsequently organized into reserve units. "Pershing Gives Finishing Blow To Baker's Bill," ran the headlines in *Stars and Stripes*.[75] Congress adjourned shortly thereafter, with the understanding that the House and Senate committees would introduce new bills during the next session.

FOUR

The future looked bright for the Plattsburgers. Not only did the hearings indicate support for their program, but there was also a feeling of real confidence that victory was

[72]Ibid., p. 1184.

[73]See Palmer to Wadsworth, March 11, 1940, Wadsworth family MSS, Library of Congress; Pogue, *Marshall: Education of a General*, pp. 107–9.

[74]Diary of John J. Pershing, October 30, 1919, Pershing MSS; see also McIlvaine to Pershing, August 5, 1919, Pershing to McIlvaine, September 17, October 24, 1919, ibid.

[75]November 8, 1919, quoted in Coffman, *The Hilt of the Sword*, p. 202.

within reach. McIlvaine's work in Washington, while not elaborate, had been effective. He made it a habit to give a copy of the MTCA bill to each person testifying before the committees and did his best to evangelize the uncommitted. His talks with Pershing seemed to be successful, as a friend reported: "The best part of his testimony was relative to the citizens' army. In this it was apparent that he had had a talk with you."[76] During October the National Security League endorsed a strong, twelve-point program for army legislation, and it was McIlvaine who drafted the resolutions.[77] The first national convention of the American Legion, held at Minneapolis, November 10–12, 1919, proclaimed itself in favor of "a national military system based on universal obligation, to include a relatively small Regular Army and a citizen army capable of rapid expansion sufficient to meet any national emergency."[78] Copies of the resolution were sent to influential congressmen.[79] *National Service* editorials (most of them written by McIlvaine) became exultant.[80] "If we can get 50,000 letters written to members of Congress in the next six weeks," one Plattsburger predicted to Wood, "it will turn the trick."[81] (At this time, also, Wood's campaign for the presidency began to build up steam; and it was Plattsburg veterans like William C. Procter, Horace Stebbins, and DeLancey Jay who headed his organization.)[82]

The prospects were not all optimistic. "There seems to be a strange indifference to military training," Wood noted

[76]E. B. Johns to McIlvaine, October 31, 1919, Wood MSS; on McIlvaine's methods, see Archibald Thacher to Kenneth Budd, September 11, 1919, Clark MSS.

[77]McIlvaine to Wood, October 31, 1919, Wood MSS.

[78]Moley, *The American Legion Story*, p. 88.

[79]McIlvaine to Senator Frank L. Greene, December 1, 1919, Greene MSS, Library of Congress.

[80]"Wanted—A Father," *National Service* 6 (October 1919): 198; "The Army Bills" 6 (November 1919): 262. See also [Tompkins McIlvaine] "The New Army Plans," *The Review* 1 (September 27, 1919): 421–22.

[81]H. H. Gross to Wood, October 15, 1919, Wood MSS.

[82]See numerous entries in the Wood Diary in the autumn of 1919; Fred M. Alger to Wood, October 15, 1919, Wood MSS; Wesley M. Bagby, *The Road to Normalcy: The Presidential Campaign and Election of 1920* (Baltimore, Md., 1962), pp. 25–31.

after his hearing. "I think the inconsistency of the administration in advocating a large standing army and military training has rather shocked the public and they are wondering what is behind it all."[83] And it was clear that the House committee, even with Julius Kahn as chairman, had less sympathy for the MTCA position than did its Senate counterpart; McIlvaine found this out during a long and antagonistic grilling from Republican Congressman John F. Miller of Washington.[84] E. B. Johns, the editor of the *Army-Navy Journal*, confided to McIlvaine that House Republicans would eventually abandon universal training. "I confirmed this," he wrote, "by interviewing several Republican leaders. . . . The excuse they give is that they fear it would not pass the House if it came to a vote. This is merely an excuse. The organization can put through anything it wants to, especially as Secretary Baker has endorsed universal training and a number of Democrats in the House would vote for it."[85] In addition, many National Guardsmen opposed universal training; laboring elements were hostile; Southerners grumbled about giving guns to Negroes; even business leaders, because of strikes and economic uncertainty, seemed reluctant to accept the expense of an adequate training program.[86]

These omens notwithstanding, the Plattsburgers meant to press their advantage. Heretofore the MTCA had not given much attention to propaganda, partly because of insufficient funds.[87] Now they mobilized. The Executive Committee on November 18 authorized a budget of $75,000 for an intensive publicity campaign. In addition to the usual letters and telegrams through MTCA branches, the principal idea was to print up an attractive pamphlet, which would include a short digest of the Kahn-Chamberlain bill, statements from General Wood, Elihu

[83]Wood to McIlvaine, October 22, 1919, Wood MSS.

[84]House Hearings, *Army Reorganization,* pp. 1400–1404.

[85]Johns to McIlvaine, October 15, 1919, Wood MSS.

[86]McIlvaine to Wood, October 31, 1919, ibid.; Mooney and Layman, "Compulsory Military Training," pp. 650–56.

[87]Previously, the MTCA had limited itself to circularizing its own membership. "Open Letter," July 1, 1919, MTCA Records (Chicago).

Root, and others endorsing universal military training, and a short history of the Plattsburg movement. These
pamphlets were to be sent to congressmen, newspaper editors, and chambers of commerce. The MTCA also planned
to circularize the 200,000 officers who had fought in the
war, urging them to join the MTCA and to make their
views known to congressmen. All efforts would be coordinated with the American Legion, the National Security
League, and other preparedness groups.[88]

The Plattsburgers also followed closely the progress of
the bill being written by Wadsworth's committee. The relationship between Wadsworth and Palmer, once the latter
was detailed as military adviser, had grown increasingly
cordial, and Palmer was able to write practically the entire
bill.[89] The MTCA kept in constant communication and
began to accumulate a special fund in anticipation of Palmer's resignation from the service.[90] McIlvaine, in particular,
made many suggestions—so many that when the Senate bill
was completed in early January 1920 he modestly regarded
himself as one of the authors.[91]

The Wadsworth bill, as finally written, was a strong
measure—"the biggest thing that has been proposed in the
line of military legislation since the beginning of our country," according to General O'Ryan.[92] Preserved intact was
the principle of a small 280,000-man standing army with

[88]Minutes of Executive Committee Meetings, December 10 and 22, 1919, Clark
MSS. The subcommittee in charge of publicity was comprised of Langdon P.
Marvin, John T. Pratt, and Charles W. Whittlesey.

[89]Palmer later recalled that Wadsworth had played politics in drafting the bill
only once. Calling Palmer into the committee room, Wadsworth said: "This time
we are *not* asking your advice. Draw up a clause giving military rank to woman
nurses!" Palmer to Wadsworth, November 29, 1926, Wadsworth family MSS.

[90]Palmer to Clark, November 24, 1919; Executive Committee minutes, December 22, 1919, Clark MSS.

[91]"Confidentially, the bill is really the work of Senator Wadsworth, Colonel
Palmer, and myself, though General O'Ryan contributed some ideas on the subject
of the National Guard." McIlvaine to Wood, January 26, 1920, Wood MSS;
compare: "I know McIlvaine of old. I acquired most of my grey hairs when I was
on duty with the Senate Military Committee and he headed your association. I was
always grateful when a day passed without some new amendment to the bill.
There were so many of them that I am surprised that Wadsworth did not fire me."
Palmer to Clark, June 28, 1940, Clark MSS.

[92]*New York Times,* February 1, 1920.

organized citizen reserves. A federalized National Guard and World War veterans would comprise the reserve at the outset, to be supplemented and replaced in time by youths undergoing universal training. Reserve officers would have access to army schools, and it was stipulated that they should constitute at least 25 percent of the General Staff and at least 50 percent of the staff committees which drew up rules and regulations for the new citizen army.[93] The selection and promotion of officers also followed along lines advocated by the MTCA. Only in regard to universal training did the Senate bill waver somewhat, the provision being for four months of training instead of six. The intent was to get the idea accepted and then extend it to the necessary six months.[94] It was all good enough for McIlvaine, who observed to Wadsworth that the bill embodied everything which "the Military Training Camps Association have [*sic*] supported and actively worked to realize since 1913." He pledged "an active campaign of its entire membership and 1200 branches throughout the country."[95]

While congressional leaders pondered the fate of universal training during the next few months, the MTCA continued to do what it could. Waiting for the Plattsburg publicity campaign to build up steam, McIlvaine wrote a strong letter in February to the Democratic and Republican national chairmen, urging that both parties support universal training before the party conventions were held that coming summer. It was laced with the usual Plattsburg philosophy, that "national defense must not be neglected on any theory that there will never again be war," that "it would be most unjust to rely on the veterans to do all the fighting for the next generation," that a citizen army based on universal training would cost less than a large professional army.[96] Women also took a hand in late February

[93]"The Senate's Draft of the Army Bill," *National Service* 7 (February 1920): 70-72.

[94]Palmer, *America in Arms*, p. 175.

[95]McIlvaine to Wadsworth, January 25, 1920, Wadsworth family MSS.

[96]McIlvaine to Homer S. Cummings and Will H. Hays, February (?), 1920, Wood MSS; *National Service* 7 (March 1920): 133-34.

when the MTCA organized a Women's League for Universal Military Training with Mrs. Douglas Robinson (Theodore Roosevelt's sister) as president.[97] The chairman of the MTCA Finance Committee, Horace Stebbins, issued an appeal early in March to raise $250,000 for propaganda purposes.[98] Several days later the MTCA Governing Committee met for the first time since 1916 at the University Club in New York and with a burst of its prewar enthusiasm resolved to devote all resources toward pushing universal training.[99] As Arthur Cosby optimistically reported, the Plattsburgers occupied "a stronger strategic position than we have been in before."[100]

In actuality, the Plattsburg position had worsened. The prospects darkened in the House when Congressman Frank W. Mondell (R.-Wyoming) confused everyone by announcing on January 27 that universal military training would cost more than a billion dollars a year, far more than anyone had previously estimated. Congressmen who opposed universal training for other reasons suddenly began making speeches in favor of economy.[101] Wadsworth, Kahn, and other MTCA supporters were disgusted, but unable to make much headway.[102] Then, on February 9, another major setback occurred when a caucus of House Democrats resolved, 106 to 17, that "no measure should be passed by this Congress providing for universal compulsory service and training."[103] Since President Wilson had publicly discouraged such a decision, Republicans accused

[97]MTCA Bulletin #5, March 1, 1920, Clark MSS; "Women's League for Universal Military Training," *National Service* 8 (July 1920): 30–31.

[98]*New York Times*, March 7, 1920.

[99]Governing Committee Minutes, March 19, 1920, Clark MSS.

[100]Cosby to Wood, March 9, 1920, Wood MSS.

[101]MTCA Bulletin #2, February 3, 1920, Clark MSS; *New York Times*, January 28, 1920.

[102]Wadsworth commented: "I know some worthy citizens, who, if they had the chance, would reduce the Army to 1,216 men, provided that the officers should be elected by the enlisted men, and forbid the general to wear a certain cut of breeches because such a garment apes the British. It takes all kinds of people to make up a world." Wadsworth to Newton D. Baker, February 26, 1920, Baker MSS.

[103]*New York Times*, February 10, 1920; Baker to Woodrow Wilson, February 7, 1920, Wilson MSS.

Democrats of rebelling against their acknowledged party leader. The Democrats in turn denied any intended rebuke, saying they had to do what was necessary because of constituent opinion.[104] For a time the MTCA and other preparedness groups found themselves in the incongruous position of applauding Woodrow Wilson.

As a result of the Democratic caucus, Republican leaders in the House decided not to press compulsory training in the current Congress, but to support it in the next. Senator Chamberlain spoke out savagely against this "taking to the woods" attitude, and Democratic Congressman Richard Olney II urged the House Military Affairs Committee to ignore faint-hearted party leaders and include compulsory training in their bill. The committee, led by Julius Kahn, did just that by a vote of 11 to 9 on February 20. House sentiment proved unyielding, however, and four days later Kahn was forced to defer any decision on compulsory training until the December session of Congress.[105] "Those spineless cowards," he muttered, "those jellyfish."[106]

Despite these defeats, the Plattsburgers were able to take some comfort in the Senate bill and the fact that Kahn was to choose a "friendly" subcommittee of seven to hold further hearings on the costs of universal training. Kahn assured Arthur Cosby: "Of course, the fight is only really begun. We are going to have no end of opposition but I hope that we will finally succeed. We are in the right and the right usually prevails."[107] Reluctantly, however, the Plattsburgers began to admit that "the effort to secure favorable legislation has passed ahead of popular education on the subject."[108] Given time, they could overcome ignorant opposition. Many veterans thought that universal training applied to them, and Mondell's arguments about cost had found many adherents.[109] Perhaps the decision

104*New York Times,* February 11, 1920.

105*New York Times,* February 25, 1920; Mooney and Layman, "Compulsory Military Training," pp. 653–54.

106As quoted in Coffman, *Hilt of the Sword,* p. 199.

107MTCA Bulletin#5, March 1, 1920, Clark MSS.

108MTCA Bulletin #6, March 6, ibid.

would have to be delayed. "What we need to do is further to educate the country . . . and Congress," Cosby told Wood.[110]

Contributing to these mixed feelings of optimism and pessimism was the widespread belief among Plattsburgers that General Wood was going to win the Republican nomination in June and thus move everything in the proper direction.[111] Indeed, as time passed, the general's candidacy became more and more the center of Plattsburg attentions. McIlvaine, Cosby, Clark, Jay, Dick and Lloyd Derby, Horace Stebbins, Ted and Archie Roosevelt, Langdon Marvin, Landon Thomas, Frederick Alger, William M. Bullitt—almost all the Plattsburg leadership was working for Wood, many as delegates to the Chicago convention.[112] This primary object tended to obscure other goals. "The least said on the subject of Universal Military Training in your speeches," one Plattsburger advised, "the better for obvious political reasons. All of your friends know that you favor Military Training, but in speaking in support of it you are likely to alienate a large number of delegates who have no use whatever for it."[113] And, as the *New Republic* noted, the candidate proceeded to do exactly as suggested. Traveling around the country that spring, Wood continued to advocate a small professional army backed by trained citizen reserves, but as to how this reserve was to be trained and organized, he became less and less articulate.[114]

---

[109]"The veterans seem to have an idea that Universal Training means that *veterans* have got to go to camp for four months. What we want to rub in is, that if we don't have Universal Training the veterans *will* have to be drafted for all future military service; that Universal Training means Universal Training for all boys who reach manhood . . . and that the *veterans will not be compelled to do anything* unless, of course, we get into such a war that every able-bodied man is needed." McIlvaine to Wood, March 5, 1920, Wood MSS.

[110]Cosby to Wood, March 9, 1920, Wood MSS.

[111]H. H. Gross, president of the Universal Military Training League, became angry "when some of the long-haired men and short-haired women get up on their hind legs and claim we are trying to Prussianize America. . . . General Wood is sound as a nut on every proposition. . . . If he is sent to the White House, the devotees of the Red flag will find short shrift." Gross to R. D. Bowen, February 10, 1920, Wood MSS.

[112]Landon Thomas interview; Hagedorn, *Leonard Wood*, 2:337–39.

[113]Hamilton Fish to Wood, March 25, 1920, Wood MSS.

[114]Mooney and Layman, "Compulsory Military Training," pp. 654–55.

The results in the Senate reflected this growing unwillingness to deal with universal training. The Wadsworth bill came to the floor on April 5, and for three days the arguments raged back and forth. Then Wadsworth "lost control of the situation." It became apparent that leading Democrats were going to oppose universal military training for political reasons. They would claim during the forthcoming presidential campaign that the Republicans "had defeated the League of Nations which would have given us peace and now wanted Universal Training so as to prepare for the wars that would come." Senator Lodge and other Republican leaders recognized the implications of such an argument, and Wadsworth had to "shift his tactics accordingly." The result was a clever maneuver suggested by Colonel Palmer; Senator Joseph S. Frelinghuysen (R.– New Jersey), on April 9, offered an amendment for voluntary universal training. Under the substitute plan the government would give four months of military training to young men between the ages of eighteen and twenty-eight who applied for it. Once trained, the youths could enlist for four years in the organized reserves, but would be under no obligation to do so. Frelinghuysen argued that if 100,000 men volunteered for such training each summer, the annual cost would amount to less than $30,000,000. The amendment "produced great consternation in the ranks of the enemy" and passed by a 46-to-9 margin.[115]

The Senate bill, passed on April 20 with the Frelinghuysen amendment intact, was a puzzle to many advocates of preparedness. The *New York Times* sniffed at the new measure and said that voluntary universal training was a contradiction in terms, that volunteers would not materialize, and thus the whole system would be ineffective.[116] Such predictions, it turned out, were accurate. Nonetheless, those who backed the Senate bill knew that they had to compromise or risk losing the entire citizen army structure.

[115] Arthur Cosby memorandum of conversation with Senator Wadsworth, April 12, 1920, Clark MSS; Cosby to Clark, April 9, 1920, ibid.; *New York Times*, April 10, 1920.

[116] *New York Times*, April 12, 1920.

"The important thing," Palmer reassured Clark, "is that the relationship of the training service to the Regular Army is established." Palmer and Wadsworth were fairly optimistic that they could obtain sufficient volunteers if the proper machinery were established. "I am firmly convinced," the colonel wrote, "that we should have compulsory training, but I am also convinced that to organize a citizen army on a voluntary basis will not only give us the best volunteer system if we never get compulsory training, but it will be the best practical step toward securing the ultimate goal."[117]

The bill then went to the House-Senate conference, where it remained for about five weeks. The House measure, passed in March, had been drafted by War Department advisers in the form of amendments to the National Defense Act of 1916. It contained features almost identical to the Senate bill with regard to the Regular Army, but lacked any provision whatever for an organized citizen reserve. This presented a problem for the Senate conferees. Wadsworth tried to persuade the representatives to accept the entire Senate version and Kahn supported him. Slowly the House conferees gave way. They argued, however, that time was too short for them to take the elaborate Senate proposals back to the House and convince their colleagues. Adjournment was drawing near, and the calendar was full of other business. If Wadsworth could condense the citizen army program into a few short sections, then they would see what they could do.

Palmer was waiting in the anteroom with the House adviser, Colonel Thomas M. Spaulding, when Wadsworth emerged with the news and told them to prepare the necessary drafts. Palmer was appalled. "It can't be done," he grumbled to Spaulding. "It would be like asking Thomas Jefferson to write the Declaration of Independence in the form of amendments to the Book of Job." Spaulding asked quietly if he might try his hand, at which point the exasperated Palmer went out for lunch. On returning, he

[117]Palmer to Clark, April 26, 1920.

discovered that Spaulding "had performed the miracle." Crammed into two new sections, plus an enabling clause, was the gist of the Senate's citizen army program. Both Palmer and Wadsworth were pleased. The House conferees indicated their approval, and within a few days the revised bill passed both houses of Congress. President Wilson, after some thoughts about a veto, affixed his signature on June 4, 1920.[118]

The National Defense Act of 1920 did not fulfill the great hopes of those persons most interested in preparedness. Advocates of a citizen army were thwarted by the defeat of universal military training, as were the Uptonians by the maximum 280,000-man limit for the Regular Army (soon to be reduced for economic reasons to fewer than 200,000 men).[119] It is even possible, as Palmer later judged, that this internal division among the preparedness forces was the major reason for the failure of universal training in 1920.[120] More likely, the inevitable "widespread apathy, the reaction from the war"[121] to things military, the overshadowing issue of the League of Nations, presidential politics, and the desire for economy were all larger causes for defeat. Until the American people decided that national interest required active participation in world politics, and that such participation required military forces sufficient to carry out responsibilities, any military policy which consisted of compulsory training or service during peacetime was doomed to failure. If universal military training had passed Congress in 1920, it probably would have met the same fate as that other notable postwar reform — Prohibition.

Nevertheless, the new Defense Act represented considerable improvement over that of 1916. Not only was the Regular Army larger and better organized, but the General

[118]Palmer, *America in Arms*, pp. 182–84; MTCA Bulletins #13, #14, May 22, June 5, 1920, Clark MSS; Newton D. Baker to Woodrow Wilson, June 3, 4, 1920, Baker MSS.

[119]Coffman, *Hilt of the Sword*, p. 211.

[120]Palmer to Wadsworth, July 6, 1942, Wadsworth family MSS.

[121]Horace Stebbins to A. G. Thacher, January 27, 1920, Clark MSS.

Staff had been streamlined and there were provisions for mobilization planning in advance of war. The "keystone" of the new system, as Palmer phrased it, rested on the citizen reserves.[122] The National Guard continued its dual status as a state-federal force, but with stronger provisions for federal training and federal pay. The ROTC and Officers' Reserve Corps were strengthened, and a new Organized Reserve Corps of enlisted men added. This latter force was a logical successor to the wartime National Army and would consist of veteran volunteers and other enlistees who trained in organized units under federal auspices. During the summer of 1920, moreover, joint War Department committees of regular and reserve officers (as constituted under section 3a of the National Defense Act) reorganized the military establishment into nine "corps areas." The new arrangement was tactical and territorial. Each corps area with its commanding general would contain one complete Regular Army division. In addition, there would be an extra allotment of officers and enlisted men to form a "training center," at which the citizen army (or "civilian components," in War Department parlance) would undergo annual training and maneuvers. Two National Guard and three Organized Reserve divisions would be attached to each corps area.[123]

Whether the civilian reserves could provide a viable military force through voluntary enlistment was problematical. Senator Wadsworth, as years passed, always maintained that the structure set up in 1920 was sound and that the only difficulty was getting enough men to flesh out the skeleton.[124] Proponents of more extensive military training had to demonstrate their position through the existing system. As one contemporary writer put it, "success with the means at hand would be the best way to persuade Congress."[125] Although the opportunities with the new system seemed greater than in 1915, the urgency was lacking.

[122]Palmer, *America in Arms*, p. 173.   [123]Ibid., pp. 187–89.
[124]Memorandum, June 25, 1941, Wadsworth family MSS.
[125]Dickinson, *Building of an Army*, p. 187.

FIVE

A week after the National Defense Act became law, hundreds of delegates gathered in the Chicago Coliseum for the Republican National Convention. After eight ballots General Wood and Governor Frank O. Lowden of Illinois had battled each other to a standstill. Then, after party leaders held conferences in smoke-filled rooms, the convention turned to Warren G. Harding of Ohio.[126] It was bitter disappointment for Wood and the men who supported him. "It is hard to relish a cheese sandwich," one Plattsburger wrote, "when we had our mouths made up for a planked steak. We may make a wry face and swallow it but just think how we would have enjoyed the steak."[127] When Harding won the election in November, there were rumors that Wood might become the new secretary of war. This too came to naught.[128]

What was the Plattsburg movement to do now? Langdon Marvin had predicted to Wood in January that "this year is to be vitally important for the country and all of us who live in it and love it; and the future of the country revolves largely about you."[129] Since the leader had failed, should his followers simply fold up tents and return home? Had the Plattsburg movement ended?

The Military Training Camps Association met in New York on July 20, 1920, to assess the future. New leaders were elected, including Grenville Clark as chairman of the Executive Committee.[130] Having stayed in the background during the recent campaign for universal training, Clark called for a return to the methods of 1915, a return to demonstrating the advantages of military training through action rather than propaganda. McIlvaine and his committee had done an excellent job, Clark observed, but their numbers were too small and they had failed "for lack of the

---

[126]Hagedorn, *Leonard Wood*, 2: chapt. 16; Bagby, *Road to Normalcy*, chapt. 3.
[127]Adolph L. Boyce to Wood, August 17, 1920, Wood MSS.
[128]Hagedorn, *Leonard Wood*, 2:374–75.
[129]Marvin to Wood, January 2, 1920, Wood MSS.
[130]Henry S. Drinker to Wood, July 22, 1920, ibid.

necessary public interest." The Plattsburgers then voted to expand the MTCA membership, to open it to any American citizen, not just the 200,000 who had attended the Business Men's Camps and officer camps. It was further

RESOLVED that a plan for a system of boys' camps beginning in the summer of 1921 be proposed as soon as possible and submitted to the War Department for its approval, accompanied by a tender of the services of this Association in assisting to promote such a system of camps.[131]

Here indeed was a return to 1913 and 1915. However much the Plattsburg movement identified itself with General Wood and universal military training, the methods used had always been voluntary. The Plattsburgers stood for civilian initiative in military matters. They had to convince the public and the army through active demonstration. Wood himself liked the idea of new training camps because they were the best form of propaganda.[132] Clark agreed. "I believe that we have got a sound start," he told the general, "and by a year from now will have things going in good shape. . . . I think the movement is a long range affair which will have to be kept up over a series of years in order to get any effective legislation, and that we ought to plan on that basis, meanwhile . . . conducting all the voluntary camps of any legitimate nature that we can."[133]

It was this policy which the MTCA would continue through the next two decades.

[131]Minutes of MTCA Executive Committee meeting, July 20, 1920, Clark MSS.
[132]Wood to Clark (telegram), July 20, 1920, Wood MSS.
[133]Clark to Wood, July 20, 1920, Wood MSS.

Epilogue

The Plattsburgers, by reviving the idea of voluntary training camps in 1920, reaffirmed their "gradualist" philosophy of the prewar years. The only way that universal
military training could possibly come to the United States
was through a process of education and demonstration.
The National Defense Act of 1920, with its provisions for
voluntary training, gave the Plattsburgers a laboratory to
test their ideas. If the camps were large enough, if hundreds of thousands of young men experienced the supposed benefits of military training, then the entire country
might be persuaded to accept the Plattsburg idea. As Clark
put it, voluntary camps were the "only method whereby the
public can be brought to consider the thing on its mer-
its. . . . I am even willing to say that if it does not work
successfully and produce a favorable sentiment, it is not
adapted to the American people and we must revise our
views."[1]

The Plattsburg effort during the interwar years was
only partly successful. Because of budget cuts, widespread
public apathy to military matters, waning enthusiasm on
the part of the MTCA, and other reasons, universal military training was no closer to fulfillment in 1939 than it had
been in 1920. Such a system, it seemed, did not suit American purposes. (One disillusioned soldier wrote that "to advocate the Swiss military system for America is just as
absurd as to advocate the yodel as a substitute for the
college yell, or goat's milk for coca-cola!")[2] But if this larger
object proved futile, voluntary military training thrived. In
the two decades following World War I, more than 500,000
young men, ages eighteen to twenty-four, underwent four
weeks of instruction in the so-called Citizens' Military

Training Camps (CMTC). Beginning in 1923, the army designated the MTCA as the recruiting agency for these camps, and select Plattsburg officials became civilian aides to the secretary of war. Not only was this quasi-official relationship responsible for high attendance at the CMTC, but it enabled the MTCA to maintain a strong organization.[3] Even in the depths of the Great Depression, when economic demands forced cut-backs in many federal programs, the War Department successfully defended the summer camps and the role of the MTCA.[4]

Despite the size and apparent success of the Citizens' Military Training Camps, they were not the same as the prewar Plattsburg camps. The CMTC was supposed to qualify graduates for reserve commissions through a three-year ("Red-White-Blue") course, but it was never very successful in this regard—only 4,630 officers were commissioned by 1934.[5] The urgency of 1915 was missing, most of the trainees lacked college educations, and so the army had to accommodate itself. CMTC training was scaled down considerably from the intensive methods of 1915 – 1916, and officers placed more emphasis on citizenship training and supervised athletics than on military instruction. The camps assumed a kind of Boy Scout atmosphere: in President Calvin Coolidge's phrase, they were "essentially schools in citizenship."[6] Less valuable than the Organized Reserves, ROTC, and National Guard in providing the country with a trained reserve, the CMTC came to be more important for its public relations. Educators endorsed the camps; President William Green of the AF of L even became a civilian aide to the secretary of war. The army's chief of staff admitted in 1930 that "the camps do not directly serve to promote any military objective. The chief

---

[1]Clark to Ralph Barton Perry, January 28, 1921, Perry MSS.

[2]Johnson Hagood to Hermann Hagedorn, December 15, 1928, Hagedorn MSS.

[3]See MTCA, *Twelve Years of the CMTC* (Chicago, 1934).

[4]John W. Killegrew, "The Impact of the Great Depression on the Army, 1929-1936" (Ph.D. diss., Indiana University, 1960), pp. 206-7.

[5]R. A. Hill, "Reserve Policies and National Defense," *Infantry Journal* (January 1935): 59-61.

[6]As quoted in MTCA, *Eight Years of the CMTC* (Chicago, 1930), pp. 7-8.

benefit to the Army lies in the increased confidence in its personnel on the part of the civilian population."[7]

As the training camps evolved, so too did the movement change its scope and purpose. To facilitate recruitment for the CMTC, the national headquarters of the MTCA moved from New York to Chicago in the winter of 1922 – 1923, and Charles B. Pike, a wealthy and ambitious Chicagoan, was elected chairman of the Executive Committee. Thereafter the influence and interest of the original Plattsburgers diminished considerably. General Wood, who left the country to become governor general of the Philippines in 1921, died six years later. Grenville Clark remained active for several years as head of a Plattsburg committee which made periodic visits to Washington, but in 1926 he suffered a severe physical breakdown, after which he cut off virtually all ties with the MTCA and involved himself in other public issues.[8] Some of Clark's friends continued to work in the New York area, helping to recruit for the yearly camps at Plattsburg, but the focus of MTCA policy gradually shifted to Chicago. Because Pike agreed with the army's emphasis on citizenship training in the CMTC, the policy of the association came to reflect his views — much to the chagrin of those who still clung to the banner of universal military training. A certain abrasiveness in Pike's personality also alienated the New Yorkers.[9] By the mid-1930s, therefore, the MTCA had evolved to the point where all decisions were made in Chicago, and these decisions usually reflected the isolationist mood of Middle America.

The coming of the Second World War brought about a full-scale revival of the Plattsburg movement. In the spring of 1940, twenty-five years after the sinking of the *Lusitania*,

[7]*Annual Report of the Secretary of War, 1930* (Washington, D.C., 1930), p. 153.

[8]In 1931 Clark became a member of the seven-man "corporation" that governed Harvard College. That same year he also helped to establish the National Economy League. A supporter of the New Deal, he nevertheless opposed the "court-packing" plan in 1937. Clark was also active as chairman of the American Bar Association's Bill of Rights Committee.

[9]There are numerous letters in the Clark MSS testifying to the animosity between Pike and the New Yorkers.

Clark watched the German army goosestep its way across Western Europe. Gathering together his aging associates of the previous war—Langdon Marvin, DeLancey Jay, Philip Carroll, Lloyd Derby, Archibald Thacher, Kenneth Budd, Anson Conger Goodyear, Tompkins McIlvaine, and others—he began a second campaign to reform American defense policy. The New Yorkers reasserted control of the MTCA by forming a National Emergency Committee which bypassed the more cautious Chicagoans. Using as an intermediary his close friend Felix Frankfurter, associate justice of the Supreme Court, Clark obtained the appointment of Henry L. Stimson and Robert P. Patterson as secretary and assistant secretary of war, respectively. With these two advocates in positions of power, and another Business Men's Camp demonstrating at Plattsburg that summer, Clark and his cohorts succeeded in writing, publicizing, and finally passing the Selective Training and Service Act of September 1940. It was under this legislation that some sixteen million Americans experienced military service during World War II, and without it the United States might have been as unprepared in 1941 as in 1917.[10]

The effort of 1940, unlike that of 1915–1917, had an enduring effect. Except for a short period after 1945, the United States has maintained a policy of selective military training and service ever since.

Whether or not the kind of military system that proved so successful in two world wars should necessarily apply to the nuclear age is a question the Plattsburgers left unanswered.[11] Having contributed much to solving the military problems of two generations, they should not be expected to settle those of a third.

Even though the Plattsburg movement did not stop in 1920, the passage of the National Defense Act of that year

[10]The story of 1940 has been well told in Samuel R. Spencer, Jr., "A History of the Selective Training and Service Act of 1940 from Inception to Enactment" (Ph.D. diss., Harvard University, 1951).

[11]Clark, who became a leading World Federalist after 1945, opposed the extension of selective service in 1948.

marked the end of a distinct and important phase. The years 1913 – 1920, one may be certain, were a time of debate and demonstration. While Europe endured the bloodletting on the Somme and at Verdun, some well-meaning Americans had set out to adapt their country's military policy to the requirements of modern warfare. If the United States should be drawn into the European war, they reasoned, the old system of volunteer armies would have to give way to conscription and selective service. Officers should be trained, not politically appointed. By emphasizing the principle of universal military obligation, the Plattsburgers tried to link modern requirements with America's historic tradition of a citizen army. If civilians trained and served under an equal obligation, there would be no need for a large professional army and little danger of militarism. Volunteers themselves, the men who attended training camps were expressing their willingness to fulfill a citizen's military duty. The fact that many Plattsburgers were romantic soldiers, naive in their enthusiasm, without large understanding of the horrors of war as it was known in Europe, does not detract from the strength of their argument. When war came and the period of discussion and argument ended, the country, if only for two years, accepted the Plattsburg philosophy.

The training camps represented more than an attitude toward national defense. The sort of men who went to Plattsburg in 1915, the publicity surrounding that famous camp, and the subsequent emphasis on officer training during the war gave a distinct elitism to the movement. The high percentage of prominent men who shouldered rifles and dug trenches meant that their efforts would have an importance beyond mere numbers. But it was a special kind of elitism. If the Plattsburgers were aristocrats, they had no fear of participating in the democratic process. Whether it be forming the Military Training Camps Association, recruiting men for the camps, or lobbying in Congress, they went about their task with confidence. In an era when Harvard and Yale could open any door, they knew the right people. There was never any hesitation in testifying before a congressional committee or telephoning the secretary of war. The Plattsburgers expected to be heard. Partly because of their background and partly because of the logic of their arguments, they were optimistic as to the final result.

It was appropriate that the movement approached its goals gradually, step by step. Beginning with the college camps in 1913, progressing to the Business Men's Camp of 1915, gaining legislative recognition and greater numbers in 1916, standing for universal training in the winter of 1916–1917, serving in the war, and sponsoring legislation again in 1920, the Plattsburgers consistently worked within the system. Although General Wood occasionally kicked up his heels, the civilian leaders proved to be patient reformers—thorough democrats seeking to advance their own and their country's ideals.

It was interesting that the Plattsburgers, notwithstanding their goal of military preparedness, often acted in opposition to official War Department thinking. By agitating for a citizen army, they found themselves in conflict with the professionals. "Plattsburg," Wood observed in 1918, "was not made by the Army . . . but by an intelligent public opinion held up by a very few men in the Army and many intelligent ones outside the Army who saw what could be done."[12] Notwithstanding all the fears he might have aroused among pacifists, Wood was regarded by his professional colleagues as an "insurrecto, a man who is outspoken in his opposition to the established order."[13] The same held true for John McAuley Palmer, whose "co-conspiracy" with the Plattsburgers in 1920 branded him as "an insurgent . . . an outlaw without credentials."[14] Clark later looked upon Plattsburg as proof that amateurs could devise solutions which experts, because they were wedded to

[12]Wood to Arthur Cosby, November 18, 1918, Wood MSS.

[13]Johnson Hagood to Hermann Hagedorn, December 15, 1928, Hagedorn MSS.

[14]Palmer to James Wadsworth, June 23, 1926, Wadsworth family MSS.

traditional methods, found impossible. It reminded him of a favorite quotation from Abraham Lincoln: "The people will save their government, if the government itself will do its part only indifferently well."[15]

The meaning of the Plattsburg movement can be seen best, perhaps, in the activities of its two central figures: Wood and Clark. An individual whose heroic stature may seem diminished to a generation which cannot accept the verities of 1915, Leonard Wood was nonetheless a man of enormous talent. Without his magnetism, the training camps never would have begun. Without his ideas on military training and his willingness to speak out, the preparedness movement would have accomplished far less than it did. If he was too impatient, too ambitious for a military officer, it was because he saw all too clearly the consequences of going into war unprepared. Singleminded to the point where he subordinated all public issues to preparedness and viewed politics in terms of black and white, the general was still subtle enough to devise a program as flexible as the training camps. Wood's main fault was indiscretion, but had he been discreet he would not have aroused publicity for his ideas. Although his punishment at the hands of the Wilson administration was inevitable and probably justified, his ideas were correct. By adopting conscription and raising a large army, the "powers that be" paid him a backhanded compliment. The general may have failed personally, but his movement was a success.

Then there was Grenville Clark, "the man who thought of it all." More than anyone else, even Wood, it was Clark who gave direction to the training camp movement. While the general stood larger in the public spotlight, Clark became master behind the scenes. He and his associates organized the committees, talked with the War Department, lobbied with Congress, publicized and recruited the camps. It was Clark who kept the movement on a gradualist course, avoiding controversy whenever possible. He accept-

---

[15]Grenville Clark, *A Plan for Peace* (New York, 1950), p. 3.

ed Wood's military philosophy and gave it his own interpretation. If there was something presumptuous about a man as young as Clark arguing with congressmen and telling off generals, he took no notice. Plattsburg marked the beginning of Clark's career as a man who "appeared, in critical or confusing times, as a lobby for particular impulses of the national conscience."[16] Although he led a revival of the Plattsburg movement in 1940, he could apply the Plattsburg motto of "national service" to areas other than national defense, such as civil rights and world peace. "He is that rare thing in America," Felix Frankfurter once wrote, "a man of independence, financially and politically, who devotes himself as hard to public affairs as a private citizen as he would were he in public office."[17] Clark and his ideal of the citizen's obligation for public service were the essence of the Plattsburg movement.

[16]Morison, *Turmoil and Tradition,* pp. 396–97.
[17]Felix Frankfurter to Jean Monnet, September 29, 1952, Felix Frankfurter MSS, Library of Congress.

Bibliographical Essay

MANUSCRIPTS

The most important source for this study was the Grenville Clark MSS at the Baker Library of Dartmouth College, Hanover, New Hampshire. When Clark died at age 85 early in 1967, his family deposited all papers at Dartmouth. Originally housed in the equivalent of 122 standard file drawers, the manuscripts were moved to Hanover in the summer of 1967. The papers are still in the process of being cataloged under the direction of Mrs. Ruth N. Wight, formerly personal secretary to Clark. The Plattsburg materials consist of one large file drawer, assorted boxes, and printed matter. Correspondence is filed according to each individual—that is, there is a Henry S. Drinker folder, an Archibald G. Thacher folder, a Leonard Wood folder, and so on. An added feature is that several of Clark's friends left their Plattsburg papers to him; especially useful was a separate box of papers belonging to DeLancey Jay. Included also were minutes of MTCA meetings, numerous printed circulars and annual reports, copies of *National Service* and *Bulletin of the First Training Regiment*, assorted brochures and publications dealing with Plattsburg, rosters, menus, congressional testimony.

The Leonard Wood MSS in the Manuscripts Division of the Library of Congress were second only to the Clark MSS in importance. Arranged chronologically according to year, Wood's correspondence for the period 1913–1917 runs to approximately thirty boxes. A prolific letter writer, the general (it seems) corresponded with practically everyone. One has to sift through much irrelevant material, but it is worth the effort. Wood also kept a diary. Neatly typed, terse, it is an invaluable source for following his daily activities. Useful, too, were the general's scrapbooks of newspaper clippings.

The Library of Congress has several other manuscript collections of importance to this study. The Hermann Hagedorn MSS contain materials that Hagedorn collected in connection with writing the two-volume "official" biography of Wood in 1931. Interviews and correspondence with such former associates of the general as Halstead Dorey and Gordon Johnston were especially illuminating. The John Purroy Mitchel MSS are also in the Library of Congress; they were not very helpful—save for a few letters and Mitchel's scrapbook collection. The Henry Breckinridge MSS, particularly his diary, threw considerable light on the relations between Secretary Garrison and President Wilson. The Henry P. Fletcher MSS contain some interesting letters from Willard Straight. Theodore Roosevelt's papers were a good source, although one wishes that his sons could have written more letters to Oyster Bay when they were at Plattsburg; the Theodore Roosevelt, Jr., MSS, also at the Library of Congress, contain nothing on the Plattsburg years. The Woodrow Wilson MSS and the Newton D. Baker MSS were important for understanding the position of the administration; both collections are divided into series of boxes, sometimes making it difficult to locate relevant materials. Supplementing the Wilson MSS were the papers of Wilson's authorized biographer, Ray Stannard Baker. Similar to the Hagedorn MSS, the Baker papers contain interviews and correspondence with many of Wilson's contemporaries. Particularly interesting was the Lindley M. Garrison folder in which the former secretary of war gave his side on the preparedness controversy of 1915 – 1916. The Baker MSS also have a "chronological file"—actually a kind of diary which Baker reconstructed from excerpts of important letters, newspaper articles, and such, giving a day-to-day summary of Wilson's activities.

Also at the Library of Congress are the papers of several military officers who were active in the 1913 – 1917 period. The Frank R. McCoy MSS were a good source in view of McCoy's close friendship with General Wood. Because McCoy did not serve directly under Wood during most of these years, his papers were even more useful, as Wood, Dorey, Johnston, and others tended to "fill him in" with lengthy, descriptive letters. The Hugh L. Scott MSS were valuable, if only because Scott served as chief of staff from 1915 to 1917. An old friend of Wood, Scott struggled in vain to maintain this friendship despite Wood's growing hostility toward the Wilson administration. It was sometimes painful to read the correspondence between the two men. Scott's papers were useful, too, in following War Department policy toward defense legislation in 1915 – 1916. Tasker H. Bliss, assistant chief of staff under Scott, has left papers, but they were more useful for his later activities during the war and at the Versailles Conference. The James G. Harbord MSS and the Henry T. Allen MSS have a few interesting letters. A similar collection is the George Van Horne Moseley MSS, which also contains a four-volume unpublished autobiography, "One Soldier's Journey."

Other collections at the Library of Congress include the papers of Frank L. Greene (senator from Vermont), James Hay (chairman of the House Committee on Military Affairs), and James W. Wadsworth (senator from New York). The Hay MSS contain valuable material on the National Defense Act of 1917, including an unpublished essay by Hay: "Woodrow Wilson and Preparedness." Also used were the Charles H. Brent MSS.

An extremely valuable set of papers were those of Ralph Barton Perry in the Harvard University Archives. A professor of philosophy at Harvard, Perry attended the Business Men's Camp of 1915 and was friendly with Grenville Clark. He and Clark served together in the Adjutant General's Office during the First World War and helped draw up the Students' Army Training Corps program in 1918. In 1920 Perry agreed to write a book about the Plattsburg movement, and Clark undertook to help him gather material. Not only are there more than a dozen letters from Clark to Perry describing his own activities with the MTCA, but there are also reminiscent letters from other training camp leaders in various parts of the country. Perry was an excellent contemporary historian who asked the right questions of his correspondents.

The Henry L. Stimson MSS, Edward M. House MSS, and Clive Day MSS, all at Yale University were of some use, as were the Willard Straight MSS at Cornell University. The Franklin D. Roosevelt Library at Hyde Park, N.Y., gave insight into naval preparedness. The Quincy S. Mills papers at the University of North Carolina Library (available on microfilm) were an excellent representation of a civilian's day-to-day routine at Plattsburg in 1915, 1916, and 1917. Mills was a reporter for the *New York Sun*, and the bulk of his papers are letters to his mother. Mills was killed in France in 1918. Anson Conger Goodyear, head of the Buffalo branch of the MTCA, has left papers in the Buffalo Historical Society; included is an unpublished autobiography. There are some records belonging to the Chicago branch of the MTCA in the Chicago Historical Society, but these related primarily to the period after 1920.

Two groups of unpublished War Department records in the

National Archives proved to be of special value. Record Group 94 (the files of the Adjutant General's Office) contains a kaleidoscope of materials ranging from the reports of camp commanders to complaints by farmers that TBMs were scaring their cows and chickens. An AGO index for the period before April 1917 helps researchers locate the numbers under which relevant documents are filed. A most fortunate discovery was in Record Group 98, entitled "Records of the Plattsburg Barracks, 1916." In actuality these papers were not the post records they were supposed to be; for the most part they constituted the official correspondence of General Wood's aide-de-camp, Halstead Dorey, for the years 1915 – 1917. Comprising seven large boxes, these materials were especially valuable on the role of the officers on Governor's Island with regard to the training camps.

The interviews of James W. Wadsworth, Langdon P. Marvin, and Henry Breckinridge, deposited in the Columbia Oral History Collection, were consulted. The Breckinridge memoir was especially informative.

An effort was also made to get as many personal recollections from participants as possible. I corresponded with approximately thirty survivors of the training camp movement and interviewed five: Landon Thomas, Thomas W. Miller, Horace Frost, John R. Tunis, and Richard A. Newhall. Mrs. Catherine Drinker Bowen conversed about her father, Henry S. Drinker. Henry Mayer, a clerk in the law firm Root, Clark, Buckner, and Howland in 1915, reminisced about Grenville Clark, Elihu Root, Jr., and Lloyd Derby. Ethel Roosevelt Derby shared memories of the Roosevelts and the Derbys, and John J. McCloy talked about Plattsburg and Grenville Clark. In spite of being an imprecise methodology, these interviews with persons in their late seventies and early eighties has been a fascinating experience. Always courteous and helpful, the Plattsburgers whom I have met bore no resemblance whatever to "snobbish aristocrats."

PRINTED MATERIALS

Government Documents

The *Congressional Record* proved most useful for the debates on the Hay and Chamberlain bills during the winter and spring of 1916. Committee hearings were also of importance: "To Increase the Efficiency of the Military Establishment of the United States," *Hearings before the Committee on Military Affairs, House of Representa-*

tives, 64th Cong., 1st sess. (Washington, D.C., 1916), contains valuable testimony on army reorganization in 1915–1916, including a long statement by Grenville Clark on the position of the MTCA; U.S., Congress, Senate Hearings, *Universal Military Training . . . S. 1695* (Washington, D.C., 1917), is also excellent. For the 1920 Defense Act, U.S., Congress, Senate Hearings, *Reorganization of the Army,* 66th Cong., 1st sess. (Washington, D.C., 1919), was most useful. The *War Department Annual Reports,* which include reports of the secretary of war, chief of staff, and adjutant general, are the basic source for War Department policy; especially revealing were the *Annual Reports* for 1914.

Newspapers and Periodicals

Used throughout the period covered in this study was the *New York Times,* with its incomparable index. The *New York Sun* and *New York Tribune* also have excellent coverage of training camp activities. Such newspapers as the *Deseret Evening News, Atlanta Journal, Chicago Tribune,* and *San Antonio Express* give good day-to-day summaries of camps other than Plattsburg. Particularly valuable were clippings in scrapbooks in the Wood and Mitchel MSS. The *Range Finder,* a student newspaper for the Plum Island camp in 1916, can be found in the Clark MSS.

The periodicals most helpful for this study were those published by the MTCA. The *Bulletin of the First Training Regiment* (published monthly from December 1915 to May 1916) gives an excellent account of local MTCA activities and contains examples of Plattsburg humor, discussion of future policy, articles on military preparedness, problems of military tactics and their solutions. The more widely circulated *National Service,* which began publication in February 1917, has a few articles and editorials which were of use, but is a better source for MTCA activities during and immediately after World War I. *National Service* ceased publication in 1922. Important, too, were the annual reports of the MTCA, the most complete collection being located in the Clark MSS.

An excellent source were the many articles written by Plattsburgers about their experiences as businessmen-soldiers. Some of the best were Lewis W. Miles, "Plattsburg," *Sewanee Review* 24 (January 1916): 19–23; Ralph W. Page, "What I Learned at Plattsburg," *World's Work* 31 (November 1915): 105–8; Raynal C. Bolling, "Opportunity in Our National Defense," *Collier's* 56 (January 8, 1916): 74 ff.; Richard Harding Davis, "The Plattsburg Idea," *Collier's* 56 (October 7, 1915): 7–9; Ralph Barton Perry, "Impressions of a Plattsburg Recruit," *New Republic* 4 (October 2, 1915): 229-31; and Frank J. Mather, Jr., "Rear-Rank Reflections," *Unpopular Review* 5 (January 1915): 15-25. Other contemporary journals with relevant articles included *Harper's Weekly, Outlook, Review of Reviews, Literary Digest, Saturday Evening Post, Vanity Fair, Scientific American, The Independent, The Nation,* and *Harvard Graduates' Magazine.* The *Army-Navy Journal* and the *Infantry Journal* reflect professional attitudes in the period 1913 – 1920.

General Studies

Well written and up-to-date, the best general history of the American army is Russell F. Weigley, *History of the United States Army* (New York, 1967). Weigley's focus is on military thought. Another useful study is Walter Millis's interpretive *Arms and Men: A Study in American Military History* (New York, 1956). Millis has also published an excellent documentary history, *American Military Thought* (Indianapolis, Ind., 1966), and his well-known book, *Road to War, 1914 – 1917* (Boston, 1935), is still a readable and highly stimulating account of America's entry into World War I. A good survey of American civil-military relations is Louis Smith, *American Democracy and Military Power: A Study of Civil Control of the Military Power in the United States* (Chicago, 1951). Arthur A. Ekirch, *The Civilian and the Military* (New York, 1956), is hostile to the army but still useful. Two provocative studies by political scientists are Samuel P. Huntington, *The Soldier and the State: The Theory and Politics of Civil-Military Relations* (Cambridge, Mass., 1957), and Morris Janowitz, *The Professional Soldier: A Social and Political Portrait* (Glencoe, Ill., 1960).

The best general account of the United States in the years leading to the First World War is Arthur S. Link, *Woodrow Wilson and the Progressive Era, 1910 – 1917* (New York, 1954). Important for the interdependence of military and foreign policies is the excellent work by Robert E. Osgood, *Ideals and Self-Interest in America's Foreign Relations* (Chicago, 1953). The best study of American involvement in World War I is Edward M. Coffman's recent book, *The War to End All Wars* (New York, 1968).

Biographies, Autobiographies, and Published Papers

By far the best biography of General Wood is Hermann Hagedorn, *Leonard Wood: A Biography,* 2 vols. (New York, 1931). Hagedorn had access to Wood's papers and full cooperation from the general's family and friends; the result is an extremely well-written, eulogistic account. It far surpasses the handful of campaign biographies which appeared in 1919 and 1920 when Wood was seeking the presidential nomination. A recent doctoral dissertation by Jack C. Lane, "Leonard Wood and American Defense Policy, 1900 - 1920" (University of Georgia, 1962), tries to cover too much in a limited number of pages.

A biography of Grenville Clark is needed. There are two short sketches: "Grenville Clark: Statesman Incognito," *Fortune* 30 (March 1946): 110 ff.; and Irving Dillard, "Grenville Clark: Public Citizen," *American Scholar* 33 (Winter 1963 - 1964): 97- 104. A full-scale study, written from the voluminous Clark MSS, would be a valuable contribution. There is some interesting material on Clark, the lawyer, in Martin Mayer's excellent portrait, *Emory R. Buckner* (New York, 1968).

John Purroy Mitchel is the subject of a short scholarly biography: Edwin R. Lewinson, *John Purroy Mitchel: Boy Mayor of New York* (New York, 1965). Henry L. Stimson and McGeorge Bundy collaborated to produce the informative memoir, *On Active Service in Peace and War* (New York, 1947). Stimson's full-dress biography is a splendid work, a portrait not only of the former secretary of war but also of the men and times he knew: Elting E. Morison, *Turmoil and Tradition: A Study of the Life and Times of Henry L. Stimson* (Boston, 1960). A biography written from private papers is James Brown Scott, *Robert Bacon, Life and Letters* (Garden City, N.Y., 1923). Roger Alden Derby, *Memoirs* (privately printed, 1959), Henry H. Curran, *From Pillar to Post* (New York, 1941), and George Wharton Pepper, *Philadelphia Lawyer: An Autobiography* (Philadelphia, 1954), all contain reminiscences of Plattsburg. Henry S. Drinker, *The Autobiography of Henry S. Drinker* (privately printed, 1931), includes some material on the training camps. Letters written from Plattsburg appear in Charles B. Davis, ed., *Adventures and Letters of Richard Harding Davis* (New York, 1917), and A. C. Denison, ed., *Letters of William C. Procter* (Cincinnati, Ohio, 1957). Although there is little on his Plattsburg activities, Willard Straight is the subject of an excellent biography: Herbert Croly, *Willard Straight* (New York, 1924). In addition to magazine articles already cited, other personal accounts by Plattsburgers can be found in class histories and anniversary reports. Most useful are the Harvard class reports, wherein the graduates often provide three or four pages of autobiographical data every tenth or fifteenth year.

Woodrow Wilson has attracted numerous biographers, the

most thorough and scholarly being Arthur S. Link. Link's magisterial *Wilson,* 5 vols. (Princeton, N. J., 1947–   ) has now reached the period of the World War. Careful, well written, and based on massive research, the Link biography cannot be ignored. Another first-rate study is the Pulitzer Prize-winning *Woodrow Wilson,* 2 vols. (New York, 1958), by Arthur Walworth. An interesting portrait of Wilson as commander in chief is John McAuley Palmer, *Washington, Lincoln, Wilson: Three War Statesmen* (Garden City, N.Y., 1930). Ray Stannard Baker, *Woodrow Wilson: Life and Letters,* 8 vols. (New York, 1927–1939), the official biography, is still worth reading. Ray S. Baker and William E. Dodd, eds., *The Public Papers of Woodrow Wilson,* 6 vols. (New York, 1925–1927), is a fairly complete collection. As for Wilson's great antagonist, the best one-volume study is William H. Harbaugh, *Power and Responsibility: The Life and Times of Theodore Roosevelt* (New York, 1956). Elting E. Morison, *The Letters of Theodore Roosevelt,* 8 vols. (Cambridge, Mass., 1951–1954), is an excellent collection of Roosevelt correspondence. The last volume contains some good examples of Roosevelt at his most militant. The best published study of his activities in the prewar years is still A. Russell Buchanan, "Theodore Roosevelt and American Neutrality, 1914–1917," *American Historical Review* 43 (July 1938): 775–90. Hermann Hagedorn's *The Bugle That Woke America* (New York, 1940), is an uncritical account of Roosevelt and the preparedness movement.

Charles Seymour, ed., *The Intimate Papers of Colonel House,* 4 vols. (Boston, 1926–1928), is a masterpiece of historical editing and reveals the relationship of Wilson's closest adviser to the preparedness movement. Another good source for administration policy is E. David Cronon, ed., *The Cabinet Diaries of Josephus Daniels, 1913–1921* (Lincoln, Nebr., 1963). Cronon is writing a multivolume biography of Daniels. Hugh L. Scott, *Some Memories of a Soldier* (New York, 1928), is a pedestrian account by the former chief of staff. John McAuley Palmer, *America in Arms* (New Haven, Conn., 1941), is also partly autobiographical. Merle Curti's *Bryan and World Peace* (Northampton, Mass., 1931) is a sympathetic study of the *bête noire* of the preparedness movement. David A. Lockmiller, *Enoch H. Crowder: Soldier, Lawyer and Statesman* (Columbia, Mo., 1955), has a good description of Crowder's role in framing the Selective Service Act of 1917. Frederick Palmer, *Bliss, Peacemaker: The Life and Letters of General Tasker Howard Bliss* (New York, 1934), and *Newton D. Baker: America at War,* 2 vols.

(New York, 1931), are two first-rate biographies. The gruff war-time chief of staff is the subject of a well-written biography, Edward M. Coffman, *The Hilt of the Sword: The Career of Peyton C. March* (Madison, Wis., 1966). Another fine piece of scholarship is the recent study by Daniel R. Beaver, *Newton D. Baker and the American War Effort, 1917–1919* (Lincoln, Nebr., 1966). Mabel E. Deutrich, *Struggle for Supremacy: The Career of General Fred C. Ainsworth* (Washington, D.C., 1962), traces the life of Wood's powerful enemy. Oswald Garrison Villard, *Fighting Years: Memoirs of a Liberal Editor* (New York, 1939), adds information about the famous speech by Theodore Roosevelt at Plattsburg. There is a short chapter on Plattsburg in Edmund Wilson's literary memoir, *A Prelude* (New York, 1967). A superb biography is Forrest C. Pogue, *George C. Marshall: Education of a General* (New York, 1963), a projected three-volume work, in which there are glimpses of Marshall commanding civilian volunteers at Monterey and Fort Douglas. Eagerly awaited is the forthcoming scholarly biography of John McAuley Palmer by Irving B. Holley, Jr.

Special Studies

No student of the preparedness movement can neglect Ralph Barton Perry's pioneer study, *The Plattsburg Movement* (New York, 1921). A Plattsburger himself, Perry treats the subject in a de-tached, straight-forward manner, using all available contemporary materials. Although the book suffers from a lack of under-standing of the Wilson administration, it offers forceful evidence that Wilson's opponents understood military matters better than he. Perry does not treat personalities in any detail. Another sketch of the Plattsburg movement is the superbly written "Plattsburg: The Camp by the Lake," in Francis Russell, *The Great Interlude* (Boston, 1964).

The best study of the preparedness movement is the thorough and balanced dissertation by William H. Harbaugh, "Wilson, Roosevelt, and American Interventionism, 1914–1917" (North-western University, 1953). Another excellent dissertation is John P. Finnegan, "Specter of a Dragon: American Military Pre-paredness in the Progressive Era, 1911–1917" (University of Wis-consin, 1969). Although written from printed materials only, two other dissertations are useful: William H. Tinsley, "The American Preparedness Movement, 1913–1917" (Stanford University, 1939), and Edward H. Brooks, "The National Defense Policy of the Wilson Administration, 1913–1917" (Stanford University,

1950). Armin Rappaport, *The Navy League of the United States* (Detroit, 1962), and Robert D. Ward, "The Origins and Activities of the National Security League, 1914–1919," *Mississippi Valley Historical Review* 47 (June 1960): 51–65, study two important preparedness groups. A careful study of public opinion and preparedness appears in Chase C. Mooney and Martha E. Layman, "Some Phases of the Compulsory Military Training Movement, 1914–1920," *Mississippi Valley Historical Review* 38 (March 1952): 637–55. The role of the chairman of the House Committee on Military Affairs is treated sympathetically in George C. Herring, Jr., "James Hay and the Preparedness Controversy, 1915–1916," *Journal of Southern History* 30 (November 1964): 383–404. The War Department side of the story is well told in James William Pohl, "The General Staff and American Defense Policy: The Formative Period, 1898–1917" (Ph.D. diss., University of Texas, 1967).

There are several studies of the National Guard: Jim Dan Hill, *The Minute Man in Peace and War: A History of the National Guard* (Harrisburg, Pa., 1964), William H. Riker, *Soldier of State: The National Guard in American Democracy* (Washington, D.C., 1957), and Martha E. Derthick, *The National Guard in Politics* (Cambridge, Mass., 1961). The Derthick account is the most scholarly. An old book but still very helpful is John Dickinson, *The Building of an Army* (New York, 1922). The role of colleges is traced in Gene M. Lyons and John W. Masland, "The Origins of the ROTC," *Military Affairs* 23 (Spring 1959): 1–12. Two studies of World War I veterans are Marquis James, *A History of the American Legion* (New York, 1923), and Raymond Moley, Jr., *The American Legion Story* (New York, 1966). A very good analysis of intellectual trends appears in Russell F. Weigley, *Towards an American Army: Military Thought from Washington to Marshall* (New York, 1962); it is especially helpful in regard to Wood's ideas. The relationship of Progressivism to Nationalism is discussed in William E. Leuchtenburg, "Progressivism and Imperialism: The Progressive Movement and American Foreign Policy, 1898–1916," *Mississippi Valley Historical Review* 39 (December 1952): 483–504. An excellent study, the first to use the Grenville Clark MSS, is Samuel R. Spencer, Jr., "The Selective Training and Service Act of 1940 from Inception to Enactment" (Ph.D. diss., Harvard University, 1951). The best account of the army between the two world wars is another dissertation: John William Killegrew, "The Impact of the Great Depression on the Army, 1929–1936" (Indiana University, 1960). Seward W. Livermore, *Politics Is Adjourned* (Middletown, Conn., 1966), is a scholarly analysis of political developments in 1916 – 1918, particularly good on the politics of preparedness.

Also of use to this study were three fictional accounts of Plattsburg: Arthur S. Pier, *The Plattsburgers* (Boston, 1917), a story of the college camps; O. N. E. [John B. Barnes], *Letters of a Plattsburg Patriot* (Washington, D.C., 1917), a humorous collection of letters; and Allen French, *At Plattsburg* (New York, 1917), a fairly sophisticated novel.

Index